TWELVE SONGS OF THE SOUL:

AN INTEGRATION OF ASTROLOGY AND PSYCHOSYNTHESIS

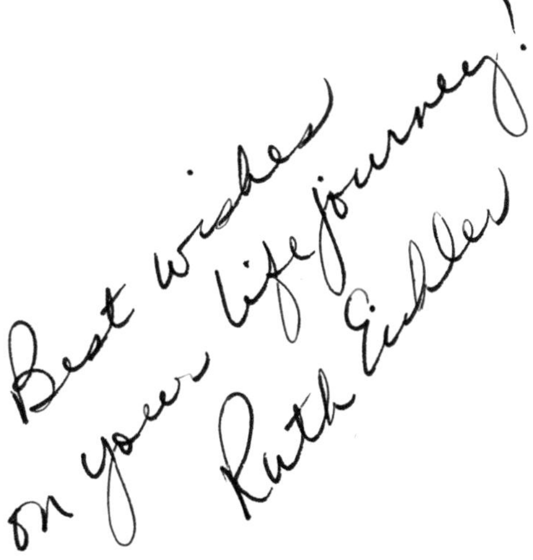

by Ruth L. Eichler, M.Ed., M.S.W.

Twelve Songs of the Soul:
An Integration of Astrology and Psychosynthesis

By
Ruth L. Eichler, M.Ed., M.S.W.

ISBN
0929915151

Library of Congress Catalog Card Number: 95-75755

For Information Address:
Ruth L. Eichler
P.O. Box 2033
Portage, MI 49081

Headline Books, Inc.
P.O. Box 52
Terra Alta, WV 26764

PRINTED IN THE UNITED STATES OF AMERICA

Table of Contents

DEDICATION

Lovingly to Vic, my husband and life partner, who has believed in me and my work since the day I met him. I am deeply grateful for his ongoing, loving support.

ACKNOWLEDGMENTS

With Sagittarius being a significant facet of my personality, my learning experiences and opportunities have been many and varied through the years for which I am deeply thankful. I especially wish to acknowledge certain teachers who have contributed to my understanding of both psychosynthesis and astrology.

I first experienced psychosynthesis at a weekend workshop taught by Harry Sloan in 1978 and knew that I was "home." This approach to psychology, spirituality, and life deeply resonated with my being and has continued to provide an uplifting lens through which I view the world. It has profoundly affected my own inner growth. Vivian King then provided an excellent foundation in a three-year training program in psychosynthesis. For the past six years, I have studied psychosynthesis and spiritual psychology with Tom Yeomans at the Concord Institute in Massachusetts. I appreciate his depth of understanding and his willingness to keep asking questions that help this work to continue growing rather than remaining static. Over the years, I have felt guided by the wisdom of Roberto Assagioli, founder of psychosynthesis, who died four years before I even discovered this subject. The many, many students who have participated in my psychosynthesis training programs and other classes over the years have also been my teachers. I am grateful to all of them, for each has added to the never ending unfolding into wholeness.

When I first met Zipporah Dobyns and took her 10-day intensive training in astrology, I had already been professionally certified by the American Federation of Astrologers. However, her psychological approach to astrology helped me to put all the pieces together into a more coherent whole. Her insistence that we choose how we play out our destinies which are reflected in the astrological chart further confirmed my own view. I am also deeply grateful to the thousands of people who have consulted with me and for the people who have participated in my astrological workshops, for I have learned much from these interactions.

I also wish to thank Ann Nunley from McLouth, Kansas, for the beautiful artwork in this book. She created these archetypal paintings representing each of the zodiacal signs a few years ago when I first began envisioning this book.

I wish to especially thank my two dear best friends, Deborah Allen and my husband, Vic Eichler, for encouraging me every step of the way and for reading and editing the entire manuscript.

And finally, I express gratitude to the Light for guiding me and to all of those who have carried the Light down through the ages.

FOREWORDS

I. Psychosynthesis

Over the years, Ruth Eichler and I have conducted many psychosynthesis workshops together, and I have delighted in her creativity and dedication to the flowering of the human potential. We have made pilgrimages to Russia together, to work with our colleagues at the Harmony Counseling Center in St. Petersburg, where I have experienced her openness to and respect for different perspectives, as well as her excellence as a trainer and guide. So I welcome this book as another expression of Ruth's wisdom, as she brings the powerful and practical tools of psychosynthesis into the esoteric world of astrology.

As a transpersonal psychology, psychosynthesis forms a bridge between psychology and spirituality. Its founder, Roberto Assagioli, believed no psychology can be complete without attention to the spiritual dimensions of life. Most psychosynthesis practitioners would also say the reverse is true: no spiritual approach can be complete without attention to the psychological dimensions of life. Personal and spiritual growth go hand and hand. Ruth bases ***Twelve Songs Of The Soul*** on this understanding, showing how we must work with and THROUGH our personalities to fully realize the qualities of soul that are latent within each of us. She challenges us to look beyond the predictive applications of astrology and to undertake a journey of self-knowledge that will bring us into wholeness. Dr. Assagioli believed in SYNTHESIS, bringing together diverse elements and qualities to form new and dynamic wholes. So he drew upon many diverse disciplines and wisdom traditions for his initial articulation of psychosynthesis. He attempted to find the underlying truth within each tradition, and those truths which seem to arise again and again, throughout the world. In his search, he studied both Western and Eastern psychology and philosophy, including some of the more mystical traditions. Ruth's study of astrology follows this treasured psychosynthesis tradition, and in this book she shares her synthesis of the truths she has found. Roberto would be proud!

In her integration of psychosynthesis and astrology, Ruth has created a comprehensive system for the self-discovery so desperately needed in our world today. As we all express more clearly and powerfully the songs of our souls, we will come together in peace and love to restore our world to wholeness.

Molly Young Brown, M.A., M.Div., teacher, workshop facilitator and author of *The Unfolding Self* and other books

II. Astrology

It is encouraging to see an increasing number of individuals who have realized that astrology is a form of psychology and who are familiar with the many attempts of both to understand and describe living beings. There are many astrologies, as there are many psychologies offering many models or personality systems, each shaped by the beliefs and values of the culture which produced them. We can map geographical space in many different projections; Mercator, Conic, Polyconic, Gnomonic, Sinusoidal, Interrupted Homolosine, and Polar Equidistant to name a few. In addition to the system of Assagioli which is featured in this work, psychology offers Skinner's operant conditioning, Freud's psychoanalysis, Perle's Gestalt, the systems of Adler, Jung, Reich, a variety of cognitive and transpersonal theorists etc. In astrology, we have the western or tropical zodiac plus many sidereal zodiacs. We have many ways to divide space into "houses," and a variety of angular distances between planets which are considered meaningful. Chinese astrology has five elements in contrast to the western four, and they do not use the "qualities." Some astrologers use the stars which are outside of our solar system, and some use the minor (small) planets which are inside our solar system.

Obviously, the map is not the territory. Models are simplified mental constructs to help us deal with the more complicated reality of life. They are not final and absolute truth. We can ask of any model, "Is this useful?" Or, better yet, "Under which circumstances is this model useful?" I have found astrology to be the most universally useful of the dozens of models which I have tested.

The basic theory behind astrology is that the cosmos is orderly and meaningful; that the sky is a convenient way to see the cosmic order, not the creator of the order but a visible part of it. Humans have been using the sky as their clock and compass to orient themselves in space, for at least 20,000 years according to archaeological evidence. But the primary gift of astrology is its use as a key to meaning. We continue to explore and evaluate astrological tools and techniques, looking for the most effective ones which will help us achieve meaningful lives. Modern computers are providing us with exciting new tools and techniques while new translations of ancient writers are providing forgotten beliefs that we can test for potential value.

As is clear in this book, every horoscope includes all of the basic principles of astrology. It is important not to overrate the zodiacal sign of the Sun. The twelve primary life drives or desires which are the basis of the astrological model or personality system are symbolized by planets, zodiacal signs, horoscope houses, nodes of the planets, dwads of the signs, and many other variables beyond the scope of this book. Each horoscope is a unique combination of the same twelve principles. Also, as this book indicates, in our search for fulfillment, each of the twelve primary drives can be manifested in many different life details, depending on our self-awareness and choices. The dangers, described as "distortions" in this text, include excesses and/or deficiencies in one or more drives, displacement when we seek fulfillment for a desire in inappropriate ways, repression when a desire is buried in the subconscious where it often leads to illness, and projection when we are attracted to other people who express our blocked desires for us but tend to overdo them as if to make up for our deficiency. Or, we may simply remain in a state of conflict between our different desires, diminishing our effectiveness and reducing our happiness.

In the astrological model, there are natural conflicts between some of the different desires. These are inherent in life and call for integration. Life is like a juggling act as we try to find a comfortable way to satisfy each of our twelve primary desires. As long as we are conscious of the natural conflicts, we can usually work out a solution by alternating between two of the contradictory desires or by finding a compromise which lets us have a little of each. For example, we can protect our own basic needs but still compromise when legitimate needs of others are at stake. Character creates destiny. I believe that we have lived before, developed a set of habits which bring us back to be born where we "fit," and that as we grow, we change our habits and the resultant consequences. Astrology is a diagnostic tool that helps us become aware of our own motivations which are driving our lives. Then it is up to us to work out the compromises, to integrate our diverse desires, to fully express our unique individuality in harmony with the Whole of which we are a part. The evolving Whole needs our unique contribution!

Zipporah Dobyns, Ph.D., astrologer, teacher, lecturer
and author *Expanding Astrology's Universe* and other books

INTRODUCTION

This book is based upon the premise that all of life--from cellular to planetary--moves toward synthesis and wholeness. Albert Szent-Gyorgyi, a research biologist twice awarded the Nobel Prize, acknowledges the existence of both an "innate drive in living matter to perfect itself," and a "psychological drive toward synthesis, toward growth, toward wholeness and self-perfection."[1] Cells unite as embryos to create more complex life. The core essence of human beings, the Self[2], continues to send out the call to parts of ourselves to come home into wholeness. People come together in groups and nations, if imperfectly, to create survival units on earth. Geosynthesis is even now being studied as the process that must occur in order for the planet to survive. As this evolutionary process towards wholeness slowly unfolds, we become increasingly cognizant of the potential that dawns, even though some of the most fully realized manifestations of Self remain only dimly in view if at all.

Interdependence is so interwoven into planetary life that we can access greater human resources than ever before in history. On the material plane, the technological invention of a Japanese inventor can be made available to the rest of the world in weeks. Centuries-old pharmacological knowledge from indigenous peoples around the world is potentially available everywhere. Acupuncture, practiced for centuries by Chinese physicians, is beginning to find acceptance by many Western practitioners.

On the psychological and spiritual planes, the wisdom of the East and the West are beginning to come together. The yoga of the East has become the biofeedback of the West. Western psychologists who have so extensively researched personality and human development up to the mental level can now incorporate knowledge of the spiritual realms which have been known in Eastern philosophies for centuries. The best can be gleaned from every culture and integrated into a more comprehensive view of human potential than has previously been possible.

This synthesis comes at a crucial time in history when we must call upon the best that is in us if we are to survive. Jean Houston states, "In this time of planetary culture, we need the full complement of human resources, wherever they are to be found. We need to bring forth and orchestrate all the Rhythms of Human Awakening that have ever been in humanity's search for what it can be."[3] The healing of the wounds of the planet--warfare, gross injustices in the distribution of wealth and resources, ecological atrocities, spiritual impoverishment--depends upon healthy individuals who are optimally integrated. The more healed and whole the individual, the more that Right relationship with the earth and all living things and beings will be possible. As the highest human potential is unfolded, peace and harmony eventually become inevitable. Dhyani Ywahoo, speaking of the prophesies of her Cherokee ancestors, says, "We have in this time an opportunity to create peace in our hearts, a peace that can resonate in every aspect of our lives."[4]

The concept of synthesis is central to this evolutionary movement toward a more integrative consciousness, incorporating awareness of the spiritual dimension. Inclusion of the spiritual does not exclude anything from the physical, emotional and mental aspects of life. We simply now have the opportunity to have bifocal vision, vision of both the sublime and the mundane. Sri Aurobindo spoke of living in both "this-worldly and other-worldly without any exclusiveness on either side."[5] When spiritual realms are synthesized with the personality dimension, the human being experiences greater inner harmony, is able to offer clear and conscious service, and is able to live with balance in the complexity of the world.

Psychosynthesis, one integrative discipline of psychological theory and practice, assists pilgrims on the journey to greater consciousness and wholeness. First formulated in 1910 by Italian psychiatrist Roberto Assagioli, M.D., psychosynthesis recognizes that each of us is more than a physical body, more than our emotions, and more than our mind. Through psychosynthesis (which is an attempt to cooperate with the natural process of growth), we can recognize, experience, and eliminate blocks in body, emotions and mind with the ultimate goal of creating a personality that is free from disturbances and has a clear awareness of its own center. That personal and transpersonal center exists as an organizing energy around which synthesis occurs. The Self, or transpersonal center, is intelligent, loving, and powerful. However, the Self often remains veiled to conscious awareness. If we feel separated from the light of the Self, life is experienced as dissonant and empty. Various aspects of the personality self can dominate, making the person less than effective, blocked and out of touch with creativity, intuition, and joy.

In discussing the journey to the Self, Assagioli states:

> "Man's spiritual development is a long and arduous journey, an adventure through strange lands full of surprises, difficulties and even dangers. It involves a drastic transmutation of the "normal" elements of the personality, an awakening of potentialities hitherto dormant, a raising of consciousness to new realms, and a functioning along a new inner dimension."[6]

In this book, I have chosen psychosynthesis as a model for how synthesis occurs and as a model of consciousness. As a facilitator of psychosynthesis training groups and as a psychotherapist, I have seen dramatic transformation in myself and others by applying psychosynthesis principles. In my work as a professional astrologer, I saw that each of the energy patterns, the zodiacal signs, form a continuum from the most ideal to the most distorted. The most ideal side of the continuum represents qualities we experience when living closer to the Self. The distortions of each sign can be seen as a multitude of subpersonalities, each with a limited view of reality, yet brought into being in an attempt to meet some unfulfilled need. Almost everyone experiences this end of the continuum from time to time; some reside there most of the time.

The wonderfully intricate and complex astrological energy patterns synthesize into a mandala representing the Self. This mandala also shows potential conflicts and subpersonalities that can be distorted from vibrant potential when basic needs remain thwarted and unmet. Dane Rudhyar states that transpersonal and humanistic astrology such as we will be discussing here requires "...a clear mind, a holistic way of facing all experiences, all life-situations--especially the birth-situation which defined our existential character and basic pattern of growth."[7]

Since transpersonal psychology and transpersonal astrology are infrequently combined, Part I of this book presents the evolutionary view of consciousness as a continuum. We are born somewhere on the continuum, often at a similar place as our family, and certain beliefs and identities must be surrendered before one is able to move to the next evolutionary level which is closer to the center, the Self. Also in Part I, psychosynthesis principles and astrological concepts will be explained to create a framework. Astrological patterns will be incorporated into the psychosynthesis model.

Part II contains chapters on the four temperaments or elements, the three qualities or modalities, and the dualities of yin and yang. Part III holds the "twelve songs of the Soul" or the twelve zodiacal signs. In each of these chapters, the energy patterns are examined as they manifest along the continuum from the most self-actualized (or closest to the Self) to the most distorted. In this presentation, I define free will as the ability to make choices that contribute to growth along the continuum. We are free to choose how we express the energy patterns, but once born, not which energy patterns we must work with in our lifetime. That is, if one is an Aries, one chooses what to do with Aries qualities; whereas being an Aries is not negotiable.

References for Introduction

[1]. Szent-Gyorgy, 1977, p. 14.

[2] The Self, explained more in depth in Chapter 2 of Part I, refers to the deepest spiritual essence within a person—sometimes called the Soul or Higher Self. Note that the Self with a capital S is differentiated from the self with a small s which refers to the personality self or the ego as defined in ego psychology.

[3]. Houston, 1982, p. xvii.

[4]. Ywahoo, 1987, p. 192.

[5]. Sat Prem, 1984, p. 147.

[6]. Assagioli, 1965, p. 39.

[7]. Rudhyar, 1975, p. 49.

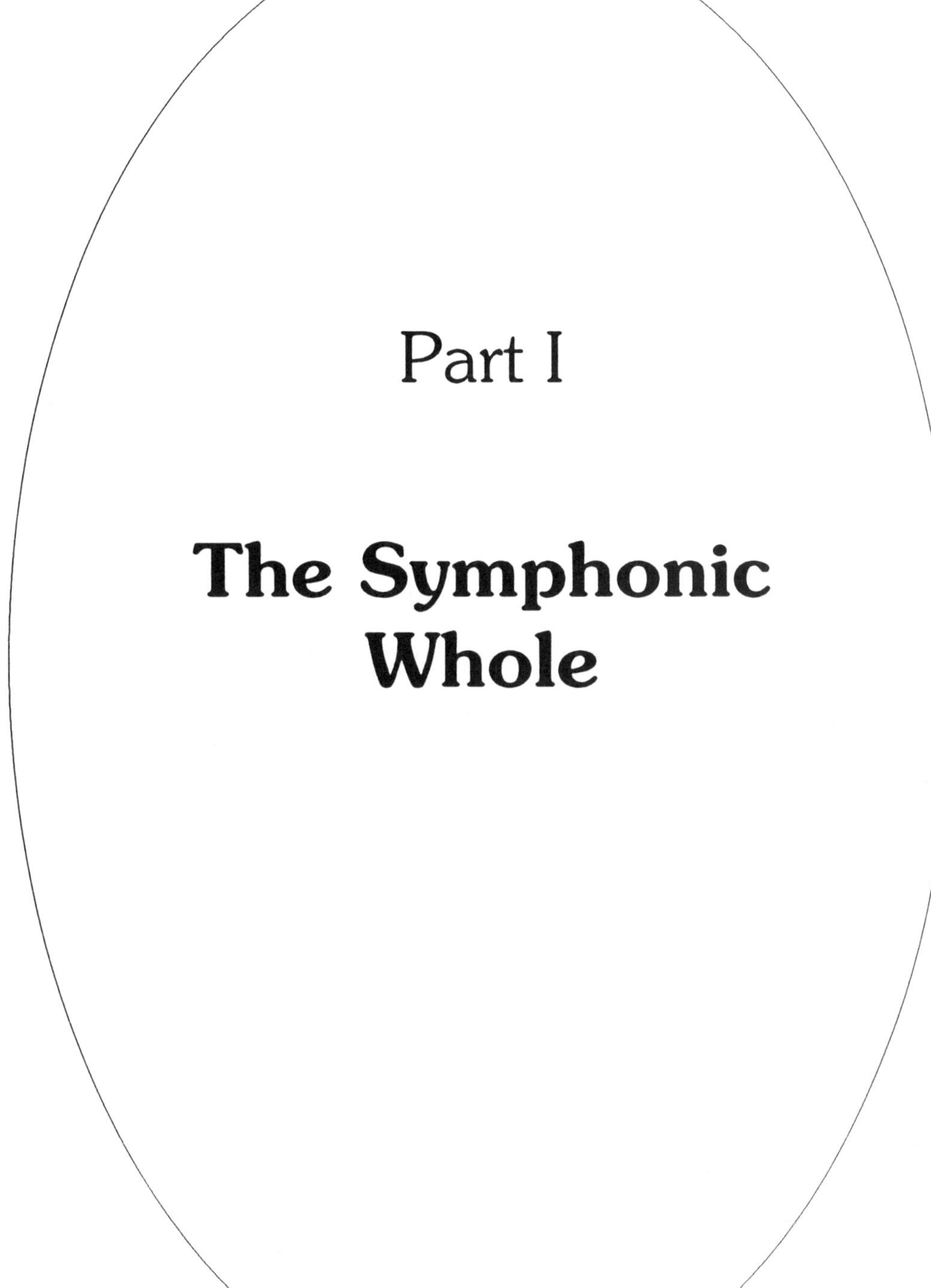

Part I

The Symphonic Whole

CHAPTER 1

The Continuum Concept Of Consciousness

Just trust Life:
Life will bring you high,
if only you are careful in selecting,
in the maze of events, those influences of those paths
which can bring you each time
a little more upward.
Life has to be discovered
and built step by step:
a great charm
if only one is convinced
(by faith and experience)
that the world is going somewhere.
—Pierre Teilhard de Chardin[1]

The Evolutionary Journey

Humanity, like a slumbering giant, has slowly, slowly begun to awaken into fuller consciousness. Theosophists suggest that in the beginning of human life on earth, the Soul consciously entered physical form in order to learn and experience. Heretofore, consciousness or spirit was individuated but not embodied, so these Souls chose to inhabit a more dense physical form, the body, for learning purposes. However, along the way, conscious awareness of Soul—divine spark or deepest spiritual essence—became lost to most human beings. Perhaps indigenous peoples have retained this connection through the ages. But, much of humanity fell asleep to this dimension and then, over the eons, began a very gradual, evolutionary process of returning to remembrance.

Although humankind as a whole has generally been unaware of a personal experience of Self or the Soul, mystics who lived with fiery passion remembered. Seeming crazy to the rest of the world, they shared their visions and cryptic messages of cosmic unity which also often included suffering along the way. Conscious awareness of the Self has been rare for ordinary persons, although some have carried the light down through the ages. Presently more of us are beginning to awaken to the radiant possibilities of living as a Self. For the vast majority, this vision remains unmanifested potential although sometimes dimly in view. The call to Unity continues. Ken Wilber suggests, "And, this finally is the ultimate Unity towards which all evolution, human and cosmic, drives."[2]

The Self as Unifying Center

What is this Self to which the awakened person is becoming aware? Ferrucci explains:

> "...the Self (is) the most elementary and distinctive part of our being—in other words, its core. This core is of an entirely different nature from all the elements (physical sensations, feelings, thoughts, and so on) that make up our personality. As a consequence, it can act as a unifying center, directing those elements and bringing them into the unity of an organic wholeness."[3]

Firman says the Self is distinct from thoughts, feelings, actions, and attitudes but not separate from these processes of body and mind.[4] The Self permeates the entire life system and is the context for that system.[5] The Self can be directly experienced and is the synthesizing center of the being, although most people remain unaware of this deepest level of Being. From the Self comes the evolutionary call to wholeness.

The Self embodies Will and holds the intention for wholeness and integration, helping synthesis to become possible. Along the way, as Firman asserts, the Self has the ability "to be fully present to us, not only in the heights of our spiritual experience, but in the depths of our isolation and pain, and indeed, in every moment of our lives."[6] As we move closer to this unifying center, we experience more choice and are less at the mercy of the whims and fluctuations of the personality. The further away from center, or Self, the less that we perceive choices as possible. Sri Aurobindo comments that without choice," ... we should have to wait for Nature to perfect (the human state) in her own ... process of evolution."[7]

This pure center of energy radiates through the personality much as the sun shines through the solar system, infusing all parts of the system with its presence. The Self provides the urge for purpose and meaning in life. Acting as the unifying center for the human being, the Self is unaffected by the flow of the mind-stream or by bodily conditions, and yet remains present to these processes. While the system is in flux and changing, the Self remains stable and eternal.

> THIS PURE CENTER OF ENERGY RADIATES THROUGH THE PERSONALITY MUCH AS THE SUN SHINES THROUGH THE SOLAR SYSTEM. . .

Although the Self is always present within human beings, Self-awareness is blocked by limiting beliefs, unmet needs, and a lack of integration. When various aspects of the personality have been integrated, barriers to growth removed, and basic personality needs fulfilled, the person then gradually deepens into a sense of Self. This process has been called psychosynthesis. The purpose of psychosynthesis, according to its founder, Roberto Assagioli, M.D., is to release the energies of the Self.[8]

As the individual personality is imbued with greater light, the evolutionary journey quickens, further facilitating integration and synthesis. Less fragmented and more healed, we then consciously reach for illumination. Yet, we need patience; the journey proceeds gradually with stops, starts, and sometimes even internal sabotage. Aspects of the personality fear losing control until they know that basic needs are going to be met. Resistance to growth comes primarily from subpersonalities, fragments within the personality, which will be further discussed in the next chapter.

As a transpersonal essence, the Self interfaces between the Universal and the individual personality. Ferrucci says that the Self, "while retaining a sense of individuality, lives at the level of universality, in a realm where personal plans and concerns are overshadowed by the wider vision of the whole."[9] Just as the Self infuses the personality, it also radiates beyond the personal, individual system. Ultimately, perhaps eons away, the individual and the Universal will blend and merge into the One. Wilber states that then "there is only that Unity which was always already the case from the start, and which remained both the alpha and omega of the soul's journey through time."[10]

Whereas the personality self carries a reflection of the Self, the Self also reflects a greater whole. Karl Pribram, Itzhak Bentov, David Bohm and others have explored the mind as an actual holographic, energetic form that has encoded all of the information of the universe. "The mind is a hologram that registers the entire symphony of cosmic vibratory events. ...The Self is a meeting place of eternity and time, the holographic mind in the evolutionary body."[11] The Self, then, may be a hologram of Universal Consciousness, interfacing between the individual and the Whole.

THE SELF IS A MEETING PLACE OF ETERNITY AND TIME. . .

The Continuum of Consciousness

The evolution of consciousness towards the Self resembles mountain climbing. As one approaches the top of a peak, the climber can both survey the path that led to this point and the path ahead, believing that only one more peak remains before the journey is complete. When what seems to be the last crest has been ascended, yet another appears. In his developmental model, Ken Wilber asserts that consciousness moves from slumber-like subconsciousness to self-consciousness or ego-awareness to superconsciousness, the realm of the Self.[12]

Western psychology excels at describing and working with individual personality and its developmental stages up to, but not including until recent times, the superconscious. The superconscious realm and the Self have been studied in depth in Eastern philosophies for centuries and now in the West by transpersonal psychologists and therapists.

Just as humanity as a whole has evolved along the continuum from slumber to awareness—from the subconsciousness to glimmers of the superconsciousness, individuals also traverse this continuum. Some are born into families with deeply embedded subpersonalities, which will be described in the next chapter, and may awaken at some time during their life. Others are born aware and move closer to the embodiment of Self throughout their lives. Yet, the development of consciousness does not always proceed in a simple, linear fashion. The plethora of books on consciousness that have been printed in the last decade attest to the fact that awareness of the transpersonal is no longer limited to a few mystics and saints. Even if people cannot live their daily lives from this dimension, higher consciousness has been born into awareness, and thought precedes action.

The Human Journey

People who experience life closer to the center are not superior to others, just more aware of choices and possibilities. Some people have been so wounded in life that options are not immediately apparent. Individuals move at their own pace, some painstakingly and gradually while others are able to move more swiftly. No cosmic race exists between souls to see which one can totally remember the Universal light first, but rather each experiences an individual journey even though it is taken with others. Several traditions claim that many paths lead to the top of the mountain. People simply find themselves at different places along diverging paths with varying lessons and choices. Self-acceptance and compassion heal wounds which accelerate, rather than impede, the journey.

This book is based upon the following premises: growth is evolutionary although not linear; movement to wholeness is a process; and choice exists along the continuum, even though not always realized in earlier stages.

References for Chapter 1

[1]. de Chardin, 1968, p. 127, quoted in Gallagher, p. 142.
[2]. Wilber, 1980, p. 75.
[3]. Ferrucci, 1982, p. 61-62.
[4]. Firman, 1991, p. 10-13.
[5]. Vaughan, 1986.
[6]. Firman, 1991, p. 11.
[7]. Quoted in A. Green, 1978, p. 46.
[8]. Assagioli, 1965.
[9]. Ferrucci, 1982, p. 45.
[10]. Wilber, 1980, p. 81.
[11]. Keen, 1982, p. 116-117.
[12]. Wilber, 1980.

CHAPTER 2

Path To Synthesis: Psychosynthesis Principles

(Psychosynthesis) is first and foremost a dynamic, even a dramatic conception of our psychological life, which it portrays as a constant interplay and conflict between the many different and contrasting forces and a unifying center which ever tends to control, harmonize and utilize them.—Roberto Assagioli[1]

Psychosynthesis

The purpose of this chapter is to present psychosynthesis principles and language which will be interwoven into the remainder of this book. In its most basic sense, psychosynthesis is a framework which attempts to consciously cooperate with the movement towards wholeness and synthesis found in all of life. Psychosynthesis postulates that a unifying center or Self harmonizes, integrates and synthesizes aspects of personal experience and that the personality organizes around this core or true Self. The Self is present to both the sublime and the suffering of our lives. Psychosynthesis provides a set of integrated principles, a map of consciousness, and an understanding of subpersonalities. Working with psychosynthesis principles, in addition to our natural unfolding, facilitates the continuing release of the energies of the Self through the personality into the world.

Subpersonalities

Whereas the Self, discussed in Chapter 1, represents unity, subpersonalities represent the multitude of lives that exist within people. "Each of us is a crowd," says Ferrucci.[2] Psychosynthesis provides a clear description of subpersonalities, explanations of their origin, an understanding of the gifts they provide, how they operate systemically, and processes for integration.

Subpersonalities may be described as parts of the personality that contribute to the whole personality; some are almost conscious while some are deeply repressed. Crampton states that subpersonalities are "structured constellations or agglomerates of attitudes, drives, habit patterns, and belief systems, organized in adaptation to forces in the internal and external environment."[3] They represent more than just roles, although a role such as "mother" or "professional" might play into a subpersonality. Each acts like a separate character in a play that has its own wants, needs, beliefs, and even subtle body language. Each speaks for its part, not the whole, and maintains its own perspective. One example comes from object relations and ego psychology: when "splitting" occurs, the person has one part that wants to be nurtured and another part that withdraws and punishes. Each part represents a subpersonality within that one person. Exemplifying another subpersonality, the Victim believes he or she is powerless. While the person is identified with the victim part, he or she fails to express power because of that belief and experiences the world as an unsafe place. This same person may hold a different view when disidentified from the victim part.

Formation

Subpersonalities are formed in the context of family and environment and affected by culture. For example, in a culture in which the woman's role is subordinate, both men and women might develop subpersonalities that harshly judge women who do not fit the expectation. Subpersonalities are generally formed in childhood when certain needs are not met in much the same way that defense mechanisms are developed. In psychosynthesis, the subpersonalities use defense mechanisms for coping and are not the mechanisms themselves.

SUBPERSONALITIES ARE GENERALLY FORMED IN CHILDHOOD WHEN CERTAIN NEEDS ARE NOT MET. . .

Gifts

Subpersonalities always contain their own gift, a valuable quality that has become distorted. Once the subpersonality has been recognized, accepted and harmonized into the personality as a whole without distortion, the gift becomes fully available to the person. For example, the martyr's distortion is that he or she must suffer while sacrificing for others. Martyr needs love which she or he mistakenly believes can only be obtained through sacrifice. Martyr's gift of compassion can be expressed in a healthy manner once what has been missing—for example, love—is provided in new ways. The more each subpersonality is recognized and accepted, the more it can make its own unique contribution to the whole.

The systemic view

Subpersonalities are interconnected into the personality system so that when one is harmonized and integrated, the entire system is affected. If the punishing, withdrawing subpersonality is able to take in the love that it needs and no longer has the urge to push away for protection from rejection, then the corresponding part that needs nurturing can receive nurturing. The personality self becomes more integrated, and qualities such as love and wisdom are released from the Self. Because change is systemic, work with subpersonalities must not be forced. The system needs time to integrate the changes before processing new ones. Often when the individual experiences the urge to grow, some subpersonalities become fearful of change and try to keep order. Synthesis is a natural, ongoing process with its own pace.

Healing

The first stage in the healing of a subpersonality requires recognition; otherwise, the subpersonality remains unconscious and uncontrollable. After recognition, the individual must then be able to experience compassion and acceptance for this distorted part, or the subpersonality will resist healing even more strongly and retrench. Disapproval for a subpersonality usually originates from another subpersonality which has set itself up as judge. One of the qualities of the Self is unconditional love.

In the next step, communication is established between the centered self and the subpersonality. Opposing subpersonalities begin to dialogue under the coordination of the self. As long as their needs are met, the subpersonalities eventually cooperate within the system.

Integration is the next stage of healing for subpersonalities. Through dialogue and cooperation, the needs of the subpersonality can be met in healthy ways, and the gifts or qualities that were formerly distorted and encapsulated can become accessible at will to the total personality. The subpersonality then no longer has a function, as it merges into the centered self.

The Will

Few theorists and writers in the field of psychotherapy have so eloquently described the function of will in the integrative process as did Assagioli. His final book, *The Act of Will*[4], was entirely devoted to this issue. Basically, the will is the ability to choose what is best for oneself, a task not always easy if subpersonalities are vociferous. From the centered position, when we are identified with the personal self or Self rather than subpersonalities, the individual has clarity.

Assagioli attributed seven qualities to the will: energy, mastery, one pointedness, decisiveness, courage, persistence, and organization. With the development of these qualities, the person can integrate what has been learned and take appropriate action. Insight is not sufficient alone; new behaviors and attitudes must become a part of the person's mode of being in the world.

Assagioli attributed seven qualities to the will: energy, mastery, one pointedness, decisiveness, courage, persistence, and organization.

Use of the will does not resemble Victorian willpower or force. While the real function of the will is to direct, it does not impose. With the development of the will—the ability to express true intention, one can regulate and direct personality functions and integration from a centered place. The will can be activated to help direct the interaction of the subpersonalities rather than being dominated by them. By invoking the will, a person can choose, and choice brings freedom. More than any other factor, the will is the key to human freedom and personal power.

The Principle of Identification/Disidentification

Definitions

The concepts of identification and disidentification are crucial to psychosynthesis work. Identification relates to who one thinks one is, usually at an unconscious level. Disidentification provides a vantage point by being able to stand back, to observe and to work with an old way of expressing oneself. The individual can be identified with a multitude of subpersonalities—one at a time—or with the personal, centered self, or ultimately with the spiritual Self. This identification determines whether the vision expands to new possibilities or limits perception. Brown concurs, "Growth may be defined as a process of disidentification from past limited perceptions of ourselves and the world and identifying with new, more inclusive integrating ones."[5] We need to identify with each new stage as a way of incorporating it before letting it go to move to yet another stage of development.

IDENTIFICATION RELATES TO WHO ONE THINKS ONE IS, USUALLY AT AN UNCONSCIOUS LEVEL.

Identification

Assagioli maintained that "we are dominated by everything with which we become identified. We can dominate and control everything from which we disidentify ourselves."[6] In other words, if someone is unconsciously identified with a subpersonality, the person acts in the world as if she or he were this character and no one else. For example, if someone has a "wild" subpersonality, he or she may dress in ways that attempt to shock others and may believe that behavior must be outrageous. Freedom to act quietly and softly is inhibited. The person, who has many other attributes and qualities, "becomes" only the "wild one." The more unconscious the process, the more that the subpersonality dominates. All subpersonalities have narrow perceptions of the world, so one's choices are consequently limited when in this identification.

With results just as restricting, the person can also identify with the body, an emotion such as fear or anger, or thoughts. When one learns to stand back from the part, one can identify with a more integrated whole and, therefore, become in charge of the part. The person can have a "wild" part that expresses appropriately and also possess and express other varying personality characteristics.

A person may even prematurely identify with a mistaken notion of the Self. That person might say, "My Higher Self told me to do this," as justification for a subpersonality's actions. When that occurs, ego inflation and grandiosity interfere with a clear view. This condition is often called "premature transcendence" in psychosynthesis, indicating that the person wants to soar above personal conflict and disharmony before the personality has been adequately integrated.

Disidentification

Learning to disidentify from the parts in order to have greater perspective is central to psychosynthesis theory and practice. In order to disidentify from a subpersonality, one may first identify with a more mature subpersonality such as "the good parent" or "the teacher." Yeomans says that most people have a subpersonality that is more mature than the others, the "relatively mature identification," which is more accessible than the personality self.[7] An example would be someone who does a good job of being a mother, a teacher or a therapist even though that person may have other parts that have greater unmet needs and, therefore, greater distortion. The "mother" may be called upon to help with a hurting, child part. In early integration work, it may be sufficient to experience that "relatively mature" identification. Eventually, one identifies with the integrated personality self and ultimately with the Self.

Disidentification generally occurs first by moving from one subpersonality to another. For example, someone with both victim and persecutor subpersonalities may switch from one to the other, first identified with one and then with the other. A man who feels he is powerless (victim) at work, where he must work long hours for low pay, may become abusive (persecutor) to his wife at home. By learning how to meet the needs of both of these parts of himself through empowerment and love, the man enlarges his perspective. Gradually, he will be able to identify with the centered self and not be dominated by either subpersonality. In any case, practicing disidentification or objectivity towards the internal parts requires will and intentionality and provides more choice and freedom.

DISIDENTIFICATION GENERALLY OCCURS FIRST BY MOVING FROM ONE SUBPERSONALITY TO ANOTHER.

Maps of Consciousness

The "Egg" Map

Any map of the human psyche is at best a crude representation of the perception of reality; yet, a map is a tool to assist the reader in incorporating knowledge. Assagioli's "egg diagram"[8] of human consciousness, depicted in Figure 1, is such a map.

Figure 1

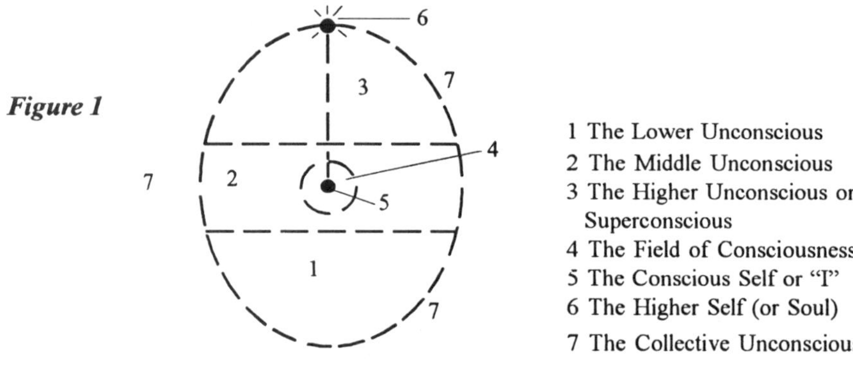

Dotted "boundary" lines indicate that contents of the unconscious can "leak" into different areas, even beyond the person into the collective unconscious which surrounds the egg map. In the collective realm (7), individuals' energy fields interpenetrate with each other, and humanity's archetypes, visions, and dreams from time immemorial abound. Even within an individual psyche the "boundaries" between dimensions of consciousness are permeable, indicating movement between these dimensions. The outer reaches of the "egg" are the most difficult to consciously access.

The unconscious, as shown on the map, has three levels: the lower unconscious (1), the middle unconscious (2), and the superconscious (3). These are, of course, only arbitrary divisions to provide clarity, and contain no judgment about one level being better or worse than another. The lower unconscious (1) mainly represents our personal psychological past in the form of repressed complexes and forgotten memories. The middle unconscious (2) resembles Freud's preconscious in that skills, states of mind, and memories can be quickly brought into conscious awareness.

The superconscious (3), the realm of the Transpersonal, inspires intuition, creativity, altruistic love, and humanitarian action. Crampton assures us that "as the energies of the superconscious are increasingly contacted, the ability is gained to approach the confusion, the pain, and the distortions of the past with clearer vision and with greater compassion and understanding."[9] The superconscious provides the ground of being for the Transpersonal Self. At this time of crisis and shifting paradigms, the planet desperately needs the transpersonal characteristics of universality, dynamic action, unconditional love and creative wisdom present in the Self.

The field of consciousness (4) within the middle unconscious represents the focus of one's present awareness. If the field of awareness were a flashlight, its beam could be shined into any area of the psyche. One could momentarily be aware of great inspiration, and the flashlight beam would be somewhere in the superconscious. One could become aware of a painful, repressed memory from early childhood, and the light would momentarily shine into the lower unconscious. As material is brought into awareness, it then often becomes part of the middle unconscious, more easily accessible than previously.

A dot (5) in the very center of the circle represents the personal self, the ego as presented in ego psychology, or the "I." The personal self is a center of awareness and purpose, and it serves an integrative and synthetic function. The personal self is responsible for personality integration, the resolution of splits, fragmentation, and conflicting tendencies within the personality. Assagioli saw the personal self or "I" as the reflection of the Higher Self (6), referred to in this book as the Self, and, therefore, connected these two aspects by a dotted line. The personal self and spiritual Self represent the same reality experienced at different levels, our real essence beyond all masks and conditioning.

THE SYSTEMIC MAP

A second diagram shown in Figure 2 portrays the systemic nature of human consciousness.

Figure 2

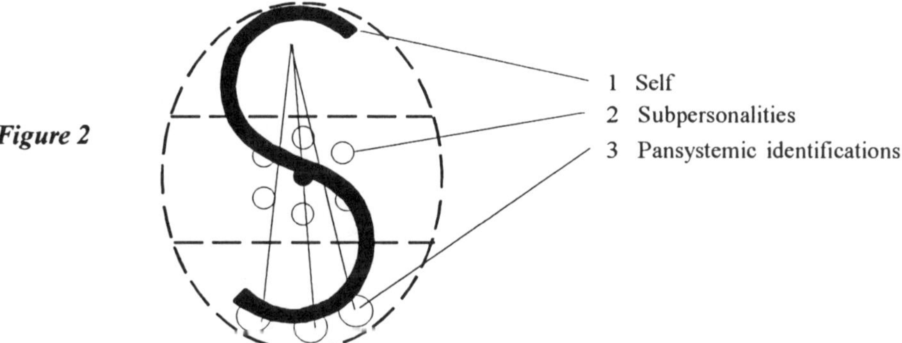

In this figure adapted from Yeomans,[10] subpersonalities (2) are represented by the ring of little circles around the "I" or personal self in the center of the egg diagram. They are all interconnected, except in the case of multiple personality disorder, in which the subpersonalities have become so dissociated and split off that there seems to be no "connecting tissue" between them. Identification moves about from one subpersonality to the other and eventually back to the center or personality self more and more of the time.

The circles at the base of the diagram in the lower unconscious represent those core beliefs that are often pre-verbal. Because these beliefs such as "I'm no good" or "life is hell" are deeply unconscious and not coalesced into a subpersonality, they seem to be pansystemic in their effect. They may be deep, parental introjects created from trauma, or they may be racial and cultural identifications that come from the collective unconscious. They bias, color and cast a shadow over the entire system. As those pansystemic identifications heal, the entire system shifts, sometimes dramatically. The deeper the healing, the greater the release of creative and spiritual energies. Yeomans has removed the Self from the top of the diagram and replaced it with the big capital S drawn throughout the map, since the Self provides the context for the whole system and acts as the organizing principle. Firman concurs, "Self can be thought of as ever-present and potentially active whether one is experiencing a traumatic memory from the lower unconscious, a peak experience from the higher unconscious, or a combination of the two. Self is always there."[11]

Synthesis

Integration and synthesis at the level of the personal self must come before deep, Transpersonal work, although glimpses may be seen of the joy and peace —or even the capacity to hold suffering—available from the Self. Aurobindo called the personality the instrument of the Self,[12] and the instrument must be in good playing order.

What, then, are the characteristics of an integrated, healthy self (with a little s)? When one identifies with the self, the person operates from a center of clear awareness and purpose. There is a sense of "being home" in one's true identity with the experience of uniqueness and individuality that feels right. Walsh and Vaughan note that "a movement toward health does not entail changing what we are but rather recognizing what we are."[13]

Just as the Self is an illumined, organizing principle, so the personality self acts as a unifying center around which the personality can be integrated. Psychosynthesis is analogous to a symphony orchestra. If the music is created by the composer at Transpersonal levels, then the conductor of the orchestra is the personality self which regulates and directs various elements and functions of the personality such as body sensations, thoughts and feelings and even subpersonalities. The conductor uses appropriate will to harmonize the personality, creating a beautiful symphony.

References for Chapter 2

[1]. Assagioli, 1965, p. 30.
[2]. Ferrucci, 1982, p. 48.
[3]. Crampton, 1981, p. 712.
[4]. Assagioli, 1974.
[5]. Brown, 1983, p. 28.
[6]. Assagioli, 1965, p. 22.
[7]. Yeomans, 1989.
[8]. Assagioli, 1965.
[9]. Crampton, 1981, p. 714.
[10]. Yeomans, 1989.
[11]. Firman, 1991, p. 92.
[12]. Green, 1978, p. 48.
[13]. Walsh & Vaughan, 1980, p. 121.

CHAPTER 3

Correspondence With The Cosmos: Astrology Principles

The human being who is willing and ready to be a self-actualized and truly individualized person must find no fault in what he essentially is. He essentially is a celestial archetype; he is born at a particular time and in a particular location because the all-encompassing Harmony of the universe dictated that such an archetypal solution to a particular need in the three-dimensional world of physical existence should take form as a human organism. This archetypal solution is "coded" in the language of the sky as the birth-chart of a particular person.—Dane Rudhyar[1]

Astrology in the Modern World

For eons human beings have been looking to the stars to orient themselves in time and space. Over the centuries, astrology evolved and changed from a system that was used to help plant crops, celebrate seasonal changes, plan warfare and advise kings to its present-day use as an in-depth psychological tool to help us understand ourselves and our lives, including our correspondence with the cosmos. As a psychological tool astrology works, not because of a cause and effect relationship with the stars and planets, but as correspondence. Jung's concept of synchronicity applies to these meaningful correspondences between who we are and the movement of the planets. "As above, so below," goes the ancient saying which we can now interpret as the synchronous correspondence between our personalities and the unfolding of our lives with the rhythms and cycles of the cosmos. The universe appears to be an orderly one in which meaningful synchronicities abound, astrology being a very significant one.

Transpersonal Astrology

Just as psychology can be understood on many different levels—from personal to transpersonal—so can astrology, depending upon a person's world view. Some people see the ancient art of astrology as a tool to predict events in the lives of people and the affairs of the world, interpreting the world from a mechanistic, cause-and-effect point of view. For them, astrology is event-centered rather than person-centered, terms coined by the late, great astrologer, Dane Rudhyar. According to Rudhyar, "The birth-chart is seen as a mandala symbolizing the whole person in the fullness of interrelated functional activities"[2] for the humanistic astrologer.

Going a step further, the transpersonal approach to astrology is open to the radiance of the Self as a unifying center. Each person is viewed with vision that includes both fragmentation or subpersonalities and at the same time a Self. In actuality, the person has always been a Self although most people do not realize this.

Transpersonal astrology holds life sacred. The person who uses this approach must try to have a thorough understanding of the unfolding of psychological and spiritual processes and keep open to intuitive perceptions as the information in the birth chart unfolds. In addition, the transpersonal approach allows compassionate detachment from the outcome and the choices that a person makes and, ideally, an attitude of unconditional acceptance. The astrologer does not determine someone's level of evolution but, rather, shares information about the continuum of possibilities.

The astrological chart, which contains the placements of the Sun, Moon, planets and other symbols in the exact position that they appeared at the moment of one's birth, represents a blueprint of that individual's potential waiting to be actualized. Every detail in the chart symbolizes an aspect of this unique individual. This vast, intricately complex set of symbols interweave and interconnect with each other in rich patterns.

The astrological chart points the way to self-actualization. Eventually, as we become more truly individuated, even cultural overlays on the personality can be transcended. The vast amount of familial, social and cultural conditioning with which we usually unconsciously identify becomes a barrier to true expression of the inner Being but can be transcended with awareness. As we reach a more encompassing perspective, we can choose to utilize the social and cultural patterns as tools rather than mandates.

. . .AS WE BECOME MORE TRULY INDIVIDUATED, EVEN CULTURAL OVERLAYS ON THE PERSONALITY CAN BE TRANSCENDED.

Even though each of us has the potential to eventually be free from these outer influences, we do not override personality patterns as represented by the aspects and positions of the planets in signs and houses. Liz Greene comments, "...people become more like, rather than less like their horoscopes as consciousness of self increases. Far from 'transcending' the birth chart, the individual seems to become more at home in it; he and it begin to fit each other; and concurrently, he is more at home in himself as what he is."[3] Of course, too little is known about the astrological charts of those few people existing at the highest rungs of personal evolution whose mode of self is "formless Self-realization and transcendent witness,"[4] to quote Ken Wilber, to know whether

her statement continues to hold true at these stages. However, this is not a practical concern of most astrologers, even those practicing from a transpersonal perspective.

Many astrology clients who are quite aware express delight as the words they hear describing their potentials resonate with their inner core. In speaking of good therapy, Welwood says, "Statements having this transforming effect are those that resonate with the implicit and allow it to unfold, either gradually or in a sudden 'opening up.'...Once the implicit has opened up,...it is never quite the same again."[5]

The Astrological Chart as Mandala

The mandala form, which universally emanates from a center, has existed in a great diversity of cultures throughout history. With the eye being always drawn back to the center, mandalas evoke latent qualities which are symbolized within it. The mandala is symmetrical and usually circular with a variety of images and forms. Often mandalas are divided into quadrants as exemplified by many of the well-known native American medicine wheels and Tibetan meditation mandalas. Jose and Miriam Arguelles, authors of a book about mandalas, state, "At the core each man (and woman) is the center of his own compass and experiences, his own **cardinal points**, North, South, East and West."[6] The astrological chart, too, is a mandala with a circular shape and four cardinal points and four quadrants. The circular astrology chart literally represents the positions of the planets, the Sun and the Moon as they were at the moment of the first breath from the perspective of the place where the person is born. From that viewpoint, every planet overhead or from one horizon to the other appears on the top half of the chart. Everything that would have appeared to have been "on the other side of the earth" would be on the bottom half of the chart. The vertical axis represents the meridian above and below, and the horizontal axis represents the horizons—all as they would have been perceived from the time and place of one's birth. Thus, the person exists at the center-point of the cross between meridian and horizon, heaven and earth, just as the Self interfaces between the earthly self and the Universe.

The Self symbolically rests at the very center of the astrological chart, that place within the chart where all of the planetary patterns come together in one symphonic whole. Sensing the wisdom, love and power that reside in that central Self evokes images of radiant light and vibrant pulsations of shimmering energy as the Self connects with the Great Mystery. Yet, the Self also has the capacity to be fully present to the wounding that inevitably occurs to human beings, ranging from minor hurts for some to horrendous damage for others.

As the Self represents a hologram of the Universe, so does the mandala. Dychtwald affirms that "One of the simplest and most functional examples of the holographic paradigm is displayed in the expression of a mandala. . . .a particular aspect of life stands as a whole unto itself as well as a storehouse of information of some grander, larger whole."[7] The holographic Self exists symbolically at the very center of the astrological chart-mandala with each of the twelve signs of the zodiac, or songs of the soul, emanating out from that center as depicted in the following diagram.

At the center of the astrological mandala, eternal potential awaits unfolding and recognition. From the center of the mandala, we are guided on how to best release the potentials that are present from birth by discovering the synthesis of the highest forms

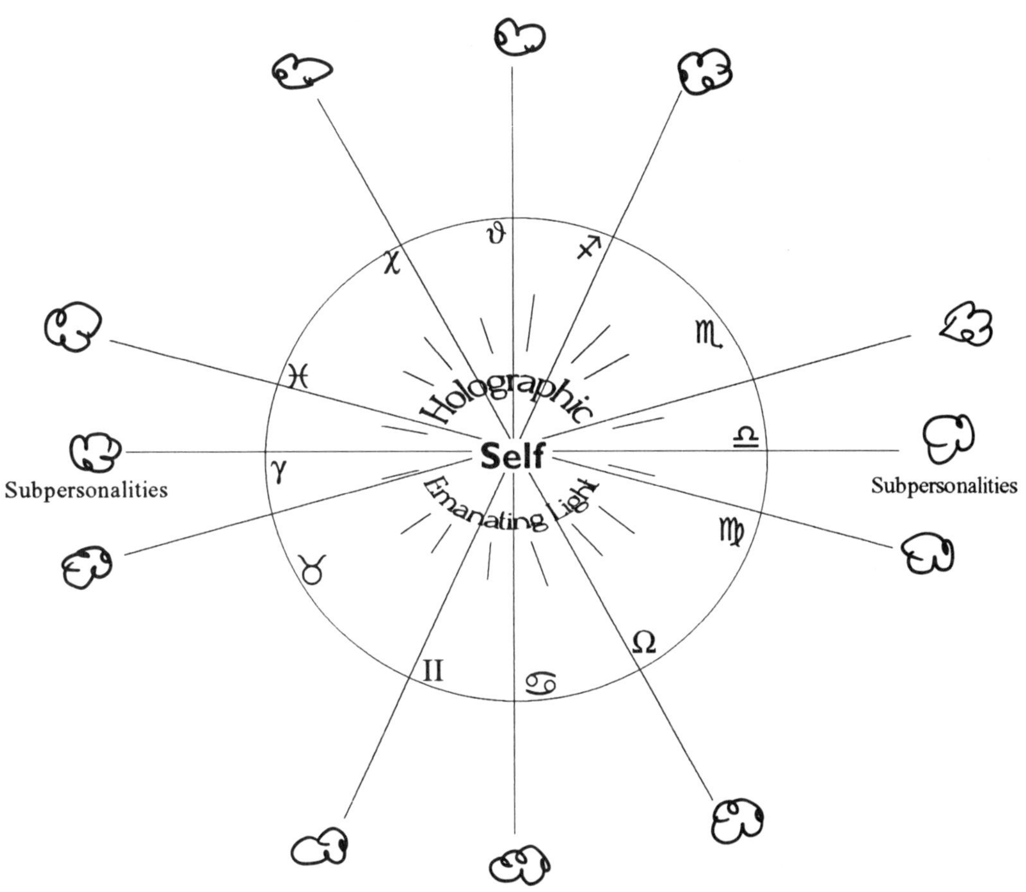

of each of the "songs of the soul." The songs of the soul refer to the various patterns which are represented by each of the twelve signs of the zodiac, each as a personality type and each with its own continuum of possibilities. All together, these "songs of the soul" represent the whole of the person. Sri Aurobindo said, "You must know the whole before you can know the part and the highest before you can truly understand the lowest."[8]

Astrological Patterns

The scope of this book cannot include a discussion of the specifics of houses, aspects or the many other details which astrologers must know in depth in order to offer consultations. However, the reader should know that each astrological pattern discussed in this book includes more that the zodiacal sign any particular planet occupies. Each "song of the soul" or pattern includes signs, houses, aspects, and groupings of planets.

The houses of an astrology chart are really divisions of space, and each one of the twelve houses corresponds with an area of our life such as home, relationships, career, etc. Each house also corresponds with the natural home of one of the signs of the zodiac such as the first house being the natural home of Aries. So, several planets that fall into the first house would create an Aries pattern, regardless of the sign that they actually occupy. The actual sign of these same planets would be another pattern.

THE HOUSES OF AN ASTROLOGY CHART ARE REALLY DIVISIONS OF SPACE, AND EACH ONE OF THE TWELVE HOUSES CORRESPONDS WITH AN AREA OF OUR LIFE SUCH AS HOME, RELATIONSHIPS, CAREER, ETC.

How the planets are configured in the chart and the mathematical relationships of one planet to another comprise what are called aspects. For example, if the planet Pluto were at the same degree in the same zodiac sign as the Sun at someone's birth, these two heavenly bodies would be considered to be "conjunct," or if they were ninety degrees apart, they would have a "square" aspect. When planets form these kind of relationships, the combination can be seen as a pattern. For example, the Sun in close aspect with Pluto will have Plutonian characteristics. Because Pluto is the planet associated with Scorpio, this combination will resonate as a Scorpio pattern as well as the pattern of the actual sign that the Sun occupies. If the Sun happened to be in the sign of Scorpio in this case, that pattern would be intensified. Therefore, the pattern or "song of the soul" called Aries would include planets and the Sun or Moon in that sign and planets which fall in the first house of the chart and planets which closely aspect Mars, the planet associated with Aries.

Each of the zodiacal patterns represents personality characteristics with its own continuum of possible expressions from the most distorted to the most integrated. Each chart may have several themes, although two or three usually predominate. For example, a person with a Pisces Sun, Neptune (ruler of Pisces) conjunct the Sun, and four planets in the twelfth house (natural home of Pisces) possesses an abundance of Pisces energy. We must examine the Pisces continuum carefully in order to understand this person. If that same person's Moon is in the sign of Scorpio and has three planets in the eighth house (natural home of Scorpio), Scorpio will also be an important continuum.

The Continuum of Astrological Patterns

The astrology chart provides a picture of the various continuums that comprise a person's destiny. Just as the experience of consciousness moves on a continuum from the most unconscious to the most enlightened, the expression of the twelve astrological signs also ranges along a spectrum of possibilities. We choose how to express Aries, Cancer, or other zodiacal patterns depending upon our level of evolution.

The most self-actualized, archetypal expressions for each of the twelve signs of the zodiac exist at one end of each of those continuums. At one end of each continuum, the harmonizing, radiant light from the Self seems to shine upon the pattern, evoking its highest meaning and purpose. On the astrological mandala, this ideal end of each of the twelve zodiacal continuums for each sign exists at the very center of the chart where all twelve converge. When personality patterns express this closely to center, to the ideal, the person experiences inner harmony. Living close to the center of the chart—the center of Being—creates wholeness and catalyzes even further synthesis.

From this perspective, crisis is welcomed, for it represents an opportunity to transform self-limiting views and pain into a greater wholeness and to consciously participate in one's own birth of Self-awareness. Rudhyar explains:

> "On the transpersonal way, everything can and should be used as the fuel to keep the fire of conscious transformation burning. All that at first produced conflicts, fear, insecurity, and. . .passionate and possessive attachments can be used. As the process unfolds, the human being within the limits of his natal potentialities, becomes the manifestation of a transcendent purpose, be it seen as a social, planetary or divine purpose."[9]

At the subpersonality end of the continuum, much inner conflict and turbulence arises. Both ends of the spectrum contain the same seed energy. However, the characteristics at the distorted end rigidify into subpersonalities, each with its myopic view of life, each scratching to meet its needs and to survive. Placed on the mandala form, these crystallized, distorted forms can be placed far outside the edge of the circle to represent their distance from the center or the Self. From this place outside, they also symbolically represent subpersonalities' difficulty in perceiving any other aspect of the individual.

Conflict and dissonance from subpersonalities appear at one end of each of the twelve zodiacal continuums. However, just because we have subpersonalities and experience the distorted end of the continuum does not mean we are doomed to misery. Through transformation, we emerge from suffering and express at a different place on the same continuum. Then the higher or deeper energy of the Self can be released. Even the most mangled manifestation of an energy pattern contains its own seed for transformation.

Sometimes a person identifies with only one personality characteristic—usually a subpersonality—with the flash light beam of conscious awareness seemingly stuck in this one focus. If a woman with an Aquarius Sun and a Pisces Moon strongly identifies with her very independent, free-spirited clear-thinking, detached Aquarian qualities, she may deny the sensitivity and feelings that arise from her Pisces Moon. She quickly tries to eradicate any surfacing emotions, considering them too "mushy" to be of value and not representative of her true personality. If she were experiencing life more from the center or Self, she would be able to own and honor both her thinking and feeling qualities.

Even though the Self is depicted in the center of the mandala, few people experience life from this perspective on a daily basis. The middle of the continuum is represented symbolically by the planets which "reside" in signs and houses inside the outer circle. From the middle of the continuum, the twelve personality types are experienced in a relatively healthy manner by our cultural standards. Most people experience these aspects of themselves in the middle of the continuum—not from the purity of Self and not from extreme distortions on the other end, although some subpersonalities are very common. At this stage of evolution, we are not "perfect," nor do we suffer too greatly from destructive impulses. We sense an integrated self, even through subpersonalities may crop up from time to time.

Choice and Free Will

Each continuum converges into the center of the mandala—astrological chart where awareness of the existence of Self may be conscious and choice is usually perceived. If we cooperate with the Universal Self and do not overly express our personal, selfish will, we become a channel for the Universal Self. If not, then we miss a great opportunity. The choice is in our hands.

The theme of personal choice and free will pervades all of the perspectives presented thus far. What is not a choice, though, once the person is born, is what personality or astrological patterns he or she will predominantly work with in this lifetime. If one is born with the Sun in Leo, one cannot decide to not have Leo personality characteristics, lessons, or gifts. The choice remains **how** to utilize these energies and where to creatively act on the continuum. The closer to the center, the Self, we live, the more we are aware of self-responsibility, self-determination and choice.

The further out on the continuum we experience life, the less we perceive choice as possible because of the distorted, defensive views of the subpersonalities. From the distorted side of the continuum, choices are made without conscious awareness. The universe may seem to provide crises, and others may seem to be the cause of our misery and suffering. Since conscious choice has been negated, most subpersonalities share an element of victim-consciousness. Even an aggressive subpersonality such as the "bully" believes he has no choice except to be a bully. Beliefs held by the subpersonalities unconsciously attract painful experiences. Rarely does a person clearly decide, "I want more suffering." For example, a person who has a strong caretaker subpersonality may continually attract people who seem to want caretaking. One woman said that alcoholics spotted her a mile away, and she could not understand why seemingly weak people continued to burden her life. She did not experience time for herself, and no one seemed to appreciate her sacrifices. She did not say, "I love taking care of people who do not want to take care of themselves." Instead, her subpersonality unconsciously believed that she would have no value if she did not rescue.

With his perennial wisdom, Rudhyar says,

> The transpersonal philosopher-astrologer...is dealing with a mystery—with man's essential freedom: the freedom to fail, and thus to begin again, perhaps wiser and more open to the Divine, because he has met in his deepest depths the experiences of fear and despair—man's greatest enemies—and he is still trying, always trying.[10]

As choices that enhance wholeness are made throughout lifetimes, the person becomes more capable of being a symphony rather than an out-of-tune band. Eventually, one becomes the music of the spheres, at one with the Universe. The holographic mandala resonates with the One Great Sound.

REFERENCES FOR CHAPTER 3

[1]. Rudhyar, 1975, p. 44.
[2]. Rudhyar, 1975, p. 76.
[3]. L. Greene, 1984, p. 317.
[4]. Wilber, 1980, p. 73.
[5]. Welwood, 1982, pp. 131-132.
[6]. Arguelles & Arguelles, 1972, p. 12.
[7]. Dychtwald, 1982, p. 106-107.
[8]. Sri Aurobindo quoted in Sat Prem, 1984, p. 247. (Original source is On Yoga II, Tome 2, p. 689.)
[9]. Rudhyar, 1975, p. 77.
[10]. Rudhyar, 1975, p. 65.

PART II

Modes of Expression

CHAPTER 1

Elemental Energies: The Triplicities

The symbolism of astrology is an attempt to portray...the basic energies behind life and behind human beings.— Liz Greene[1]

Central to all life on this planet are the four elements of fire, air, earth and water. Ancients from many cultures knew about the elements, and modern physicists cite four states of matter: radiant and ionized energy (fire); gaseous (air); solid (earth); and liquid (water). Indeed, astrology itself cannot be understood without a thorough knowledge of these elements as they are expressed through the zodiacal signs. Whether the astrologer is interested in the mundane or the transpersonal, an understanding of the elements provides insight and perspective. Arroyo states:

> The four elements are not merely 'symbols' or abstract concepts, but rather ... they refer to the vital forces that make up the entire creation that can be perceived by the physical senses. This is why the zodiac was referred to in ancient times as the 'soul of nature.' The elements are therefore not only the foundation of astrology ... but they comprise everything we can normally perceive and experience.[2]

The elements are interwoven into the fabric of nature and of the human experience. We can literally be nourished by our predominant element which is the experience of "being in one's element," whether that be abundant sunshine for the fire person, time beside oceans, lakes and streams for the water person, a few hours in a beautiful garden for the earth person, or a tantalizing discussion or hot air balloon ride for the air person. One's very approach to life is reflected in the elements: those who are receptive, yielding and introspective express the yin energies of water and earth; those persons who are active, assertive and outwardly expressive reflect a predominance of the yang energies of fire and air. The terms, "yin" and "yang" seem less gender-oriented than feminine and masculine which are traditionally used in astrology to describe these two sets of elements.

Even our mode of perceiving and relating to others is highly correlated with the elements, as is our personal style of problem solving and conflict resolution. Persons with a lot of water and earth in their horoscope expect their fire friends to be more gentle and sensitive, less exuberant. Air and fire people often become annoyed because water people avoid confrontation and respond indirectly. Without realizing that each individual is composed of a unique, intricate pattern of energies, even the most perceptive and astute of us often make assumptions that the rest of the world should experience life the same way. Not so.

Each of the twelve signs of the zodiac is classified as either fire, air, earth or water, each element being an integral part of how the sign is expressed. Jung, himself an astrologer, utilized the four elements in his four personality types: intuitive, sensation, thinking and feeling.[3] These types are closely allied with the four elements, essentially, different semantics for the same phenomena. Jung's personality types, in turn, are incorporated into the Myers Briggs Personality Inventory and the Keirsey Temperament Sorter, measures known to a large number of psychologists, social workers and counselors.

Elements	Jung's Temperaments	Astrological Signs
Fire	Intuitive	Aries, Leo and Sagittarius
Earth	Sensation	Taurus, Virgo and Capricorn
Air	Thinking	Gemini, Libra and Aquarius
Water	Feeling	Cancer, Scorpio and Pisces

According to Jung, by the age of thirty, most people have consciously developed two of the functions, one a "superior" function and the second an "auxiliary" function. A third function is often partially developed by mid- life, and the fourth is rarely fully developed, thus generally remaining unconscious. Usually, early in our development, we begin to identify with one mode of being over the others. For example, one person might identify as a "feeling" type rather than being a "thinking" type. The "feeler" often believes that this mode of being in the world is superior to that of "thinkers" who seem too aloof and detached for the water person's comfort. On the other hand, the air person may be disdainful of the perceived over-emoting by the water person.

The "inferior" function, as Jung called the undeveloped fourth mode of being, is often projected onto another person. That is, while seeing another person as wrong or defective for having a certain quality, a person disowns that same quality which he, in truth, also possesses. Instead, he sees only his own supposedly sterling qualities which are unlike those that are projected.

Conversely, sometimes the individual overcompensates for an element that is lacking. For example, a person who lacks water may try too hard to be emotionally expressive, although coming across as inauthentic and stylized. With enough developmental years, though, the inferior function may become more conscious and, therefore, more natural although never as fully as in someone in whom that element predominates.

In certain cultural or family groups, one element may be highly prized, and those persons whose natural element is different may try hard to be like everyone else. The shy, quiet, water child may try to be more exuberant in a fiery family, the result being strain and a feeling of inferiority for not being more outgoing. In a healthy family, the parents recognize that differences exist in the makeup of each individual and that differences are acceptable. In that way, each member of the family is encouraged to fully express his uniqueness and not be forced unnaturally into a group mold.

IN A HEALTHY FAMILY, THE PARENTS RECOGNIZE THAT DIFFERENCES EXIST IN THE MAKEUP OF EACH INDIVIDUAL AND THAT DIFFERENCES ARE ACCEPTABLE.

Assagioli, the founder of psychosynthesis, recognized the human characteristic of becoming too identified with one way of being and developed a dis-identification exercise which, condensed, states: "I have a body (earth, sensing), but I am more than my body. I have emotions (water, feeling), but I am more than my emotions. I have a mind (air, thinking; and possibly fire, intuition), but I am more than my mind. I am a center of pure self- consciousness. I am a center of will, capable of mastering, directing and using all my psychological processes and my physical body."[4] Therefore, even though we may more closely identify with one element, we must recognize that our real essence goes beyond fire, air, earth and water characteristics. The key, then, in working with our own elements within is not to think that one is better than another but to be able to honor our most dominant mode as our way of being in the world and at the same time to dis-identify from thinking it is our whole essence. From the more centered position, choices are possible. We can choose when to fully embrace an element and when to consciously develop another, when to nurture ourselves by "feeding" our predominant element and when to pull back. Sometimes, a fire person needs to be nurtured by lying in the sun, fully "soaking up" the element of fire. At other times, this fire person may need to learn more about the emotional sensitivity of water, momentarily backing away from the predominant element of fire.

In determining how the elements are distributed within an individual personality, the astrologer first counts how many planets reside in each sign, by element. For example, Sun and Mercury in Taurus, Mars and Jupiter in Capricorn, and Saturn in Virgo equal five planets in the element of earth. Next, the astrologer counts how many planets fall in fire, air, earth and water houses. For example, a planet in the first, fifth or ninth houses, natural fire houses, counts as fire. Therefore, even though each person has some of each element, some individuals may possess an overabundance of one element and lack another. A person with the Sun in Capricorn (earth), the Moon in Virgo (earth) and six planets in the second house (an earth house) has a great preponderance of earth energy and considerably less of the other elements. This person may be so rooted in the material world that he forgets there is a spiritual dimension to life. Other individuals, however, have a more proportional balance of the elements.

Too much or too little of an element usually manifests in subpersonalities or distortions. For instance, the very earthy person may express disdain for intellectual persons, considering them too idealistic to be of value, and calling them "pointy-headed intellectuals." The aggressiveness of someone with an abundance of fire might be difficult to cope with in a work situation. More of these distortions, as well as the most ideal expressions, will be explained in following chapters.

Just as the signs of the zodiac express on a continuum of possibilities, so do the elements. How does fire express at the level of Self? How does the expression of fire become distorted? What characterizes fire as it is expressed at the personality level in a human being? What gifts does a fire person possess? We can ask these questions for each of the elements. The more we are aware of the spectrum of possibilities, the more tools we have to assist us in the integration into Self.

A brief imagery experience to assist in capturing the essence of the energy of the element begins each of the chapters on the four elements. Any of the following suggestions may help deepen your experience: 1) read the imagery over several times so that you can recite it with your eyes closed; 2) have another person read it softly while you listen; 3) read it into a tape recorder so that you may listen with your eyes closed; 4) read it slowly with your eyes open. In any method, pause long enough at the dots to allow images to register.

Your own impressions can add a richer and more fuller understanding to what is written here. Essentially, all of our experiences are valid, for they transcend rational, linear understandings. Messages about "essence" come through intuitive means. Art, movement, dance, poetry, visions, images, and pure "knowing" often serve as a bridge to our understanding of this non-linear essence to the conscious mind.

References for Chapter 1

1. L. Green, 1980, p.15
2. Arroyo, 1975, p. 87-88.
3. Jung, 1971.
4. Assagioli, 1965.

CHAPTER 2

Fire

The element fire refers to a universal radiant energy, an energy which is excitable, enthusiastic, and which through its light brings color into the world.—Stephen Arroyo[1]

Affiliated Signs:	Aries, Leo, Sagittarius
Affiliated Houses:	1, 5, 9
Ruling Planets:	Mars, Sun, Jupiter

Imagery Experience for Fire

I invite you to close your eyes to get in as comfortable position as possible to experience the following meditation upon the essence of fire. Take a few moments to allow your breath to return you to center. ... Be aware of the vitality and the sparkling life force in the breath as it is expands throughout your body. ... From the highest point of wisdom and safety, sense the Spirit that is Fire. Allow an image to come to your mind for fire in its most pure essence. ... What are its qualities? ... Allow your body to move as if it were this fire. Experience the qualities of fire as you move. ... When you have completed this experience, allow some time to write or draw what you learned to further deepen your experience.

Essence End of the Continuum

At the heart of fire is the urge to express universal, radiant energy into the world. Fire signs represent the spiritual side of our natures.[2] Joy and exuberance leap forth from fire. Fire is an irrepressible love for life that uplifts, inspires, warms and heals those it touches. The fire person is a channel for the life force itself, radiating it into the world as an expression of Divine Spirit. Images of golden, red and orange colors passionately flare as the Self flames into an active livingness. The "Lord of the Dance," a title of a song, represents the essence of fire. In all of these metaphors, Jung's words hold true: "Intuition (fire) is not mere perception or vision, but an active, creative process that puts into the object just as much as it takes out."[3]

Middle of the Continuum

Several key phrases for fire qualities emerge as they are expressed at the middle of the continuum:

- Creative and expressive,
- Courageous and self assertive,
- Direct and honest,
- Ardent and strong,
- Generous and warm,
- Freedom oriented, and
- Intuitive.

Creative and expressive

Fire's action-oriented creativity is expressed through a childlike spontaneity and exuberance. When the fire person experiences creative ideas, the urge to express is usually immediate and may seem impulsive to less fiery types. The fire person becomes impatient with delays in expression, and if a delay is necessary, she or he may become excited about newer plans and drop the old idea. The fire person seeks fresh, new opportunities to express the upwelling creativity and may lose interest in old projects that have lost vibrancy and newness. They love exploring new possibilities and feel suffocated by old, stable conditions. Liz Greene states, "It is more important to him to experience life dramatically than to accept the apparently drab and sometimes threatening world that more pragmatic types insist he recognize as the real one."[4] They are colorful in personality and in dress, for the inner color seeks constant expression.

Courageous and self-assertive

Perhaps because fire continually seeks expression in the world, fire signs are noted for strength, courage, and the ability to consciously direct their will power. The closer the fire person is to her or his own center, the more the will serves as an expression of what is best for the innermost Self. To the fire person, deciding and acting upon this inner wisdom may not even seem like an act of courage but, rather, simply doing what needs to be done. Throughout history, the finest warriors, whether male or female, have demonstrated willpower which emanates from the Self. On the other hand, many fire people gratify their egos by exerting their wills upon the outer world and even upon their own inner psyches, unaware of the needs of others or of their own gentler, quieter side.

To the fire person, deciding and acting upon this inner wisdom may not even seem like an act of courage. . .

Direct and honest

They communicate directly, honestly and openly and prefer the same treatment from others. Fire people often speak of "laying their cards on the table," meaning openness and honesty in communication. They have difficulty understanding why everyone is not similarly direct. With less integration, the fire person may try to force perceptions down other people's throats in the name of being truthful.

Ardent and enthusiastic

Arroyo notes that fire signs are proud of being channels for life.[5] High spirited, fire people are noted for their exuberance and zest for life. Any project requiring a cheerleader needs a person with some fire to enthusiastically propel it ahead. As the fire rises, the person has the urge to follow the vision of what is possible. For Aries, the dream might be wanting to pioneer a project for other-planet-inhabitation or of winning the next race; for Leo, the call might be to create a visionary theater piece or to lead a rousing march; the Sagittarian might teach others how to reach their highest potential. The person filled with soaring Fire, not doused with water or snuffed out by earth, exudes confidence, unmarred by doubt—of self or others. All is possible to these high-spirited folks, and they offer inspiration and optimism to others. Even though fire people hate routine and become bored with dogged perseverance, they remain faithful to the ideal.

> The person filled with soaring Fire. . . exudes confidence. . .

People with an abundance of fire energy require physical activity in order for the juices to flow and to feel alive. They love being out of doors, especially in the sunshine. Sometimes, though, these confident, impulsive types push through life as if they were speedboats, oblivious to surroundings, aware only of the thrill of the speed, the wind rushing through their hair, and the excitement of another adventure. These qualities appear early in life. One fire child is even known to have confidently toddled more than half a mile, headed for her grandmother's house many miles away.

Generous and warm

Fire people often lavish warmth and affection on others, even though they are not always sensitive as to how it is being received. In a group setting, they frequently speak first, breaking through the barriers of shyness and protectiveness, reaching out to others in an open, ingenuous way. Some people bask in this warmth and sunshine, finding their fire friends endearing and uplifting. Others experience them as too much, too soon and too overpowering. Dobyns notes that the generosity of fire is born out of the confidence that they always have the capacity to obtain more,[6] so why not give this away?

Freedom oriented

Fire types hate being imprisoned by anything, anyone, anywhere. They strongly prefer being their own bosses and not being told what to do. In relationships, they want space to move about so that they don't feel tied down. They need room in which to express their exuberance and creativity without feeling restrained. Some fire persons even report that they dislike wearing hats because of not wanting to feel confined.

Intuitive

Jung used "intuitive" as a synonym for the expression of fire. Yet, fire types often consciously mistrust the intuitive process even while unconsciously acting upon hunches based upon perceived undercurrents. Used to responding quickly, the fire person acts instinctively upon gut reactions, confident that something will provide a solution. Their intuitive perceptions are focused upon objects, not of a direct sensory nature, but rather, more of a seizing and shaping of the object. Jung talks about extroverted and introverted intuitives, and by definition, pure fire in astrology is the extroverted type as has been discussed in this chapter. Jung's introverted intuitive would be a person with both a predominance of fire and a lot of water or earth as well. With this blend, the introverted fire person's objects become internal images rather than external objects, this being especially true with a water and fire combination. Jung said that, for this type, "unconscious images acquire the dignity of things."[7] Out of this combination is born the mystic, the prophet, or the weirdo if badly distorted. For both extroverted and introverted intuitives, perceptions of inner or outer objects directly influence their actions.

Lack of fire

If no planets are placed in fire signs or the natural fire houses and no close aspects to other planets are made from the Sun, Mars or Jupiter, the chart lacks fire. When fire is lacking, the person lacks spirit, inspiration, and a zest for life. Confidence and enthusiasm may be low, and digestion may even be poor. This person mistrusts life, and his personality may be lackluster. The person so born may increase inner fire by exercising moderately. Energy enhancing exercises like chi gong, tai chi, and special breathing practices help create internal fire. Confidence can be increased by learning affirmations and other practices designed to inspire, and a deeper sense of spirit can be touched by finding a belief in a higher power.

WHEN FIRE IS LACKING, THE PERSON LACKS SPIRIT, INSPIRATION, AND A ZEST FOR LIFE.

Subpersonality End of the Continuum

The multitude of distortions of fire qualities is countless at the subpersonality end of the continuum as is true for each of the elements and signs. The descriptions which follow represent only samples of the many possibilities. Some subpersonalities remain rather harmless, easily healed and integrated into the personality. Other subpersonalities may be extremely distorted if bio-psycho-social-spiritual supports were chaotic or minimal in childhood. As described in Part I, Chapter 2, subpersonalities only become distorted because certain basic needs remain unmet. Natural qualities such as enthusiasm or high spiritedness twist as the person unconsciously grasps at the most feasible means to meet deep needs. The following subpersonalities could be milder or more extreme than described depending upon factors influencing the person's personality development.

The Zealot

Many people yearn for love and recognition, both basic needs. When either of these needs is unmet for the fire person, he may unconsciously attempt to meet those needs by leading an impassioned crusade of some kind. He is desperate for recognition, yearning even for God's approval. The fire qualities of vision, enthusiasm, courage, and strength become hardened, the person single-mindedly championing a cause. The Zealot, filled with flaming zeal, develops an unrelenting sense of his own point of view. Only by finding alternative ways of meeting these needs and by consciously experiencing self-love can the Zealot heal enough to release those fire qualities in a more compassionate way.

Fire Truck

The Fire Truck might also be looking for love, or she might be compensating due to lacking a sense of safety. Perhaps others pushed too hard on her, inflicting their will upon her, and she, with her fire qualities of strength and self-assertiveness, learned to push her way through life. She is often unaware of the pain she inflicts through the imposition of her own will and authority on others. She can be ruthless, often destroying the efforts of others. When she has learned love for self and others, she will know that she is safe. Then, even without imposing her will, she can reclaim the gifts of this subpersonality: true assertiveness, containing compassion for self and others.

Don Quixote

The idealistic and impractical hero of Cervantes appears in some fire folks' repertoire of subpersonalities. The quest for the ideal, for that next greener pasture, for life itself, becomes a desperate search. He may become overwhelmed by physical passions and dash off to the next lover thinking "this is love," yet avoiding true intimacy. He may dart from continent to continent, fueled by his passionate dreams and free spirit. Yet, the life force may be dissipated and the ideal remain elusive in "this glorious quest." He needs a greater sense of self so that his dreams may be grounded more in reality and that he may experience joy in the present.

Burned Out

When a sense of Self, the integrating center, is missing, the fire element may burn out of control with nothing providing boundaries or inner control. In some senses, the freedom that the fire person so desperately seeks is gone because he is controlled and consumed by the fire itself. Her life can become so fast paced and hectic, her zeal so exuberant on any project, that she literally burns out, recklessly wasting the life force. In order to renew and replenish, this fire person has to learn a sense of self that goes beyond the raging fire, a sense of self that can provide a context in which the fire can burn brightly and creatively, not destructively.

Insensitive Egoist

To those familiar with the elements, this is probably the most famous of fire's subpersonalities. Most astrology books warn of fire's selfish, egocentric side that comes out when the fire person is intent upon gratifying his needs at the expense of others. Most likely, his needs remained unmet as a child, and he unwittingly fails to meet anyone else's needs. Sometimes the expression of his own creativity dominates his vision, and he becomes so absorbed in whatever he is doing that he is childlike, oblivious of his insensitivity to others' needs. He may not notice that everyone else is thirsty and that he has the only glass of water. He may not be aware that someone on his staff has a valuable idea as he pushes for his own. His boasts about conquests even in front of the defeated may simply be his way of increasing inner confidence, and he may be oblivious of the effect on others. Healed, this insensitive one becomes more aware of his surroundings and is able to use confidence and zest to inspire and uplift others as well as himself.

References for Chapter 2

[1]. Arroyo, 1975, p. 95.
[2]. Hickey, 1970, p. 56.
[3]. Jung, 1971.
[4]. L. Greene, 1978, p. 79.
[5]. Arroyo, 1975.
[6]. Dobyns, 1972.
[7]. Campbell, 1971, p. 259.

CHAPTER 3

Earth

An attunement to this element indicates that the individual is in touch with the physical senses and the here-and-now reality of the material world.—Stephen Arroyo[1]

Affiliated Signs:	Taurus, Virgo, Capricorn
Affiliated Houses:	2, 6, 10
Ruling Planets:	Venus, Mercury, Saturn

Imagery Experience for Earth

Become as comfortable as possible and close your eyes if that is right for you. Be aware of how your body is supported by the chair/floor and how the earth supports you. You can simply rest upon the earth. ... As you become aware of the breath, note how the breath carries sustenance to every cell of your body. ... Note how peace begins to fill your legs, the trunk of your body, your arms, your neck and shoulders and your head. ... Sense the Earth's presence with you. ... Allow an image to emerge for earth in its most pure essence. ... What are its qualities? ... Allow yourself to move as if you were totally Earth energy. ... When you have completed this experience, allow some time to write or draw what you learned to further deepen your experience.

Essence End of the Continuum

The rhythms of life itself beat at the heart of Earth energy. Earth connects us with natural, grounded processes born from the Earth and of its place in the cosmos. "To everything there is a season," states the sage in Ecclesiastes. Seasons change; women's menstrual cycles follow a rhythm; certain rhythms found even in insects change with the rising and setting of the moon; Jung talked about the developmental "seasons" that occur in human lives; astrology is the science of cosmic rhythms. Nikos Kazantzakis must have known the wisdom of inner patterns when he said, "Find the absolute rhythm and follow it with absolute trust."

Earth energy, at its essence, provides an awareness of the consciousness that exists in all of nature and in natural objects. Many teachers of Native American practices and crystal healing have a predominance of earth energy in their astrological charts. Earth Mother becomes a spiritual reality for those so attuned. In pure form, Earth energy is yin and receptive, absorbing information about life from the five senses. What is received is used both as an experience of being in the moment and as information for the service of others.

Middle of the Continuum

Several salient qualities hallmark Earth's expression at the personality level:

- Sensing;
- Practical and realistic;
- Stable and dependable;
- Deliberate and reserved;
- Enduring and self-disciplined;
- Preserving and protective;
- Productive.

Each of these qualities differ significantly from those of fire; yet each quality from all four of the elements is essential to our lives. No one person can embody all of the qualities. Rather, the planet itself includes the collective whole of these elements.

Sensing

Jung's sensation function in which the person directly experiences the universe through the senses is synonymous with Earth. Arroyo states, "The earth signs tend to rely more upon their senses and practical reason than upon the inspirations, theoretical considerations, or intuitions of the other signs. They are attuned to the world of 'forms' which the senses and practical mind regard as real."[2] Jung differentiates introverted and extroverted in a type.[3] Extroverted sensation involves perceiving and absorbing just what is on the surface. Extroverted sensation, by astrological definition, requires a blending of some fire or air into the earth element. Introverted earth people, on the other hand, see beyond the surface of nature, sensing the consciousness within all of nature. Some Earth types are even able to sense the presence of nature spirits or

> SOME EARTH TYPES ARE EVEN ABLE TO SENSE THE PRESENCE OF NATURE SPIRITS OR TO "SEE" THE ENERGY PATTERNS THAT INTERPENETRATE THE HUMAN FORM SUCH AS THE AURA, THE CHAKRAS, AND THE "SUBTLE BODIES."

to "see" the energy patterns that interpenetrate the human form such as the aura, the chakras, and the "subtle bodies."

Even in sensing of such beyond-the-surface properties, the Earth person still relates to what is tangible, even if not discerned by the naked eyes, ears or fingers. Earth people value tangibility. When they are artists, they often create functional and beautiful objects rather than getting lost in the abstract. In relationships, they like to give tangibly whether the gift is affection (mostly a Taurean concern), material things, or overt gestures of service. As bankers, managers, or executives, they like black and white results from their assets.

In touch with the material world, Taureans and Capricorns are especially at home with money and property, usually managing each with ease and common sense. Virgo, also very much in touch with the "real" world, concerns itself more with service than with material things, except details. All of these earth signs sustain life through natural processes. Even their humor is earthy, coming from their sensory experience of the world about them.

Practical and realistic

"Down to earth," sensible, practical, and realistic are the adjectives most often used to describe Earth persons. Uncluttered by wishful thinking, they see the world as it is and sense when to do things. They are cautious in making changes and will almost always have another job secured before leaving even hated employment. This practicality and frugality can range from solid, common sense to overly fearful caution, depending upon where on the continuum the person experiences life.

The Earth person considers necessities of life to be food for the belly, fuel for the furnace, and assets for the bank account, whereas other elements have different views.

> THE EARTH PERSON CONSIDERS NECESSITIES OF LIFE TO BE FOOD FOR THE BELLY, FUEL FOR THE FURNACE, AND ASSETS FOR THE BANK ACCOUNT. . .

A watery Piscean might believe that necessities are music and poetry, while an airy Gemini might think that essentials are yet another magazine subscription and another class to attend.

Earth people, especially Virgo and Capricorn, may even sacrifice their own emotional needs for practical concerns.

Stable and dependable

Often the backbone of family and community, these solid, dependable types are like rocks that others can lean on in times of crisis. They deal with real circumstances with a dependability that reassures others. While the fire person has galloped on to new vistas, the water person has swum in a sea of emotions, and the air person has become lost in the clouds, the Earth person is still there taking care of business at hand, comforting those still with him by his sheer, unmoving presence.

Deliberate and reserved

Carefully putting one foot in front of the other, one step at a time, the Earth person carefully makes his way through life making sure that he has stopped at the red light and proceeded at the green light. Although Virgos and Capricorns are slightly speedier than Taureans, all three Earth signs prefer not wasting their energy rashly. They like to know where they are going, why, and how.

In the same spirit, they are reserved with their emotions, generally emitting neither exuberance nor discouragement. Golda, the obviously Earth wife in *Fiddler on the Roof*, answers her husband's question about whether she loves him by saying that she has washed his laundry and darned his socks for twenty-five years. With this practical expression of devotion, she cannot understand why he even asks the question. Clearly, her husband Tevya's dominant element was one other than earth.

Enduring and self-disciplined

Whereas Fire types "rush in where angels fear to tread," Earth types sometimes stay in one place longer than even angels could bear. If they have reasonable material security and perhaps a somewhat satisfying sexual relationship (the latter especially true of Taureans), they can endure relationships that others would have long since abandoned. Perseverance may in the end prove wise for many, and, for others, self defeating if endurance is really another name for fear of giving up security. Their placement on the continuum will determine whether or not the choice to stay proves wise.

Earth folks know how to manage time and resources, and this skill carries them to the end of projects and whatever needs to be done. "Their innate understanding of how the material world functions gives the earth signs more patience and self-discipline than other signs. They rarely have to be told how to fit into the world of making a living, supplying basic needs, and persisting till a goal is reached,"[4] says Arroyo.

EARTH FOLKS KNOW HOW TO MANAGE TIME AND RESOURCES. . .

Preserving and protective

Security for an Earth person comes from knowing that resources are available and accessible. Those resources can range from money to property to vocation to family. In this sense, Earth persons are the true conservationists, protecting resources in the same way that a mother lion protects her cubs. Earth people may otherwise be fairly quiet and unassuming until their security is threatened. They may also desire to preserve the past as evidence of life's continuity. Capricorns, in particular, are noted for maintaining antiques and being historical buffs.

Productive

With all of the qualities so far discussed, Earth persons certainly have the tools for productivity. They are organized, industrious and often have management skills. Besides, being productive makes sense to the Earth person so that he can provide the continued resources for maintaining a secure place in the world. Earth urges to produce something in tangible form. They like to be of service, and they have a gift for actualizing desires in the material world. Isabel Hickey says that Taurus is the concentrator, Virgo the discriminator, and Capricorn the practical idealist,[5] all assets in dealing with producing in the "real" world.

Lack of earth

If no planets are placed in earth signs or natural earth houses, are unoccupied, and Venus, Mercury and Saturn make no close aspects to other planets, the chart lacks earth energy. Without the grounding that earth provides, people who lack this element may act "spaced," for they are not concerned with practical or material aspects of life. They may even seem out of place in the "normal" world, and others may refer to them as being from a different planet. Passionate journeys of the mind and spirit may seem more real to them than eating muffins and marmalade for breakfast. They may dream impossible dreams and lack the understanding of limitations that seems common sense to the Earth person. Paying bills and maintaining steady employment may not seem relevant because the material realm seems meaningless. Even their physical bodies may suffer from neglect while they are thinking of other important matters. Many who lack earth actually have to learn how to live in the body, rather than living a short distance from the body, or for some, a long distance. A healthy dose of Earth energy reminds us that we live in bodies on this earth plane for a purpose and how to do it well.

Although never experiencing life like a person born with an abundance of Earth energy, the person born with a lack can learn to compensate. Certain meditation practices such as Vipassna which focus upon awareness of the here-and-now help provide grounding. Any methods which focus on awareness of the body and the natural environment are helpful in becoming more earthy. Some people walk barefoot, learning to absorb more Earth energy.

Subpersonality End of the Continuum

The "If-I-Can't-See-It, It-Doesn't-Exist" Materialist

Perhaps growing up in a rigid home in which safety was only found in seeing everything as black and white, this subpersonality takes practicality and realism to the extreme. She trusts only her immediate environment, physical body and senses and demands that everything have material proof before grudgingly admitting validity. She may accumulate facts, but she usually misses the connections. She is so bound to hard science and predictability that art and music have no redeeming value to her. She needs to learn to trust that she will survive with a grey or colored universe rather than just a black and white one in order to reclaim the gift of practicality.

Feet-in-the-Mud

For Feet-in-the-Mud, the need for security becomes all consuming. He demands proof for everything before proceeding one inch ahead. Meanwhile, he becomes almost immobilized by his caution and over-pessimism. While originally finding safety in his practicality, he now is stuck, unable to see anything except what exists right in front of his face. He lacks spirit and perspective. Sometimes he merely slogs slowly through the mud, eyes to the ground. At other times, he becomes stuck in the quagmire. He needs to develop a sense of trust of his own intuition, although he would never label his gut reactions as such. He needs to lift his sights so that he can use the valuable gifts of common sense and perspective.

> HE DEMANDS PROOF FOR EVERYTHING BEFORE PROCEEDING ONE INCH AHEAD.

Scrooge

Substituting things for love, Scrooge hoards her resources, fearful that someone will take something, leaving her barren. The truth is that she already feels barren inside although she may not be conscious of that fact. She has probably always had to turn to things as a solace for her unmet and unacknowledged emotional needs. She may even become a tycoon, accumulating business after business, growling as she protects her hoard. Only when she opens her heart to love and learns that loving can be safe can she, like Dickens' Scrooge, find a more balanced life.

Ultraconservative

Fearing change, Ultraconservative overdoes Earth's natural quality of stability. He digs in his heels, opposing anything new that even slightly changes the status quo. He contracts, shrinking away from any expansion. He is narrow minded and sometimes even bigoted. He, too, needs to learn that the world can be a safe place and that change is a natural process rather than one to be feared and tightly guarded against. As he heals, his gift of conservation can be used effectively in the world rather than squeezing him to death.

Nose to the Grindstone

Certainly hard work and effort is required for survival by a large percentage of the world's population and joyful play remains a luxury. However, many people seeking approval have not realized that they now have a choice: they now can both play and work, each in its proper place. Nose to the Grindstone, though, is addicted to routine, order and work and probably does not even realize that she has a delightful, natural inner child. Instead, she has become so responsible and capable, good Earth qualities that have become distorted, so that the joy is gone even when completing excellent projects. Her inner child needs to heal in order to play safely and joyfully. When that occurs, even work can be effortless.

References for Chapter 3

[1]. Arroyo, 1975, p. 99.
[2]. Arroyo, 1975, p. 99.
[3]. Campbell, 1971.
[4]. Arroyo, 1975, p. 99.
[5]. Hickey, 1970.

CHAPTER 4

Air

We refer to air as the "collective" element, for all men and women of this planet are connected to each other through the air we breathe.— Alan Oken[1]

Affiliated Signs:	Gemini, Libra, Aquarius
Affiliated Houses:	3, 7, 11
Ruling Planets:	Mercury, Venus, Uranus

Imagery Experience for Air

Become as comfortable as possible and become aware of your breath which carries the life force, prana. As you take the next several breaths, experience the peace and clarity that come from breathing prana in and out of your body. ... Imagine the air that surrounds and supports you, every molecule filled with sparkling prana. ... Allow an image to emerge for air in its most pure essence. ... What are its qualities? ... Allow yourself to move as if you were totally Air energy. ... When you have completed this experience, allow some time to write or draw what you learned to further deepen your experience.

Essence End of the Continuum

Sparkling wind, filled with divine Spirit, carries the essence of the Air element just as the air itself carries prana, that life force spoken of by yogis for thousands of years. Moving lightly and gracefully as if social relationships were an exquisite ballet, Air signs represent relationships. Only air signs are symbolized by non-animal figures. Instead, a set of human twins, a balancing scale, and a human water bearer represent Gemini, Libra, and Aquarius.

In its most archetypal form, Air represents the mind of God. Even in human form, the mind must first conceive of an idea before it can manifest on the earth plane.[2] Cosmic, archetypal patterns arise in thought forms long before they materialize on the earth. In that sense, Air people create seeds that scatter on the earth taking root with nourishment from earth, sun (fire), and rain (water).

Middle of the Continuum

Light and free, Air persons primarily identify with mental and interactive qualities. The following attributes comprise the mental qualities of air:

- ♦ Thinking;
- ♦ Intelligent and alert;
- ♦ Detached and objective; and
- ♦ Fair and just.

Air people possess the relational qualities of being

- ♦ Sociable and interactive;
- ♦ Communicative; and
- ♦ Cultured.

Thinking and Mental

Often when first encountering Assagioli's disidentification exercise,[3] Air people become quite perplexed when they come to the sentence, "I have a mind, but I am not my mind." Mentally identified, Air people find difficulty in realizing that their real self could be anything other than the mind. Jung classified Air people as the "thinking type,"[4] in which predominant mental functioning overrides feelings. Thinking types often repress feelings into the unconscious, sometimes causing relationship problems. Often Air people are unaware of both their own and others' feelings. They tend to intellectualize and rationalize feelings. They respond to the question, "How do you feel?" by answering, "I think ... ." Any true Air person generally avoids the dark, emotional side of life, not quite comprehending how others become so involved in something so irrational and sticky.

They relate to life from a rational framework of ideas that has been extrapolated from much thought, and their actions follow thinking. They find the fire person's "plunge first, think later" tactic annoying. After taking action, the Air person rehashes the experience in his mind. All of this thinking appalls fire people. Earth people consider too much thinking frivolous, and water people quiver because feelings—the "real stuff of life"—are ignored. Thinking is so important to Air people that they may even forget to eat while in the midst of theories and ideas. The extroverted thinking type thinks about things such as politics, creative plans for projects, art, science and philosophy in the objective world. The introverted Air person, one who also has water or earth elements in combination with air, thinks more about internal processes and reflects more, although still more objective than water types.[5]

Intelligent and Alert

With all of this thinking, Air people possess qualities of being intelligent, questioning, and alert. With highly developed minds, they are insulted if others criticize their ideas, theories, or intelligence. They gather knowledge[6] as some Capricorns collect antique furniture. Not only do they gather and categorize information, they also synthesize diverse ideas into new patterns. They specialize in creating and playing with theories and concepts which later emerge into material form in the world. They enjoy the creative process of working with ideas much more than actually creating the final product. Certainly, think tank employers who know astrology would insist that all of their staff be predominantly Air. These employers need not worry if they do not know astrology—only Air types, especially Aquarians, would apply anyway.

Detached and objective

Air people possess the gift of standing back, observing, and seeing clearly. They remain unfettered by the distortions caused by watery emotions, earthly security needs, or fiery impatience. The ability to be objective and detached brings a clear, rational perspective. Because of non-attachment, Air people can work with a variety of people. Remaining detached, they do not become too involved in others' problems, especially emotional issues. Their non-attachment is sometimes interpreted as aloofness by others. Even though their own lives are based upon preconceived ideas, they appreciate and enjoy others' viewpoints which differ from their own. They play with the ideas as a child would play with a box full of toys.

Air people possess the gift of standing back, observing, and seeing clearly.

Fair and just

Impersonally assessing situations through observing and thinking, Air people arrive at clear ideas of what seems fair in the world and speak out for these ideals. Liz Greene says that they possess "courageous adherence to principles."[7] With the scales of justice as Libra's symbol, judges often have planets in this sign. Aquarians champion political causes in the name of justice, fairness, and equality. Air people, sometimes called the most "civilized" of the elements, generally care about humanity.

Sociable and interactive

"People who need people are the luckiest people in the world," a line from a popular song a few years ago, certainly could refer to Air people. However, Aquarians sometimes remain aloof in the crowd. However, they need others for interaction and conversations, not for emotional support as do water people. Air signs socialize more than any other of the elements. The three houses affiliated with air—three, seven and eleven—are classified as relationship houses, ranging from siblings and relatives to partnerships to friends and associates. Air people revel in thoughts and concepts, especially when they share them with others.

Communicative

Air people's gifts of communication and the use of language contribute to their social talents. Exquisitely eloquent, they articulate clearly. They can speak brilliantly and coherently to present a point of view, inspire an audience of salespersons, expound on a candidate's qualifications for mayor, educate the masses on the dangers of AIDS, or explain the theory of relativity. Their rapid and fluid speech sparkles with clarity. They love disseminating knowledge and sharing ideas with others. The evening news anchor person, without a doubt, is imbued with Air qualities. Even in love and sex, they prefer lively and stimulating conversations that create a connection with their partners before experiencing stirred passions, something hardly understood by Earth persons.

Cultured

Having interests in education, lifelong learning, the humanities, arts, and sciences, Air represents a cultured element. They love to share cultural appreciation with others, though for some Aquarians the counterculture may have more appeal. Almost as if carried by the wind itself, Air people move lightly in social settings. Even their features are frequently more refined than other signs, especially Librans.

Lack of air

When a chart lacks planets in air signs and houses, that person must learn to compensate. The person so lacking finds alternate methods to communicate rather than the clear, articulate spoken and written messages of people gifted with Air. March and McEvers cite Helen Keller, Vincent Van Gogh, Edgar Cayce, and Marlon Brando as examples of people who lack air in their chart but who found ways to compensate effectively even if expressed differently from an Air person.[8]

With a lack of air, the person also lacks rational objectivity and may be much more ruled by heart and feelings than the head. Their attachments and fears overly guide them. However, they may not realize that this is a problem, because they will not likely reflect. Instead, they may be quite attached to their feeling, impulse, or security-dominated life-style. Generally, people lacking air mistrust anyone who is too intellectual and adjust with difficulty to new ideas, concepts, people and places.

Subpersonality End of the Continuum

Ivory Tower Professor

As with all subpersonalities, Ivory Tower Professor's distortion of living too much in the head came about because of trying to meet a need. Perhaps he only felt safe in the realm of ideas where rationality made sense of life. Perhaps feelings terrified due to painful or chaotic circumstances in his early childhood. Bright and intelligent, the professor becomes so attached to his theories and opinions that he recoils if someone disparages his ideas. He interprets this kind of insult as an attack on his very identity. He lives in the mind, devoid of awareness of feelings. His overactive mind endlessly entertains him in the intellectual realm. His theories and ideas remain untested in the "real" world. He may collect piles of research data in order to satisfy his curiosity. He never writes or publishes the material, being bored with such mundane tasks. Ivory Tower Professor considers the real world to be ideas. To be more fully integrated, he will have to learn that the world of senses and feelings can be trusted and satisfying.

The Mad Inventor

A close cousin of the Professor, Mad Inventor also lives in a head filled with dreams and schemes. One can almost imagine looking inside her brain at a surrealistic view of gears, springs, coils, intermeshing at tremendous speeds. New formulas for new inventions spew forth every few days. She makes a good character for a science fiction story. Lost in a maze of plans and ideas, she loses touch with the outer world. She exhibits eccentric and imbalanced characteristics and minimally affects the practical world. She, too, needs to learn that she can live in the physical world <u>and</u> still find life interesting. Both she and her professor cousin need to learn to contact their feeling nature in a safe environment in order to release the gift of a creative mind in a more constructive manner.

Aloof Computer

The less they experience life from their center, the more deeply they push feelings away from awareness. As with other forms of repression, the repressed material actually dominates them, for they unconsciously fear the feeling realm. The deeper the fear, the more exclusively they try to live in their heads. Run by fear, Aloof Computer tries to rationally categorize life into black and white choices. He differs from the Earth subpersonality who sees life in black and white in that the Earth person's choices are based upon what can be seen, heard, smelled, tasted, and touched. The Air person's choices are based upon logical, rational concoctions of the mind. He takes the gifts of detachment and objectivity and makes them into gods to govern his life. Life becomes a series of clear choices among the many alternatives that can rationally be written into pro and con columns. Then, regardless of feelings or other considerations, choices are based upon logic. He, too, needs the heart's wisdom to go with the head in order to become a fully integrated person. Then he reclaims the gift of detachment as a tool rather than as the determiner of his life.

The Socialite

For whatever reasons arising from her past, Socialite becomes externally motivated. Her self esteem is bound up with how many names she can drop, how many cocktail parties she attends, and whether she appeared at the right places with the right people. She has lost her sense of inner self and has defined herself by an outer, superficial world. She dabbles in life as if life itself were a table of appetizers from which to sample, but she never tastes the main banquet. Even though she thrives on social connections and interactions, she remains impersonal. Though she gossips, she disconnects from her own heart and from a deeper sense of purpose and meaning in her life. She has seen every new play and gallery opening and has visited acquaintances far and wide. Her gifts of being cultured and refined now consume her life. She continues to run faster and faster, talking glibly, so that the underlying, unconscious feelings do not catch up with her. In order to heal, she needs to learn how to connect with her inner self so that she can find value, meaning and life from the inside out rather than from the outside in.

SHE DABBLES IN LIFE AS IF LIFE ITSELF WERE A TABLE OF APPETIZERS FROM WHICH TO SAMPLE, BUT SHE NEVER TASTES THE MAIN BANQUET.

The Babbler or The Orator

At first glance, these subpersonalities might seem to be different. The Babbler brings to mind images of a fourteen-year-old talking for hours on the phone, fearful that he will cease to exist if not connected by voice to his friends, or of the neighborhood gossip. On the other hand, the Orator brings to mind images of politicians speaking at rallies or Toastmasters Club presidents waxing loquacious in front of an audience. Somehow, the Orator seems more sophisticated, but really, they differ only in audience and perhaps level of education and sophistication. Orator entertains with quotations from Plato and Socrates while Babbler entertains with quotations from friends and foes. Both can talk for hours, generally disconnected from feelings and often paradoxically detached even from the content itself. Their minds propel their mouths until both they and their audiences exhaust themselves. Orators and Babblers seek connection with others and ultimately with themselves. Both distort the gift of communication so that it becomes merely a tool to meet personal needs resulting from emptiness. Like the Socialite, the Babbler and Orator need to find a deeper sense of Self so that communication becomes truly meaningful and purposeful, a source of true pleasure to themselves and others.

References for Chapter 4

[1]. Oken, 1973, p. 43.
[2]. Oken, 1973.
[3]. Assagioli, 1965
[4]. Jung, 1971.
[5]. Jung, 1971.
[6]. Hickey, 1970.
[7]. L. Greene, 1978, p. 63.
[8]. March and McEvers, 1977.

CHAPTER 5

Water

Water can dissolve more substances than any other liquid known to man.—Alan Oken[1]

Affiliated Signs: Cancer, Scorpio, Pisces
Affiliated Houses: 4, 8, 12
Ruling Planets: Moon, Pluto, Neptune

Imagery Experience for Water

Allow yourself to become comfortable. ... Imagine that you hear the waves of the ocean. Each wave gently cleanses away any tension you feel. ... Continue breathing as you take in the images, sounds, and feelings of the ocean. ... Allow an image to emerge for water in its most pure essence. ... What are its qualities? ... How do you feel as you experience these qualities? ... Allow yourself to move as if you were totally Water energy. ... When you have completed this experience, allow some time to write or draw what you learned to further deepen your experience.

Essence End of the Continuum

Like the ocean, the element of Water cleanses, soothes, and heals. Countless persons through the eons have healed pain and suffering while sitting in the presence of ocean spray, the sounds of gulls, and the ever-present rhythm of the waves. The soul seems to resonate to the eternal rhythm of the ocean. Yet, the ocean can rage, consuming those who dare traverse her during storms, just as deep, unconscious emotions can consume their owner. At a spiritual level, as Arroyo states, "the water element corresponds with the process of gaining consciousness through a slow but sure realization of the soul's deepest yearnings."[23] Water yields, goes around obstacles, washes away the earth, seemingly passive. As an 11th century Chinese scholar, cited by Arroyo, states, "Water gives way to obstacles with deceptive humility, for no power can prevent it following its destined course to the sea. Water conquers by yielding; it never attacks but always wins the last battle."[4]

Middle of the Continuum

As Water people submerge beneath the ocean surface, floating as if in amniotic fluid, they remain oblivious to what is above the surface. These people resemble fish who do not even know that they swim in water because they have no experience of earth or dry air. However, as they become conscious, they raise their head above the water to see new horizons and find a different perspective. Lest they become dry and brittle, they relish keeping the remainder of the body submerged. This image exemplifies the experience of water. As the feeling element, water is associated with the emotions and with the astral dimension.

Besides being feeling and emotional, water possesses the following qualities:

- Cleansing and healing;
- Sensitive and compassionate;
- Dependent and vulnerable;
- Protective and private;
- Preceptive and absorptive;
- Yielding and conquering.

Feeling and emotional

Most astrology texts relegate the unconscious expression of Water to the lower unconscious which is replete with memories, fears, and conditioning from the past. Certainly Water people express this dimension, for inner storms do sometimes leak into their daily lives. However, in psychosynthesis, as in some other psychologies, the lower unconscious represents only one aspect of that vast realm of experience that remains beneath the surface of awareness and yet impacts daily actions. Assagioli discussed the higher unconscious which provides the impetus for higher intuition, inspiration, illumination and a sense of oneness with the universe.[5] At this level, rather than experiencing raging storms, the Water person accesses calm, healing seas. Both realms of the unconscious comprise the world so familiar to Water people, even though the lower unconscious perhaps impacts more for many people than does the higher unconscious. With continued evolution, perhaps one day the experience of the higher unconscious will be as common in daily life as the lower unconscious is at present.

In either case, Water people lack objectivity, and they color their evaluations by deep, unconscious feeling responses. Whether experiencing the higher or lower unconscious, Water people verbalize their experiences, especially motivations, with difficulty. When pushed, they usually come up with some plausible, yet flimsy, reason which may change with the next passing wave. Often, Water people remain unaware of the contents of their own unconscious even though they realize the power this realm holds.

Assagioli said that developing consciousness "prepares for easier assimilation of unconscious aspects."[6] We slowly realize that we can observe our own functions, including emotions, and gradually gain mastery. Mastery comes from awareness of inner processes and the recognition that one is a Self rather than just a body, emotions, mind, or a subpersonality. Until that time, the Water person is dominated by moods which shift with the wind and tides.

Cleansing and healing

Many people feel cleansed simply by listening to ocean waves lapping or by wading in a crisp, clean mountain stream. Crying often helps to cleanse the body of stored emotions such as grief, sadness, and hurt. Most medical authorities recommend drinking lots of water each day for optimum health because of the purifying quality of good water in the system. Similarly, water as an element in the personality heals and cleanses when people experience their feelings in a healthy, constructive manner. Awareness of feelings provides connection with others. Unconditional love and joy, imbued with feelings from Self, deeply connect us with others.

Sensitive and compassionate

Water people sense others' pain, suffering, joy, love, tenderness, and hardness by internal "radar" which scan the emotional field around them. Water people do not require physical proximity in order to accurately sense another's feelings. This "radar" can go to anyplace in the world, as Water's psychic abilities result from emotional fields reaching out and connecting. Stories abound about people sensing danger when a loved one is in peril.

Sensing so deeply the feelings of others, Water people possess enormous capacity for compassion and empathy. They intuitively know about "walking a mile in another person's moccasins." However, Water people must learn boundaries so that they do not inappropriately take on the feelings of others as their own. Because they respond so easily, they often excel as care-givers, whether as friends, parents, or professionals such as teachers, healers, and counselors. Sometimes, others take advantage of this great gift of sensitivity.

Dependent and vulnerable

Sensitivity leads to vulnerability. The Water person almost always lives with a soft underbelly that is prone to hurt and wounding. Lacking objectivity, the Water person tends to personalize experience. At the same time, this softness taps at the very core of being human, for feelings intangibly connect all of life. Water people can teach others the value of gentleness as a strength rather than a weakness. At other times, they are overwhelmed by their own raw belly.

> WATER PEOPLE CAN TEACH OTHERS THE VALUE OF GENTLENESS AS A STRENGTH RATHER THAN A WEAKNESS.

James Cavanaugh once wrote a book entitled, *Some Men Are Too Gentle to Live Among Wolves,*[7] a title which certainly describes Water, whether or not Mr. Cavanaugh had ever heard about astrological elements. Because of cultural conditioning, many predominantly Water men have more difficulty being true to their inner nature than do predominantly Water women. They resemble teddy bears disguised behind lion's and tiger's masks. Although many Water men are at peace with their feeling natures and many Water women are not, the culture still provides more encouragement and support for women being emotional and men being rational.

THEY RESEMBLE TEDDY BEARS DISGUISED BEHIND LION'S AND TIGER'S MASKS.

Water people connect through feelings to others so much that they become dependent upon others' responsiveness to validate themselves and in order to feel alive. The closer that they live to their own center, the less they need external validation, although they still appreciate connection. The further away from their own center, the more that Water people do anything, even create crises, in order to evoke emotional responses from those around them.

Protective and private

Whereas some air and fire signs, notably Gemini and Sagittarius, resemble open books available for anyone to read, Water people are like fine, rare books which reveal their secrets only to those who promise to handle with care. Once Water people feel safe with a trusted other, they may blurt out their story for hours, before once again retreating into the land of quiet. Water people sometimes appear shy when, in reality, they may just be self-protective. They need protection from outside influences "in order to assure themselves the inner calm necessary for deep reflection and subtlety of perception."[8]

Unlike fire and air counterparts, Water people prefer indirectness, thus better assuring protection of their vulnerabilities. Like a river, they move around rocks rather than demanding that the rock move. A little secrecy provides a sense of safety so that they do not have to openly defend an action, thought, or feeling.

Receptive and absorptive

The only three signs in the zodiac symbolized by cold-blooded animals are the three water signs: Cancer—the crab, Scorpio—the scorpion, and Pisces— two fish. Cold-blooded animals, by biological definition, respond to the temperature of their environment. That is, when they lie in the sun, their body temperature literally warms. When they submerge under icy water, their inner temperatures drop lower than would be life-sustaining to warm-blooded animals. Water people, then, often respond like a sponge to their environments as if the environment and those around them determined their own responses. The more conscious we are, the more we realize that we have choices as to response even though we will always be somewhat affected by our surroundings.

Absorbing unconscious perceptions that go beyond physical senses and logic, the Water person often finds guidance from these impressions. As Water people become more conscious and centered, they know more accurately whether the material received can be trusted. Much that comes from the astral level filters through in a distorted fashion. The less conscious we are, the more the unconscious rules us.

Because of the need for reflection in order to assimilate and process what is received, Water people need times of solitude—at least peace and quiet. In these reflective times, they "wash" off extraneous impressions that they have absorbed from others and return to their own sense of Self. They can reflect on the Truth of their experience, although it will always be based upon feeling perceptions.

Yielding and conquering

Yielding and pliable, Water takes on the shape of its container, whether that be a river bed, an ocean bottom, a drinking glass, or a human being. Therefore, Water appreciates someone or something providing banks or a container. They often experience difficulty in providing form for their desires and needs. Water's fluidity, unless it is ice as sometimes happens with Scorpio, gives the appearance of changing at whims. It shifts with the winds and tides. Water needs a true connection with the Self which provides a connection with the higher Will. When Self-directed, Water people pursue a course true to inner wisdom.

However yielding Water may be, it also conquers in the end. It extinguishes fire, erodes entire mountain sides, and even cuts through rock. Even though Water may not appear persistent, we can strongly feel its force.

Lack of Water

People without planets in water signs or houses have problems with the feeling realm of life. They lack the capacity to feel deeply or to have true compassion and empathy. They lack sensitivity for others and perhaps even themselves, so relationships often pose problems. Water cleanses and heals, so people lacking this element may experience excessive toxicity. Their environment has little impact upon them, and they distrust anything resembling psychic knowledge or gut reactions. Life may seem brittle and cold without a feeling nature.

THEY LACK THE CAPACITY TO FEEL DEEPLY OR TO HAVE TRUE COMPASSION AND EMPATHY.

Subpersonality End of the Continuum

Moody Blues

Many Water people experience being overwhelmed by feelings from time to time. However, Moody Blues, who received little emotional support and safety as a child, is consumed by her emotions. Moody Blues exaggerates feelings all out of proportion to the point that she totally immerses herself in her own experience with no awareness of anyone else's plight. Sometimes hysterical, she swings wildly from one emotion to the next. She allows the environment and other people to determine her moods by reacting to everything rather than acting from her own center. She takes personally most things that are said and done, regardless of the intention of the other person. When someone inadvertently scowls in his own reverie, Moody Blues assumes that he frowns because of her. She identifies so much with her emotions that she rebels when hearing, "I have emotions, but I am not my emotions" from Assagioli's disidentification exercise. Addicted to emotions, she must learn a deeper sense of Self so that she may use the great feeling gift of Water as a tool rather than allowing emotions to rule her life.

The Great Caretaker

In popular parlance, this supreme caretaker expresses co-dependent characteristics. His needs often went unmet as a child, and he learned that being very responsible for others earned at least a modicum of safety and attention if not nurturance. He expertly knows what others need and attempts to meet those needs. He knows others' requirements far better than his own. In the service of unconsciously trying to meet his own inner needs, he exaggerates compassion. Unfortunately, the cravings of his own inner child remain unmet. Although the healing process occurs gradually, he must first come to terms with his inner child and find new ways of meeting its needs. Then the gift of compassion can be released in a more wholesome manner—both for himself and for others.

Needy Nelly

Related to the Caretaker, Needy Nelly tries to meet her own deep need for security by maintaining very close, unhealthy connections with significant others. Indirect by nature, she manipulates relationships so that enmeshment continues, hoping that she will not be abandoned. The more she fears losing the relationship or forfeiting control, the more she tightly clings. She may even threaten suicide if left alone. Unlike her cousin, the Great Caretaker,

THE MORE SHE FEARS LOSING THE RELATIONSHIP OR FORFEITING CONTROL, THE MORE SHE TIGHTLY CLINGS.

Needy Nelly sometimes becomes so depleted that she nurtures no one, especially not herself. Even if treated badly, even if she only receives crumbs, she holds on as though she would die without the relationship. With considerable work on her self worth and esteem, Needy Nelly can learn to believe in herself as a capable, resilient person who can be alone <u>or</u> in relationship. She realizes that she can make viable choices, of which she is unaware while totally identified with this subpersonality.

Psychic Sponge

Distorting the gift of absorption and sensitivity to others, Psychic Sponge retains no boundaries. Without discernment, Psychic Sponge soaks up anything and everything from everybody. Every thought form and every feeling that floats around in the astral plane is subject to being sucked in by the Sponge. At the far end of the continuum, Psychic Sponge exhibits psychotic characteristics, totally unaware of where he ends and others begin. He may hallucinate and be overwhelmed by psychic overload. If not psychotic, Psychic Sponge just absorbs the feelings of others, including their emotional sufferings and physical ailments. Often he develops a headache when walking into a room in which someone else suffers a headache.

The sense of oneness with the universe can be a gift when the individual is fully integrated at the personality level with an intact sense of Self. That experience of oneness provides a true glimpse of the spiritual realm. To be "at one" without a solid, integrated core and without a sense of Self invites disaster. His work involves learning who he is, a being contained in a body and personality, so that he has a basis for making discerning choices about what to absorb and what to leave in the floating garbage dump.

Isolate

Using tactics just the opposite of Needy Nelly, Isolate hides under her shell — whether that be crab, scorpion or fish scales — afraid of the vulnerability of her underbelly. She builds walls around herself, figuratively and literally, and tells the world, "I can do it alone!" The fear of exposing her weaknesses outweighs her desperation for connection which she denies even to herself. Lonely and afraid, she lives out a hollow existence, never savoring the joys of her gift of feelings and connection. Although the work may take a long time, she needs to develop a relationship with her inner child. Now she does not even know of its existence. Over time she can learn to provide safety and love for the inner child. Only then, will she feel safe enough to reach out to others for the sustenance she so very much unconsciously yearns.

References for Chapter 5

[1]. Oken, 1973, p. 46.
[2]. Arroyo, 1975, p. 99.
[3]. Arroyo, 1975, p. 99.
[4]. Arroyo, 1975, p. 98, cited from John Blofeld's *The Wheel of Life,* p. 78.
[5]. Assagioli, 1965.
[6]. Assagioli, 1965, p. 69.
[7]. Cavanaugh, 1970.
[8]. Arroyo, 1975, p. 98.

CHAPTER 6

Qualitative Energies: The Quadriplicities

The quadriplicities are aspects of force manifesting in matter. —
Isabel Hickey[1]

In addition to being divided into the four elements, the zodiacal signs fall into three modes of operating in life called the quadriplicities: cardinal, fixed and mutable. These different qualities color each sign's presentation, and each mode contains one each of the four elements:

	Cardinal	Fixed	Mutable
Fire	Aries	Leo	Sagittarius
Earth	Capricorn	Taurus	Virgo
Air	Libra	Aquarius	Gemini
Water	Cancer	Scorpio	Pisces

Each of the zodiacal signs in the same element expresses qualitatively differently depending upon whether it is cardinal, fixed, or mutable. That is, the cardinal, fire sign of Aries operates with more initiatory action than fixed Leo or mutable Sagittarius. The qualities represent yet another rich overlay of astrological meaning.

Cardinal

Qualities: initiatory action

The four cardinal signs each initiate new seasons, the beginning of each occurring either at an equinox or solstice: Aries—spring; Cancer—summer; Libra—autumn; Capricorn—winter. Similarly, people born with cardinal signs prominent in their charts like to start things, although each takes action distinctly differently due to its elemental energies. Dobyns uses the metaphor of cars meeting in an intersection for each of the modes and says cardinal cars crash into each other with irresistible momentum.[2]

Cardinal signs all can deal energetically, quickly, and ambitiously with situations, for they know how to assert themselves when needed. The yin signs of Cancer and Capricorn assert more quietly and less directly than Aries and Libra. Nevertheless, all four of these cardinals make their needs known. They sometimes are too impulsive and impatient. Their enterprising and forceful manner leads to executive abilities, and they thrive in the midst of activities and projects.

Subpersonality: Pushy

Pushy becomes so caught up in taking action that he impatiently rushes, unaware of others' desires or feelings. Like a whirlwind, Pushy involves himself in such a frenzy of activity that he loses sight of his own center and forgets the underlying purpose. When Pushy has reconnected with his Self, his gift of initiating and accomplishing again can be expressed to the benefit of himself and others. Then everyone wins.

Fixed

Qualities: stable and determined

The fixed signs—Taurus, Leo, Scorpio, and Aquarius—continue to build and construct what the cardinal signs initiated. They contain reservoirs of power and energy and an enduring will that leads them to complete whatever they set their minds to, for they all possess a strong will. Once a course of action has been chosen, they do not deviate from the path unless someone thoroughly and completely demonstrates a better path. Even then, they remain noncommittal for a long time, not easily revealing their thought processes or motivations. Generally, they resist changing any established pattern. They prefer remaining loyal and reliable to people and plans, offering determination and stability as their gifts.

> . . .THEY RESIST CHANGING ANY ESTABLISHED PATTERN. THEY PREFER REMAINING LOYAL AND RELIABLE TO PEOPLE AND PLANS. . .

Subpersonality: Set-in-Ways

Set-in-Ways stubbornly refuses to budge from her own opinions or ways of doing things even if in her best interests. Like Zip Dobyns' cars meeting in an intersection, she remains in an impasse without giving an inch.[3] Her behavior patterns are so deeply ingrained and she seldom looks at her own shortcomings, so she becomes stuck many times in her life. She inflexibly digs in her heels, willfully balking against any change. Set-in-Ways cannot overcome her inertia unless she is willing to perceive the problem from a new level, like climbing to the top of the mountain for a view rather than just remaining at one base camp. Eventually, she must be willing to allow the higher Will to flow through her which then releases her considerable gifts.

Mutable

Qualities: flexible and changeable

Again using the cars-in-the-intersection metaphor, Dobyns says that mutable cars weave in and out in a kind of dance, circling, going around each other, and never touching.[4]

The most adaptable of all signs, the mutables of Gemini, Virgo, Sagittarius and Pisces all exemplify versatility and bendability. They like to have Plan A, B, and C lined up for any situation, and then if those do not work, they try Plan Q, R or Z. With this kind of pliability, they are fairly easygoing, free flowing, and open to suggestion. They go with the current rather than against the tide.

Although Gemini is the only air sign among the mutables, they all contain a mental quality of experiencing vicariously through reading, thinking, and observing. The mutables generally have the ability to see many points of view. They learn new methods easily, for they thrive on constant change and variety, gifted with flexibility.

Subpersonality: Scattered

Scattered has trouble discriminating between the many options, possibilities, and plans available. Sometimes he chooses them all, wondering why he can never complete anything. Perseverance and persistence do not count among his gifts. Sometimes he cannot decide, not knowing what to do, what to trust or where to go. He lacks direction and fluctuates from one thing to another. Having lost himself by responding to every whim offered by the external environment, Scattered needs to return inward for a sense of Self. Although he retains the gift of flexibility, he needs to make choices from a more grounded center. Then he can dance joyfully through the changing seasons of life, thrilling at the movement and variety.

REFERENCES FOR CHAPTER 6

[1]. Hickey, 1970, p. 53.
[2]. Dobyns, 1973.
[3]. Dobyns, 1973.
[4]. Dobyns, 1973.

CHAPTER 7

Masculine And Feminine Energies: The Polarities

In the further explanation by early Chinese authors, the Yin and Yang components never became fully separated, but at each stage only one is manifested and dominant, while the other is latent and recessive. Through the discussions of the wavelike operations of these forces, there is no undertone of good and evil.—Herbert Guenther[1]

The twelve zodiacal signs are divided into yet another category: the polarities of masculine and feminine, or as some people prefer calling them, yang and yin. Angeles Arrien has called the masculine energy "dynamic" and the feminine energy "magnetic" which further delineates these two energies. In reality, these polarities represent two sides of a unified whole. Fire and air signs comprise the yang or masculine energies, and earth and water signs constitute the yin or feminine energies. Even though given the appellations of "masculine" and "feminine," these energies go far beyond gender identification as will be explained later in this chapter.

Yin	**Yang**
Taurus	Aries
Cancer	Gemini
Virgo	Leo
Scorpio	Libra
Capricorn	Sagittarius
Pisces	Aquarius

Jung said that every man contains an anima or female energy and that every woman possesses an animus or male energy. Jung believed that men repress their anima while women repress their animus. Certainly cultural expectations and norms, even in a changing society, support this possibility. Also, these archetypes from the collective unconscious profoundly affect everyone on the planet at some level. Yet, some men are born with considerably more yin energies if earth and water signs predominate in their charts, and some women possess more yang than yin energies from fire and air in their charts. Perhaps as the culture liberates itself from restrictive gender roles and expectations, both men and women can more comfortably express their true natures.

We all contain both yin and yang qualities within us, although one of these polarities usually remains less dominant. When we repress either the yin or yang side of ourselves, our relationships become skewed. If a woman with strong yang energies represses her animus, she attracts men to her to play out that quality in an exaggerated, macho fashion. When she trusts both her masculine and feminine sides, her outer world mirrors this shift. She attracts more gentle and whole men, for she can now express her own assertiveness.

Each quality complements the other. As we allow both sides of our nature to find expression, and as we relate more harmoniously to others, we can live in delightful interdependence. The creative union of yin and yang allow both intuition and action, right and left-brain functions.

Yin

Qualities: Inward and Magnetic

Water and earth signs express more introversion and introspection than do the yang signs. Seemingly pulled by a centripetal force, they turn inward. Symbolically at home in caves or underwater, they prefer the soft folds of night and darkness to the harshness of daylight. Thus, they find lunar qualities more appealing than solar. They await gestation, inspired by creative impulses. Yin energies support dependence more than independence, for they move towards union and oneness rather than separation. They prefer some form of security from the outer world unless they always live from the level of Self. True yin people receive inner guidance which comes from dreams, metaphors, emotions and body wisdom.

SYMBOLICALLY AT HOME IN CAVES OR UNDERWATER, THEY PREFER THE SOFT FOLDS OF NIGHT AND DARKNESS TO THE HARSHNESS OF DAYLIGHT.

Subpersonality: Super Security

Super Security becomes fearful of losing either emotional or material security. She often proceeds at a snail's pace, constantly testing the water before making a move. She may ask for proof after proof before making a decision. She fears that there will not be enough and often operates from a scarcity mentality. She has lost sight of her inner wisdom to guide her in discerning who and what can be trusted in the world. As she connects with her innermost Self, she becomes more free and secure, able to move forward once again.

Yang

Qualities: Outward and Dynamic

Extroverted, yang signs exert a dominant force as they go forth into the world. They prefer taking action to inaction. They assert themselves in the world by thinking, speaking, and moving their bodies. They find dark places aversive, favoring light and sunshine. All of the yang signs move towards independence and find dependence confining and, at times, appalling. Therefore, they see themselves as separate individuals acting upon the world. Inspiration arises from their interactions and actions in the world rather than from more internal yin promptings.

Subpersonality: Insensitive

Insensitive brashly thinks out loud or takes action in the world without considering the desires or feelings of his more quiet yin friends or relatives. He runs quickly when anyone depends too much on him, for he wants to remain independent at all costs. Always acting or talking in response to the outer world, Insensitive seldom listens to his own inner wisdom. Even though he moves his body a lot, he fails to listen to body messages on what is required for optimum health. Like Super Security, Insensitive must learn to balance his masculine and feminine energies within himself in order to experience wholeness.

References for Chapter 7

[1]. Guenther, 1984, p. 176.

PART III

The Twelve Songs

ARIES

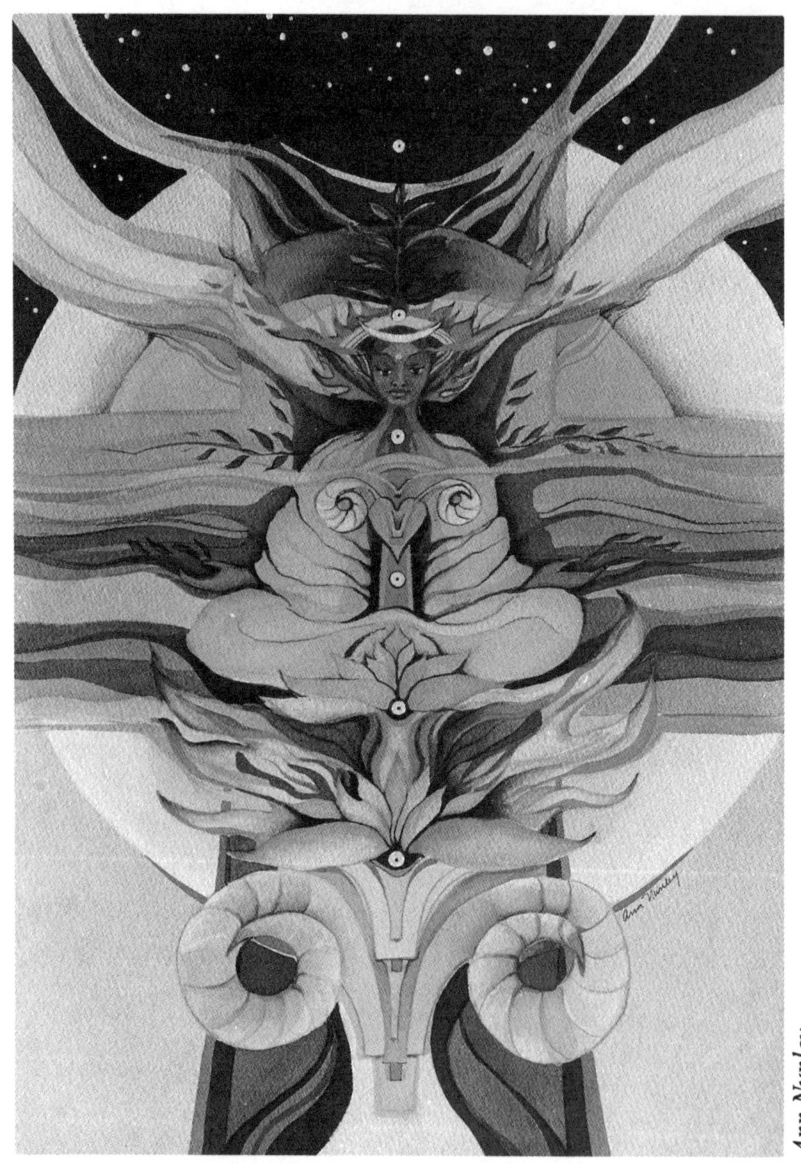

Ann Nunley

March 21 - April 21

CHAPTER 1

ARIES

In Aries, the "pulsing of life"—the creative Breath—is felt. It passes through. It surges forth—and is gone. — Dane Rudhyard[1]

In Aries, self-becoming has its beginnings, here with the zodiac the great cycle of struggle towards self-expression starts. — Louise Huber[2]

Affiliated House:	1
Ruling Planet:	Mars
Element:	Fire
Quality:	Cardinal
Polarity:	Yang
Dates:	March 21 - April 21
Key Words:	I AM
Symbol:	Ram
Anatomy:	Head, face, brain, upper teeth

Imagery Experience for Aries

As you take deep, slow, relaxing breaths, become aware of your physical body, allowing it to be as comfortable as possible. ... Become aware of your emotions, allowing them to become peaceful. ... Allow your mind to become still. ... Imagine that you are an Aries ram in the springtime, ... bursting with vitality, life, and energy. It seems as if you are the first and only ram that has ever existed. ... Become aware of your power and aliveness, ready to spring forth into action. ... Take as much time as you need to really experience being a ram. When you are ready, write or draw your images. Or, you may want to move or dance, expressing the experience of being a ram.

Essence End of the Continuum

As the egg suddenly cracks open, the chick bursts into the world, fresh, new, and alive. At first, the chick just IS in this moment, totally oblivious to the hundreds of others also chirping with life in their brand new environment. This new babe remains unaware of the millions of others who have preceded him, and he certainly is unconscious of the suffering and death that necessarily occurs in order for new generations to be born. He only knows of himself in this moment. He irresistibly rushes forth to express the creative power rising within him. The protective pre-birth covering no longer contains him; he has emerged into the world. Frances Moore writes, "Aries is the outpouring of Living Energy—undisciplined, unfocused, undirected. Aries is youth, unafraid, optimistic, eager to experience everything."[3]

At the most integrated end of the continuum, Aries moves from "I am" to "I will" to "I can," sweeping aside all obstacles. Aries expresses the will to make life sacred. Out of this push for the sacred fire comes the will to transform selfishness into service, the will to participate cooperatively in life, and the will to unite the soul and personality. Few people at this time in history express with such purity, untainted by distortion. Nevertheless, the expression of divine will remains a potential and from time to time, manifests fully conscious within the Aries person.

Mars, as the exoteric planetary ruler of Aries, provides the impulse to actively create and express at the physical level. Although the impulse begins in the mind, little time elapses between thought and action. Mercury, as Aries' esoteric ruler, provides insight into the divine for those who are ready. In spiritual writings, Aries represents the birthplace of divine thoughts. With Mercury's presence, purpose and inspiration infuse action. The esoteric seed thought for Aries states, "I come forth and from the plane of mind I rule."[4]

Middle of the Continuum

The whole requires gifts from each of the zodiac signs. Each sign focuses upon its own dimension of human existence beginning with the birth of the individuated self in Aries and ending with the merger into oneness with the Universe in Pisces. As the first sign of the zodiac which also launches the first day of spring, Aries represents beginnings and the newness and excitement that accompanies birthing.

In addition to self-becoming, Aries expresses these qualities:

- Pioneering and creative;
- Exuberant and physically vital;
- Spontaneous and action-oriented;
- Assertive and self-expressive;
- Daring and adventurous;
- Self-assured and confident;
- Competitive;
- Freedom-loving and independent.

Self becoming

Aries pulses with new life, bursting forth as freshly and vibrantly as colorful flowers, tree leaves and baby animals do in springtime. In actuality, an individuated personality self or ego is being birthed. A strong, healthy ego must exist "so that spiritual energies can flow into a usable vessel."[5] The development of spirituality must await the building of a healthy self at the personality level. Otherwise, the person prematurely transcends, denying very real issues, and enormous spiritual energies can short circuit the undeveloped system. The personality self or ego must be excited enough about whatever it must accomplish in the world in order to fully cooperate with the divine impulse, this being especially true for Aries. The key words, "I AM," celebrate the birth of self, no matter where on the continuum the person experiences life. In the process of developing a vibrant self, Aries people become self-absorbed and remain unaware of others or what is happening around them.

THE KEY WORDS, "I AM," CELEBRATE THE BIRTH OF SELF, NO MATTER WHERE ON THE CONTINUUM THE PERSON EXPERIENCES LIFE.

Pioneering and creative

Throughout history, people with strong Aries energy have sailed to new lands, charting new territory, crossed frontiers, and explored new possibilities. Their occupations have ranged from discovery voyagers to pioneers headed West to cartographers mapping uncharted lands to astronauts headed for outer space. They have planned and brought into form innovations in marketing strategies, athletics, organizational management, and nearly every dimension of life. In the process of creating, Aries people strip away anything that confines or limits them or the project. They find the creative act more interesting than the actual creation. Therefore, many pioneering Aries need other people to complete their projects, for they become bored once the thrill of implementing the vision ebbs. Once the previous idea has been set into motion, they leave it behind to charge onwards to the next project. They throw seeds to the wind, many of which land in fertile soil and grow, nurtured by someone other than the sower.

Exuberant and physically vital

Unless hampered by other planetary combinations or illness, abundant physical energy and vitality bless the true Aries person. They experience the world kinesthetically. Throughout history, they have wiggled more than other children in places where wiggling was prohibited such as churches and synagogues. They even require less sleep than the average person, this being especially true when Mars conjuncts the Sun. Often, these dynamic, high-energy folks feel disgusted with eight-hour-a-night sleepers deciding that anyone who needs more than four or five hours of sleep must be lazy and ill-equipped for life. They cannot comprehend nappers.

Spiritually-oriented Aries people often experience their sport—whether running, weight lifting, swimming—as a meditation. They store excess energy as tension in their bodies which demands release. They need to physically move about; sitting at a desk for more than a few minutes seems tortuous. Even at a sedate senior citizen picnic, the Aries octogenarian sets up the volley ball net or slings frisbees to anyone who will play. Generally, they love to exercise or play sports which acts as a release for pent up energy. When they have finished a workout, they feel fresh and revitalized, ready for the next challenge. More than any other sign of the zodiac, Aries people consider sex as either recreation or physical release, perhaps oblivious that their partners want long, sensuous caresses and emotional connection. Exuberance wins out over slowness every time.

Spontaneous and action-oriented

Although thoughts precede action, Aries people move so quickly that, practically speaking, they act first and then think. Their first impulse in any situation is to act: a fight breaks out on the street, and they either jump into the middle of it, yell at the scufflers, or grab the nearest object they can find and shake it in the fighters' faces. A little blood never concerned an Aries, for regardless of consequences, Aries believe in immediacy. They can even be addicted to the adrenaline rush that comes from constant, speedy action. Burt tells us, "So often, it's a lifetime of going, doing, and taking action to prevail against mediocrity and sameness."[6]

Their spontaneity benefits or destroys, depending on the person. Many paramedics, fire fighters, and police officers, whose ability to act immediately often makes the difference between life and death, have strong Aries energy. They feel stifled and bored if they have to sit behind a desk or to work at a job which requires lengthy deliberation or copious paperwork. One accountant remained in his profession longer than most Aries would because he worked as an auditor which involved frequent moves from one location to another during the week.

> Impatience and impulsiveness describe most Aries people at some point in their lives.

They expect instant success at whatever they do and have no patience for delays, ignorance, or mistakes on the part of others. Impatience and impulsiveness describe most Aries people at some point in their lives. Many astrologers notice that Aries clients often nod their heads or move their hands, motioning the astrologer to hurry the explanations and more quickly move on to the next piece of information. They act with such alacrity that they rarely realize the impact of their actions upon others. Huber warns, "The ability to measure out and to moderate his powers is an exercise with which the Aries person is usually occupied for his whole life."[7]

Assertive and self-expressive

At the core of their being, Aries people need to decisively and surely express their needs to the world. They want to do what they want when they want. When clear and direct, they stand their ground without interfering with others' rights, and they prove to be excellent models for the end goal of assertiveness training. Before they learn the finer points of assertiveness skills, they can express too aggressively. Their tempers flare, maybe even lashing out in violence. After all, the planet Mars traditionally has been associated with warfare. They often take instant offense at any limitations put upon them. Generally, though, the Aries temper flares as quickly as a flash fire in a trash can full of paper on which has been sprayed lighter fluid. The anger dissipates just as quickly as it came. They then puzzle as to why the object of their anger, usually another person, still reels from the outburst an hour later. Aries has long forgotten the trigger for the flare-up.

On the other hand, some Aries persons inhibit their urge to assertively stand up for themselves, much as if a lid were put on a burning fire. Some of these people choose to express passively because of cultural conditioning such as most women experience. Others do not declare themselves because some other part of their personality wars with the assertive part, such as people with Saturn aspects to Mars or to Aries planets. Headaches often result from squelching fiery assertiveness in this manner. Even then, fire can only be contained for so long before an explosion occurs. By learning to express needs assertively rather than aggressively or passively, the Aries ram learns to live in the world with others <u>and</u> retain individuality. The placement of Mars, by sign and house, and its aspects to other planets indicates how assertiveness and anger are expressed.

Daring and adventurous

Fearless and courageous, Aries people thrive on adventure, rocketing through one experience after another. Test pilots, hang glider enthusiasts, rock rappelers, and race car drivers all certainly possess a big dose of Aries energy. Any parent of an Aries toddler can tell stories of the child's escapades: the little tyke fell off of the refrigerator top trying to get the cereal long before dawn or before the par-

> ARIES PEOPLE LOVE ANY SPORT OR OCCUPATION THAT INVOLVES SPEED, DANGER, AND RISK-TAKING.

ents had awakened. She crawled over the fence to get a closer look at the cute tigers in the zoo while the diligent parents turned their backs for a split second. His tricycle wheels wore out from careening around the driveway. Aries people love any sport or occupation that involves speed, danger, and risk-taking. They express fearlessness even in hopeless situations, charging through experiences until the thrill of the challenge subsides.

SELF-ASSURED AND CONFIDENT

Imbued with confidence to tackle any challenge, Aries people see the world as something to conquer. They attribute their successes to their own powers and abilities. Whether the task be parenthood, playing a football game, climbing a mountain or starting a new job—innate confidence provides an extra boost of energy for whatever action needs to be taken. They say "yes" out of the self-certainty they can accomplish any risk-invoking task. One man moved from one city to another without an awaiting job because he knew he had the ability to easily find one. This action would mortify his Earth or Water cousins. In his perception, he had not even taken a risk. Sometimes Aries people promise more than they can deliver, because they do not consider the consequences of tackling more than any human being could complete. They confidently know they can do it.

COMPETITIVE

Aries people blend their exuberant self-confidence into their competitive nature, always seeking to be first. They consider the position of first in the zodiac as their rightful place anywhere. They love to win at whatever they do. However, Rudhyar reminds us that the Aries person "does not seek power in order to satisfy himself, but to demonstrate himself to himself—the power necessary for him to become a personality."[8] Even though he loves to lead, he often does not even notice who follows. They thrill just to be in front. Many kinds of businesses offer an outlet for natural competitiveness. Athletics also provide the opportunity for healthy competition whether they be team sports or solo events in which Aries strive to beat their own records.

FREEDOM-LOVING AND INDEPENDENT

Like a bright, red racing car, Aries hate any kind of road blocks or speed limits. They need to keep expressing creativity and their emerging self in the world. They could lead seminars on how to eliminate limitations in one's life. Not introspective by nature, Aries may never know that they secretly fear routine and tradition because it would limit growth. Instead, Aries surge forward, constantly seeking new experiences and new options. If blocked, they may even impulsively harm themselves, although they normally lash out at others who stand in the way.

Their fear of restriction and love of freedom affect relationships with others. They prefer independence over connections when they must choose between the two. They resist any kind of dependence on others that limits their expression. Ultimately, an Aries must learn how to be a free self who maintains an identity and who can also be interdependent. Then reaching for the highest good for the individual contributes to the highest good of those in their environment. Aries no longer competes with others for the freedom to be.

> ARIES MAY NEVER KNOW THAT THEY SECRETLY FEAR ROUTINE AND TRADITION BECAUSE IT WOULD LIMIT GROWTH.

Subpersonality End of the Continuum

Daredevil David

The old saying, "Fools rush in where angels fear to tread," applies to this subpersonality. He may unintentionally hurt others in his haste to get to his destination. Taking confidence and courage to the maximum, sometimes beyond realism, Daredevil walks a tightrope over Niagara Falls or drives cars over canyons as Evel Kenevil, the stunt driver, did a few years ago. He dashes into battle—and maybe dies—without thinking, preparing, or carrying any weapon other than his flaming bravado. Daredevil needs another method in which to express his inner creativity and zest; he needs other ways for obtaining the respect of others. Healed, with these adventurous qualities integrated, David retains his excitement, incorporating it with common sense and purpose.

Hot Head Hilary

Hilary explodes with little provocation, spewing forth her fire on whoever or whatever happens to be in the way. If a server at a restaurant brings the wrong entree, everyone in the restaurant immediately hears her explosion as she berates the server for making an error. Unwilling to control her impulses, she almost never thinks ahead of time about the fallout from her angry outbursts, yet her hair-trigger temper wounds many. She first needs to develop a sensitivity to consequences and then learn methods to manage her impulses more appropriately. Trapped in the confines of the Hot Head subpersonality, the gift of assertiveness becomes grossly distorted. She needs to redefine what "standing up" for herself means and to learn new methods of asserting herself that produce constructive results both for herself and others.

Macho Joe

Joe resembles the movie characters played by John Wayne. In the movies, men swagger into saloons exuding confidence and manhood. Any frail, helpless person immediately knows that protection and safety have arrived and that guns will be fired and tables overturned if necessary. In real life, Joe also swaggers. He does not need to boast of his conquests and fearless courage, although he secretly gloats that everyone knows. If he quakes inwardly at the sight of blood, he hides this fact even from himself. If called to war, he bravely marches off with gun in hand telling everyone how eager he is for combat. Macho Joe's persona prevents him from admitting to even the slightest sensitivity; therefore, he feels lonely. Robbing himself of the capacity to embrace any of his gentler qualities which would make him more whole, this tough guy always takes charge and pretends that he needs no one. Locked into a subpersonality, Macho Joe must first learn that he is acceptable as a whole human being, not just a one-dimensional character. Then his gifts of courage and assertiveness can be used in wholesome ways.

Roadrunner

This subpersonality thrives on adrenaline, darting hither and yon, sometimes even confusing herself as to where she is going. The speedy race itself intrigues her much more than the destination. Going into withdrawal if she ever sits still for longer than twelve minutes, she instantly mobilizes her energy and dashes away again. She races so fast that taking the time to acknowledge or experience inner feelings of any kind—joy or despair—proves to be impossible. Her adrenaline excitedly rises in response to any new project, so she often agrees to more than she can possibly accomplish. Starting projects thrills her more than the slow plodding sometimes required to pick up the pieces and complete the task. Although usually not deliberately, she appears untruthful at times because she promises more than she can deliver.

ALTHOUGH USUALLY NOT DELIBERATELY, SHE APPEARS UNTRUTHFUL AT TIMES. . .

She needs to learn how to channel her energy productively and how to rest from time to time. In spite of her high physical energy, she usually remains unaware of her body's needs and may push it beyond its limits. She must learn ways to experience inner joy rather than being addicted to adrenaline which will occur if she taps into a more cohesive sense of self. Being in charge of her activities rather than being run by them, she still accomplishes more than the average person. Then, she can participate in her true gift, creative expression.

Cocky Kevin

A kinfolk of Macho Joe, Kevin convinces only himself of his heroism whereas others believe in Macho Joe's heroism, so public is Joe's bravery, courage, and strength. Kevin resembles a feisty little rooster, loudly crowing while pretending to be king of the barnyard. He brags of his accomplishments and abilities, masking his inner fears and insecurities. Like Macho Joe, Kevin feels lonely, for he has walled himself off from meaningful, truthful interaction with others. His desperation for acceptance prevents him from receiving the very thing that he most wants. His wounds can be healed, although he finds difficulty in accepting any guidance for this journey. Perhaps only in the depths of crisis will he be able to permit his vulnerabilities to surface long enough to allow true, unconditional acceptance from another to penetrate his feisty shell. When his inner pain is exposed to the light of day, he can learn to accept himself, thus replacing cockiness with the gift of genuine confidence.

Poor Loser

The sense of healthy competition becomes so distorted in Poor Loser that "to win at all costs" becomes the motto. While playing basketball, she thinks nothing of tripping her opponent who drives to make a basket. In a sales contest, she gleefully sabotages her competitor's performance in any way she can devise. She yells at the umpires while watching her child's Little League baseball game and pouts and complains for days when the team loses. When she loses any battle—she sees all competition as a battlefield—she slams down any handy object, stomps away, and stormily forgets to even acknowledge her opponent. At the deepest level, she wants acceptance and acknowledgment. She becomes less driven to win as she learns to provide these qualities for herself. She then turns her natural, competitive gift from a self-defeating behavior into an asset in business or sports or any other area of her life in which striving for excellence is appropriate.

Me First

This subpersonality distorts the process of self becoming so that he is only aware of himself to the exclusion of everything and everyone else. Even when his family calls, he talks exclusively about himself and forgets to even inquire about them. He remains unaware of anyone's feelings but his own. He acts as if the universe revolves around him, oblivious to his own narcissism. When he speaks, every sentence begins with "I." Just as a small child learns to relate to a broader world than himself, so too must Me First learn to expand his horizons. Slowly, he can experience satisfaction that comes when more of his needs are met by including others in his world. He transforms selfishness and self-centeredness into appreciation for his unfolding potential in the greater world.

Impatient Irma

Patience remains one of the hardest lessons for Aries people to learn, regardless of their evolution. Woe to those living with an Aries whose impatience as the driving force becomes encapsulated into a subpersonality. Irma wants everything to happen instantly, and she abhors waiting in lines of any kind. She tolerates no mistakes or slowness on the part of anyone else. Yelling in disgust at anyone who causes roadblocks or delays, she is incensed by anything that gets in her way. She blares her car horn if someone cuts in front of her, perhaps shaking her fist and yelling a few obscenities. Being outer-directed, she expresses more intolerance for others than for herself. However, when she accidentally cuts herself while impatiently chopping salad vegetables, she curses her own stupidity. As she learns to find her center core or true self, she gradually learns patience and inner peace. While still moving more quickly than the average person, impatience no longer dominates her. Then her gifts of exuberance and quick accomplishment can be available in a more ideal form.

References for Chapter 1

[1]. Rudhyar, 1970, p. 35.
[2]. Huber, 1984, p. 32.
[3]. Moore, (no date given), p. 3.
[4]. Bailey, 1951.
[5]. Huber, 1984, p. 35.
[6]. Burt, 1988, p. 24.
[7]. Huber, 1984, p. 32.
[8]. Rudhyar, 1970, p. 32.

TAURUS

Ann Nunley

April 22 - May 1

CHAPTER 2

TAURUS

The question is: Will the bull of desire or the bull of divine illumined expression succeed? — Alice Ann Bailey[1]

In the life of one attempting to walk the Path of Light, this desire is transmuted into the spiritual aspiration which surfaces in the urge to liberate oneself and others from the attachment to matter. — Alan Oken[2]

Affiliated House:	2
Ruling Planet:	Venus
Element:	Earth
Quality:	Fixed
Polarity:	Yin
Dates:	April 22 - May 21
Key Words:	I HAVE
Symbol:	Bull
Anatomy:	Throat, neck, ears, vocal chords, thyroid, tongue, mouth, tonsils, lower teeth

Imagery Experience for Taurus

Allow your awareness to follow your breath, gently being aware of breathing in and breathing out. ... As you continue breathing, imagine that the exhalation moves through your body, out your feet, and deep into the earth. As you inhale, imagine that you are breathing in earth energy through the bottoms of your feet, through your body and to the top of your head. Continue this circular breathing a few times. ... Imagine now that you are Taurus the Bull out in a beautiful place in nature. Sense what you see, hear, taste, touch, and smell from this perspective. Be aware of the power within you as you slowly move about. ... Take as much time as you need to really experience being Taurus the Bull. When you are ready, write or draw your images. Or, you may want to move or dance, expressing the essence of this experience.

Essence End of the Continuum

Earth Mother softly sings as she slowly walks among the newly sprouted plants nestled in protective straw in the fertile valley. Her song comes from her deepest sense of being, for Taurus is associated with the throat. Flowers splash the land with color, fragrantly nodding in a gentle, spring breeze. Earth Mother listens to everything in nature as one would listen to a wise elder, learning how to best steward this rich, verdant land. In its most spiritual form, Taurus represents Earth Mother—connected both with the earth and with earth's spirit.

At any level on the continuum, Taurus desires to plant fertile seeds. Taurus symbolizes will and power, both required for manifestation into physical form. The closer to the most integrated end of the continuum, the more desire transforms to aspiration to bring into being what the Self urges. The stamina of the Taurean to bring about what is needed is phenomenal. "Taurean stamina is the stamina of Mother Earth herself into which the crops were planted every spring to be watered by Father Sky. This endurance or loyalty is more characteristic of Taurus than any other quality," says Burt.[3]

On the personality level, Taureans usually seek to satisfy material desires and to accumulate more and more. The Buddha, who allegedly was born under the sign of Taurus, spoke often about the problems caused by desire—for material things, for security, for recognition, for whatever. The Buddha stated:

> If you are filled with desire
> Your sorrows swell
> Like the grass after the rain.
>
> But if you subdue desire
> Your sorrows fall from you
> Like drops of water from a lotus flower.[4]

Thus, free from grasping, the spiritual Taurean gradually understands that everything is good, beautiful and pleasant. As the esoteric seed thought for Taurus states, "I see, and when the eye is opened, all is illumined."[5] Taurus then relinquishes its material hold and awakens to a life on this earth that transcends baser desires.

Middle of the Continuum

As the second sign of the zodiac, Taurus builds upon what Aries initiated. Taurus nourishes what has been seeded and rests after all of the hyperactivity of Aries. As a fixed earth sign, Taurus demonstrates practicality and groundedness, budging only when ready.

Taureans possess the following qualities:

- Organic and earthy;
- Practical and productive;
- Sensual and affectionate;
- Traditional and security-oriented;
- Possessive and protective;
- Determined and strong-willed;
- Steady and deliberate;
- Unrushed and patient;
- Kind and generous.

Taureans struggle to moderate, for they tend to overdo each of these qualities.

Organic and earthy

According to Rudhyar, the purpose of Taurus is organic.[6] As the first earth sign in the zodiac, Taurus emerges from nature and from the Earth herself like the archetype of Earth Mother. Isabel Hickey, the late, spiritual astrologer, said that Taurus resembles "freshly plowed earth of springtime, ready for the seed."[7] As the ruler of Taurus, Venus seeks harmony by being attuned to the natural forces of nature. Herbs and natural healing processes which cooperate with the living organism, human or otherwise, interest many Taureans. Like the fruitful surface of the earth, Taureans attract bounty and abundance. They adeptly and resourcefully earn money and provide finances and substance for others as well as for themselves. Thus, one can see how the second house, affiliated with earthy Taurus, has become known as the house of "resources," whether these be financial and material assets, personal attributes and skills, or spiritual values.

LIKE THE FRUITFUL SURFACE OF THE EARTH, TAUREANS ATTRACT BOUNTY AND ABUNDANCE.

Practical and productive

From this organic base, Taureans desire practical and concrete results. As the "salt of the earth," they build and settle. Razzle dazzle performances do not interest them. Rather, they find the most simple, direct way in which to obtain the fruits of their efforts. They prefer tangible expressions in the material world. Even Taurus artists produce beautiful pottery or sculpture that also serves a functional purpose. Like other Earth signs, Taureans experience reality as coming from the concrete world, and they need tangible proof before they believe or accept something. "If you really love me, you will be affectionate." "I will buy a new computer when I see that it works and saves time." "I will look at your idea if you can show me what purpose it serves in my life."

Sensual and Affectionate

Earthy Taureans fully immerse "into the world of physical matter and the physical senses,"[8] and they gratify the senses with great satisfaction. Pure, sensual delight and joy sparkle at the more integrated end of this continuum, and sensuality coalesces into gluttony and indulgent pleasure-seeking as the continuum moves closer to the distorted end. They experience pleasure and comfort in manipulating and experiencing the physical sense world. Their eyes drink in beautiful sights, colors, forms whether in art galleries, arboretums, or meadows. Ferdinand the Bull exemplifies Taurus as he munches daisies and green grass, basks in the sun, smells the fragrant meadow flowers and casts an appreciative eye towards the contented cows.

No self-respecting Taurean would admit to enjoying McDonalds hamburgers, for their epicurean tastes tend to the gourmet side. Over the years, their bodies often accumulate weight because of indulging the taste buds once too often with a second chocolate eclair, strawberry mousse or chicken cordon bleu. However, their love of comfort usually prevents them from eating to the point of nausea as sometimes happens with Cancers who try to fill an "empty" space inside.

> No self-respecting Taurean would admit to enjoying McDonalds hamburgers. . .

Taureans love sensual fabrics such as velvet and other soft textures that provide pleasure to their skin. The car in the parking lot with soft, lambs wool seat and steering wheel covers probably belongs to a Taurus. Plush, comfortable furniture provides a relaxing environment. Probably no one appreciates the scent of the oil and the touch of the masseuse's hands more than a Taurean. The cosmetics industry undoubtedly loves Taureans in that they probably use more skin softeners, moisturizers, perfumes, and bubble baths than most other signs. Cosmetologists usually have Taurus or Venus placed prominently in the career house of their charts.

Their ears seem to be more finely tuned to sound than many other types and demand the finest sound equipment for listening to the best music. One man even refused to continue to date a woman who thought a tinny sounding album was "good enough." His sensibilities were insulted by her lack of appreciation. Taureans also love to sing and create music. Beethoven and Schubert had Taurus Ascendants, and Brahms and Wagner both had Taurus Suns, as do singers Barbra Streisand and Glen Campbell.

Calling upon the best of all five senses, Taureans love the sensuality of physical affection—pats on the back, hugs, a kiss on the cheek—and of sexuality. Physical magnetism emanates from their earthy nature. Once again, they may indulge the physical appetites too often, or they may prove to be exquisite lovers whose crude raw edges are as refined and honed as a fine musical instrument.

Traditional and security-oriented

The solid Taurean prefers sticking with the known and tested over seeking newer truths. They generally gravitate to orthodox religious faiths and to conservative political stances. Rudhyar reminds us that "Taurus is the reaction which follows Aries action."[9] Averse to change, the Taurean can either become rigid and stuck in the mud or develop fine-tuned skills of knowing what makes practical sense.

Deeply rooted in tradition, Taureans value security and stability. They like the continuity of regularly feeding the ducks at the pond, of attending the same church, and of vacationing at the same cottage. They also value security experienced from material acquisitions, domesticity and loyal connections.

Unlike the Capricorn who finds security in prestige from material possessions, the Taurean experiences security through meeting the needs of the five senses through material possessions. Taureans relish domesticity because of the comfort and security afforded by the delights of the home—a gourmet omelette cooked to perfection in a cast iron skillet, family puttering about the house, a hammock in the back yard, and a fragrant rose garden. World traveling which requires effort and sacrifice of known comforts does not entice them. However, Taureans enjoy pleasant visits from friends and family—provided the company travel to the Taurean's home.

Possessive and protective

The key words, "I HAVE," relate to Taurus' propensity to be quite aware of "my possessions and my resources," with which they feel they have the right to do as they please. Many Taureans even consider their partners, friends and spouses as their possessions, closely protecting them. Rudhyar explains that the typical Taurus traits of taking, accepting, and possessing, come "as a result of the deep sense of an inner need which must be satisfied."[10] They carefully protect anything they consider theirs and have a hard time letting go. Depending on the level of inner security, the Taurus person can anxiously cling to possessions or realize that the most valuable possessions are spiritual motivations and goals.

Determined and strong-willed

The expression of will can range from absolute stubbornness to divinely inspired choice. In discussing will as choice, Ferrucci, a psychosynthesis writer, states, "We can truly and freely choose, bearing the full responsibility of self-determination. It is to this evolutionary acquisition, still very much in development, that we give here the name of will."[11] For the average Taurus, however, outright stubbornness enters their personality from time to time. Even Taurean babies exhibit a strong will, as any parent knows who has tried to place a stiff-legged, unwilling Taurus baby into a car seat. Anyone who wants to work effectively with Taureans must learn the art of gentle persuasion rather than force. Force applied to Taureans only increases their resistance and determination to dig in their heels. Most Taureans consider strong determination to be one of their best qualities. One twelve-year-old was taken on a trip by his grandmother who scolded him, saying that he was the most bullheaded person she had ever known. He matter-of-factly, yet proudly, told her that he was bullheaded because he was a Taurus.

The ability to apply concentrated will allows most Taureans to obtain almost anything they really decide that they want. From a spiritual perspective, Taureans apply this fixity of purpose to evolutionary growth.

Steady and deliberate

Taurus demands practical results which are gained by repetition, set motions, stubborn insistence and undeviating effort. Like the turtle in the fable of the turtle and the hare, Taureans steadfastly persevere no matter what competitors do. They plod along their paths, not deviating an inch unless they find a good reason to do so.

In any kind of relationship, Taureans provide loyalty and constancy. They stay with partners through all kinds of storms and adversity, even when their partners find them boring. As letting go proves difficult for Taureans, they do not easily end relationships. They stand as solid as the Rock of Gibraltar. If a major catastrophe occurs, let us hope that many unwavering Taureans are present to provide strength, support and reassurance to other survivors.

Taureans' thinking processes follow the same steady, deliberate pattern. To those used to thinking like a popcorn popper, the Taurean may seem slow. They need time to assimilate facts and to adjust to new ideas. If they don't understand, they push the material aside and steadily continue the known path.

Unrushed and patient

More than any other sign, Taurus knows how to stop and smell the roses and to rest on the porch swing. They can curl up on comfortable pillows and watch movies, unmoved by the rushing and scurrying of the rest of the world. They savor quiet contentment as if it were an exquisite after dinner drink. The Taurean must know the purpose for any action. "Sooner or later, the outrushing life of Aries will be checked, controlled, channelled and held to Purpose. This is the work of Taurus."[12] Some Taurean children are known to balk at parents' insistence that they participate in after-school activities, for these children would rather follow their own rhythm and their own time. Their hidden talents need stillness in order to unfold.

Enamored by inactivity, Taureans can easily relax. They have even been called lazy by more active types. At times, they become as inert as a freight train that has come to a dead standstill. At these times, they may just rest until they find purpose to move again. Conversely, they may have become stagnant, in which case they need a shaking experience or inspiration in order to find the motivation to move again. Like the freight train, they start slowly, and once they roll with powerful momentum, they do not stop easily, for they are fueled by mighty purpose.

Generally composed and placid, Taureans exhibit the patience of Job. Appearing calm and unmoved on the outside, they can be cajoled, pushed and nudged by others for a long time, for they anger slowly. However, once the Taurean has finally had too much, he breathes the explosive force of a raging bull and charges at his matador. Woe to those who push the Bull too far, for he never forgets once he becomes angry.

GENERALLY COMPOSED AND PLACID, TAUREANS EXHIBIT THE PATIENCE OF JOB.

KIND AND GENEROUS

Believing deeply in an abundant universe, the Taurean exhibits calmness, quiet kindness and benevolence. The greater their own satisfaction and thankfulness, the more they give generously to others. They supply loved ones with gifts, comfort, possessions, and even an understanding ear in time of need. When connected with their own inner essence, they are truly harmless, "borne by the recognition and esteem of the Divine in all things and by the knowledge of the good and beautiful in creation."[13]

SUBPERSONALITY END OF THE CONTINUUM

Lazy Lil

She makes a life style of sitting on the sofa, watching old movies and indolently avoiding any kind of physical exertion. She carries relaxation to such an extreme that her body resembles the posture of wet spaghetti. Sloth and torpor predominate the day, for Lazy Lil has lost her inner sense of purpose. She apathetically squanders her gift of being present to the moment and smelling the roses. She needs to find motivation to moderate her life. In order to be inspired to find balance and purpose—both in activity and inactivity—she needs to connect again to her true Self.

Merlin, the Magician

Merlin distorts Taurus' natural gift of bringing desired things into form by selfishly creating results that put him in a powerful position over others. He now not only covets material possessions but power as well, and others may fear him. As if he were an amateur sorcerer, Merlin plays with dangerous forces in trying to manipulate nature itself. Cut off from his natural benevolence, he fears the world and believes that he must overpower nature and others in order to survive. He needs to learn that personal safety can exist while working in harmony with the world, sharing the resources, and that his ego can be gratified by expressing the positive qualities of Taurus. Then Merlin once again accesses the natural ability to ethically produce results.

Setting Hen

Setting Hen is so possessive of anything she deems hers that she clucks disapprovingly at anyone who comes too close, fearing that they may threaten her precious chicks. Not realizing the abundance of the universe, as more integrated Taureans do, she believes that she must carefully guard her possessions. At times she extremely overprotects family members, employees, friends or co-workers. She believes that without her protection that life would be a shambles and that others would fall apart. She needs to learn to trust others' capacity to know what is best for themselves and to trust the universe to provide resources. As she more fully integrates, she realizes her true resources reside within.

Boring Plodder

His eyes focus on his feet slowly slogging through the mud. Plodder even forgets to look around at the wonders of nature. He has lost contact with the joyful, inner child that would allow him to truly enjoy being an Earth person. Instead, he fixes his intention on taking one step after another, after another, after another. Bound by routine, he has even forgotten the purpose of the routine—and the purpose of his life. Dulled by a lack of inspiration and color, he trudges through life not even enjoying his natural propensity to sensuality. He needs to find healing for and reconnection with the natural child within his own being. Then he reconnects with inner purpose, releasing his gifts of steadfastness and deliberateness.

Squandering Sarah

Like a spoiled child, Sarah wants more and more things, demanding greater and greater satiation from the material world. More chocolates, better stereo equipment, plusher furniture, a more expensive car, finer clothing, a larger expense account—she voraciously consumes pleasures and material goods hoping for satisfaction which never arrives. She constantly throws away the not-even-outworn objects, replacing them with more expensive versions, oblivious of her wastefulness or of her unconscious striving for love. She believes she has a right to these possessions always hoping that they will make her feel good. Only when she has realized her own inner worth will she again find true pleasure in simple comforts. Then squandering transforms to sensing.

Balky Mule

This character acts stubborn for the sake of being stubborn. He strongly identifies as a person who cannot be pushed around by anybody and wears "obstinate and mulish" as badges of honor. He perversely hangs onto opinions, possessions, points of view, and purpose regardless of reason or outcome. He would rather retain his identity of stubbornness than he would to have a positive outcome. He has distorted Taurus' natural gift of expressing conscious choice into willfully and mindlessly choosing. While stubbornness helped him survive by not being manipulated and pushed by others, he has given up true choice. He needs to learn ways in which he can be safe with others without extreme balkiness. He needs to cooperate without sacrificing himself, which he unconsciously fears. As he eventually learns to trust his inner self, then he surrenders some of the strong personality will and allows an expression of divine will to move through him.

The Boss

With strong opinions about how things should be done most productively, The Boss takes control to protect her own interests.

She focuses her fixed purpose upon those around her, getting them to comply with her orders. Being a fixed Earth sign, even she as a subpersonality, bosses others with a quiet and calm force unless they persistently do not comply. She exerts greater and greater pressure without losing her cool unless she is pushed to the limit, and then she becomes very angry. As the boss, she solidifies ownership—she feels she "owns" all of those she bosses. She, too, needs to learn cooperation and a higher expression of will in order to be whole.

Hedonist Henry

Henry revels in the senses, overindulging every appetite known. The old expression about spending his life on "wine, women, and song" applies to him. His animal nature rules his life as he searches for greater and greater sensual pleasures. He does not realize that he, like his cousin, Squandering Sarah, really searches for deeper meaning and purpose. He has distorted the natural gift of sensuality into oversatiation. He needs to learn how to find pleasure in moderation and to find true appreciation for the exquisiteness of the senses. He may even learn new methods of expressing sexuality that provide a more satisfying energetic union with his partner. He does not have to give up earthly pleasures. Rather, in order to come from a more centered place, he must incorporate reverence for life into his experience.

HIS ANIMAL NATURE RULES HIS LIFE AS HE SEARCHES FOR GREATER AND GREATER SENSUAL PLEASURES.

NOTES:

References for Chapter 2

[1]. Bailey, 1951, p. 378.
[2]. Oken, 1990, p. 167.
[3]. Burt, 1988, p. 51.
[4]. Byrom, 1976, p. 128.
[5]. Huber, 1984, p. 46.
[6]. Rudhyar, 1970.
[7]. Hickey, 1970, p. 14.
[8]. Dobyns, 1972, p. 4
[9]. Rudhyar, 1970, p. 38.
[10]. Rudhyar, 1970, p. 43.
[11]. Ferrucci, 1982, p. 73.
[12]. Moore, no date, p. 4.
[13]. Huber, 1984, p. 53.

GEMINI

Ann Nunley

May 22 - June 21

CHAPTER 3

GEMINI

Through his ability to turn intellectually in any direction with ease and to differentiate between the many objects in the physical world and to order them correctly, the Messenger of the gods appears in his true nature, capable of combining extremes together in a higher way. — Louise Huber[1]

His whole being now yearns for a vivid extension of the sphere of his experience. — Dane Rudhyar[2]

Affiliated House:	3
Ruling Planet:	Mercury
Element:	Air
Quality:	Mutable
Polarity:	Yang
Dates:	May 22 - June 21
Key words:	I THINK
Symbol:	Twins
Anatomy:	Lungs, collar bone, hands, arms shoulders, nervous system

Imagery Experience for Gemini

As you gently follow the breath in and out, allow your body to relax and release. When thoughts arise, quietly note them and then return your awareness to your breath. ... Experience the sparkling vitality that is carried on the breath revitalizing every part of your body, emotions and mind. ... Imagine now that you are both Gemini Twins, one masculine and one feminine. ... First imagine the perspective from one ... and then from the other. ... Allow any thoughts, images or perceptions of Gemini to emerge into your awareness. ... When you are ready, write or draw your insights.

Essence End of the Continuum

In its most spiritual expression, Gemini radiates both outward, gathering information and awareness, and inward, realizing more and more of the light of the true

Self. As the Self illumines the personality, synthesis occurs—of soul and personality, of masculine and feminine, of light and dark. While Mercury, as exoteric ruler of Gemini, gathers and disseminates information and ideas, Venus, the esoteric ruler, helps synthesize the diversities brought together. Huber says that Venus "resolves the duality with her unifying quality and transforms it into a 'fluid synthesis' as it is expressed esoterically."[3]

The esoteric seed thought for Gemini, "I recognize my other Self and in the waning of that Self, I grow and glow" addresses this synthesis. When the "other Self" directs the personality and transmits soul energy through the personality, duality ceases to exist. Separation ceases. Therefore, the great light "grows and glows." Huber further says that "The other Self disappears as its substance flows over into us and we ourselves become inner illumination."[4]

> "I RECOGNIZE MY OTHER SELF AND IN THE WANING OF THAT SELF, I GROW AND GLOW"

In Aries, the individual first exerts the impulse to BE. In Taurus, the desire body carries the impulse which then moves to the mind in Gemini. At the spiritual end of the continuum, Gemini transcends the lower mind, although utilizing it for conceptualization. Gemini operates from the intuitive higher mind in which diversity synthesizes into a whole. Gemini, the Twins, then merge into the one dazzling light of the Soul.

Middle of the Continuum

Gemini, bored with the slow and grounded pace of Taurus, accelerates speed and expands into the world, curiously seeking knowledge. Burt refers to Gemini as Hermes who "...is a catalyst, a messenger. He communicates information and brings people together."[5] At the personality level, the mind dominates in the sign of Gemini, so being rational and emotionally detached are salient qualities of the sign. Since the personality usually experiences separation from the Self, Gemini also represents dualism.

The following qualities also express in the Gemini personality:

- Connective and integrative,
- Self-educated and curious,
- Adaptable and versatile,
- Communicative and verbally expressive,
- Sociable and outgoing,
- Noncommittal and freedom-oriented,
- Lighthearted and playful.

Rational and emotionally detached

The key words, "I think," find constant expression in Gemini, and people with a predominance of this sign's energy strongly identify with the mind and often erroneously think that the mind is the Self. As a mutable air sign, "Gemini, more than any other sign, must realize that the mind is not the supreme commander of the Self, but just a tool of that Self," says Oken.[6] While Taurus immerses itself in the senses, Gemini observes and thinks about what the senses perceive.

> GEMINI . . . MUST REALIZE THAT THE MIND IS NOT THE SUPREME COMMANDER OF THE SELF. . .

The Gemini mind loves to classify, play, and be in constant motion. The native of this sign yearns to order and categorize the multiplicity of information that it gathers, so expect overflowing filing cabinets in the Gemini person's office. They want logical proof for everything, which provides some security in the swiftly changing tides that swirl around this mutable person. Logical Geminis provide the gifts of objectivity, clarity, and detachment. However, when Geminis over-identify with the mind, they rationalize everything with their self-created logic. Feelings remain submerged in the subconscious; true sensory and feeling experience remains remote when they operate only from above the neck. They may become cold and aloof when out of touch with their feeling nature.

The mind of Gemini resembles popcorn popping—each thought randomly and quickly tumbling out of the popper, sometimes spilling out of the container. The mind dances with a variety of thoughts and topics from dawn till long after going to bed. Even with just one eye open in early morning, Geminis have already experienced 763 thoughts. While gifted with wonderfully creative minds, Gemini people must learn how to relax and to be in charge of thoughts which otherwise take control and wreck havoc with their nervous systems.

Because of the rapidity of their thoughts, Geminis do not realize the repetitiveness of their mental processes. If they kept a diary of every thought, they would be surprised to see how many times the same thought popped out of the popper. They need to learn how to select the thoughts which require concentration and learn to observe and dismiss the rest.

> EVEN WITH JUST ONE EYE OPEN IN EARLY MORNING, GEMINIS HAVE ALREADY EXPERIENCED 763 THOUGHTS.

From babyhood until death, the Gemini needs mental stimulation. Reading to the tiny Gemini in utero is not too early.

By the time their little fingers can hold the pieces, they love mentally-oriented board and card games. Geminis likely even prefer to be buried with a few magazines just in case it gets boring on the "other side." Their mind penetrates through everything, and highly developed Geminis combine the intuitive mind with regular mental gymnastics.

Dualistic

From the perspective of the Self, dualism is an illusion, for only one light interpenetrates all of life. As Emmanuel explains, "There are, in fact, no direct opposites. They only seem so in that one is speaking of Divine Law perceived from different areas of understanding."[7] However, from the perspective of the personality, pairs of opposites exist: light and dark, love and fear, male and female, selfish and selfless, higher and lower, even the Self and personality. Emmanuel further explains, "The duality of your earth has a Divine purpose. . . .Though you may live in it, you are not trapped in it. It is not your prison but your schoolroom. You are using duality to help you find unity."[8]

The symbol for Gemini, the Twins, heralds from Castor and Pollux of Roman mythology. One twin represented heaven and the other earth, symbolic of Self and personality dimensions of the human experience. Mercury, the Messenger of the Gods, mediates between the two until synthesis eventually occurs.

In a lighter vein, Geminis experience dualism in humorous ways. If possible, they would clone themselves in order to be in two places at once. They buy two of everything, perhaps in different colors, and they often wear two pins or ornaments at once. They sometimes even relate to two lovers at once—or, if the lover is versatile and creative, perhaps just one. The Gemini may be the only person who walks down the wedding aisle checking out the attendees to see if he or she would rather have another bride or groom.

Connective and integrative

Gemini, the thinker and weaver of ideas, creates "patterns which will emerge finally as visible forms."[9] Civilizations exist because language allows ideas to connect, weave into patterns, and express into form. Geminis build with words. At their best, they synthesize and see the whole even with scanty information. They conceptualize thought systems, adding meaning to experience.

Human beings connect with each other through the air itself, Gemini's element. Rudhyar explains, "We are all, actually and in concrete fact, united with every breathing organism."[10] However, some Geminis believe that they will die unless connected with words to others, and hence, some talk compulsively.

Self-educated and curious

From the moment the wee, little Gemini leaves the birth canal until death, he explores the world and becomes aware of everything around him, including a legion of ideas. He longs for knowledge and experience of the world, and Dobyns asserts that "knowledge is the prerequisite for freedom."[11] The Gemini learns, snapping up ideas as quickly and deftly as a toad catches flies.

Quick witted and intelligent, the Gemini easily suffers boredom when hearing the same material twice or experiencing one set of material too deeply. Loving variety in learning, they are addicted to books, magazine articles, classes and workshops. No self-respecting Gemini reads less than seven books at once—one in the bathroom, one in the car in case of delay due to a train crossing, one in a purse, one or two in the living room, and another three or four beside the bed. They do not finish every book, for Geminis search for key ideas and then bounce to another subject. Many Geminis prefer magazine articles over books, because the articles can be read more quickly on a greater variety of subjects. One Gemini professor reported that she loved to learn all kinds of information in doing research, but she hated to write about the findings because she quickly lost interest once she learned what she wanted to know and was already exploring new ideas.

Geminis possess insatiable curiosity. Why is the sky blue? Why do lady bugs have spots? Why does the cat prefer tuna over chopped liver? Why did Sally kiss Joe? Where are the people in the television set? What did John say to Mary during class? What is for dinner? Who won the basketball game? How many jelly beans are in one bag? Where do butterflies sleep at night? They possess as much curiosity as a baby learning to explore the world by touching and feeling everything it can reach and popping nearly every new-found object into its mouth for another delightful learning experience. Many Geminis drive dozens of miles on a whim just to hear a lecture on some topic they find fascinating at the moment. They certainly need a varied education in order to remain satisfied and intrigued.

While a more retiring person might relax at home, one Gemini reported that on her afternoon off, she relaxed by first visiting a friend, then shopping, then attending a concert in the park—definitely not a boring day! They resemble butterflies flitting through a beautiful meadow of flowers, first tasting the nectar of one flower, then another, then another. However, if they do not monitor their "yes's" to activities, people, books, and educational pursuits, their energies scatter to the four winds.

THEY RESEMBLE BUTTERFLIES FLITTING THROUGH A BEAUTIFUL MEADOW OF FLOWERS. . .

ADAPTABLE AND VERSATILE

Out of their curiosity comes a love of variety and the ability to do many things at once. Their versatility and dexterity find expression in being "Jack of all trades." Most prefer work in which they can do a variety of tasks or have two jobs which allows greater stimulation. Adept at getting along with many types of people, Geminis see each new contact as interesting.

As a mutable sign, Gemini is adaptable and flexible, changing either on a whim or as needed in order to be at the right place at the right time. As changeable as quicksilver—simply another name for Mercury—Geminis rapidly shift mental moods and opinions as new information appears. This shifting and changing unsettles more fixed types, for Geminis appear to be inconsistent and unstable when Mercury rises and falls too quickly. On the other hand, they make wonderful teachers and salespeople who need to constantly shift with the needs of the situation.

Their flexibility allows them to adapt to new environments and to accommodate to new circumstances and ideas. The gift of adaptability is sorely needed in these rapidly changing times when the average person will have four or five significant career changes, when the total amount of information in the world doubles every five or less years, and when skills needed to survive in a modern, technical world increase every day. Perhaps every baby would do well to ask for a little dose of Gemini to guide them through these changing times.

Communicative and verbally expressive

While some students cringe in their seats before giving their first presentation in Speech 101, Geminis bask in the opportunity to share their natural-born gift of communication. The Gemini credo states, "I see, conceptualize and talk."[12] A Gemini's hand fits onto a telephone receiver as if it were a piece of equipment that emerged from the womb with him, and many Geminis spend hours on the phone. Some Geminis fall into the trap of gossiping, for they love to give and receive tidbits about other people. They can write witty, clever letters, and they take notes consummately.

> THE GEMINI CREDO STATES, "I SEE, CONCEPTUALIZE AND TALK."

Loquacious and diplomatic, Geminis provide skill in any marketplace where ideas are exchanged. They excel at occupations that require expertise in communication: education, sales, marketing, radio and television, advertising, writing, public relations. They love to express with words, "words that are rooted in images of the living and in personal experience, rather than in the search for universal meanings (as Sagittarians do)."[13] Many writers of and lovers of poetry and literature have Gemini prominent in their charts. For example, Tennyson had Moon, Venus, and Ascendant in Gemini. William Butler Yeats had Sun, Mercury and Uranus in Gemini, and Ralph Waldo Emerson had Sun, Mercury and Midheaven in Gemini.

Sociable and outgoing

Gemini emerges as the social butterfly of the zodiac with the capacity to enjoy, understand, accept, and interact with a wide variety of people. Geminis welcome the new neighbor before anyone on the block and quickly show the new foreign exchange student around town. They could win prizes for congeniality, for they can charm and fascinate others with their ingenuous, friendly demeanor. They establish immediate rapport with others, although the contact may be superficial and temporary. Geminis do not always keep deep, dark secrets, for they resemble open books, wanting to share every thought.

Relationships stimulate and interest Geminis, and they love being in the midst of people. Something can be learned from neighbors, siblings, relatives, acquaintances, and classmates — all people represented in the third house of an astrological chart, Gemini's natural home.

Noncommittal and freedom-oriented

Geminis prefer having an arm's length between themselves and the world just to make sure that they remain unfettered and untrapped. They resist settling, and according to Isabel Hickey, are like "the light changeable breezes of early summer. Here today and gone tomorrow but you are better for the contact."[14] Unlike Taureans who want to own and be owned, Geminis fear boredom and monotony if they stay in one place or one relationship too long. Kathleen Burt, a Jungian astrologer, calls Gemini the "puer," the Peter Pan who refuses to grow up and take responsibility.[15] They like a variety of friends and acquaintances so that they always have choice. If they do leave a long-term relationship, they generally do not mourn for too long. Instead, they focus on the interesting sights and experiences ahead. Like an adolescent leaving home to see the world, they refuse to experience bondage or too close ties to family or environment. Trying to tie one down is like trying to hold onto a wisp of air.

Restless by nature, Geminis hate to begin at the beginning. They hastily assume that they already know the material at the beginning anyway. With their mind racing ahead ninety miles an hour, they need to be in constant motion—never sedentary. They prefer situations and occupations in which they have a variety of experiences and are free to move quickly from place to place. The urge to rush sometimes causes tension and anxiety, and they need to learn methods of relaxation and focus so that purpose clarifies.

Lighthearted and playful

Of all of the signs of the zodiac, Gemini most naturally exhibits childlike characteristics. Their playfulness and ability to delight in fun reminds everyone to be more lighthearted, laugh more, and not take life so seriously. They dance lightly through life providing surprise and paradox, sparkling the lives of others. Silly and inane at times, they love mischievous pranks. They may teasingly pit two people against each other, secretly laughing at the trouble they instigate. Their great gift remains in their ability to greet life lightly, objectively, and cheerfully.

Subpersonality End of the Continuum

Peter Pan

Entire books have been written about this subpersonality who never grows up. He fears real-life responsibility and relationships. The perennial child, he flits from relationship to relationship and experience to experience, never quite grasping the meaning of adulthood. He plays, chatters, and occasionally pretends to be serious, but his true life purpose eludes him. He believes danger results from being adult and that he must continue to live in never-never land. When his hair begins to thin and his friends have grandchildren, he somehow vaguely realizes that something is missing in his life. The sterility and seeming choicelessness that comes from being stuck in one developmental stage of life eventually causes him to ask, "Is this all there is?" He must contact inner life purpose and face his fears of adulthood in order to truly free his gift of lightheartedness.

Scatter-brained

Scatter-brained is involved in countless committees, organizations, community activities, evening classes, little league games, and correspondence courses. She forgets what sitting down for a five-minute rest feels like. Her mind is so cluttered with lists of things to do and places to go that eventually she forgets everything. "Where is Johnny (her five-year old)?" she asks. With the baby sitter? At Grandmother's? In the living room? She shows up out of breath at church for a meeting only to discover it was held last night. After she locks her car keys in her car for the fifth time, she wonders if she is losing her mind. While versatility is her gift, she has sold her soul to activity forgetting the purpose of activity. Her mind, also her gift, has become fragmented and overloaded, unable to coherently organize her life. She needs to remember how to be the director of her orchestra rather than frantically jumping from one instrument to the next.

Gossip Gary

Gary knows tidbits of tantalizing information about nearly all of his acquaintances and friends and shares these morsels with anyone who listens. He gleans information about others as skillfully as a newspaper reporter. Sometimes he secretly chuckles to himself as he watches the rumors spread. How much will the messages change as they circulate, he muses, out of touch with any damage they may cause. Instead of writing novels or teaching great literature, Gossip Gary entertains himself by gathering and disseminating petty details about others. Some circles which voraciously await gossip welcome him. Eventually though, he wears out his welcome because people realize that no one is immune from being celebrated in his stories.

He yearns for recognition from and connection with others and erroneously believes that gossiping achieves this goal. His methods work for awhile, and then he feels lonely and rejected. He must learn more satisfying ways to have his needs met. Most of all, he needs a connection with his innermost being so that his true gifts of communication and the ability to relate to others can be released in a healthy manner.

Motor Mouth Mary

Mary talks nonstop from the time she awakes in the morning until she falls asleep at night. She versatilely talks about gossip, the weather, the football game, new scientific discoveries, what her children are doing, where she is going on vacation, information she has gleaned from reading while not talking. She compulsively talks to anyone who listens and probably even to herself when no one is available. Although never quite reaching conscious awareness, she believes that unless she is connected by words to others that she exists all alone in the world. Unaware of emotional connections with people, she experiences words as her lifeline to humanity and to love. She does not realize that the overdose of words actually cuts her off from the very people she wants to relate with the most. Like Gossip, she needs to first experience connection with her Self.

. . .SHE BELIEVES THAT UNLESS SHE IS CONNECTED BY WORDS TO OTHERS THAT SHE EXISTS ALL ALONE IN THE WORLD.

Imp

Imp sees himself as the life of the party and a joy to be around. He loves to tease and to play pranks on others. Proud of his sense of humor, he wonders why everyone else acts so seriously. Even at age 36, he loves to repeatedly make the garage door go up and down with the garage door opener, thinking how cute he is. Like his cousin, Peter Pan, Imp remains stuck in childhood. Perhaps as a child he acted as the "mascot" of his family and was rewarded for being the joking, funny one. He kept his family laughing so that they could focus on Imp rather than family tensions. "That imp!" they chuckled, applauding his antics right through chronological childhood, adolescence and adulthood. He wonders whether his family will still love him if he fails to tease and act silly. He never learned how to find safety or to gain recognition for being serious and adult. He needs to learn how to disidentify from this role so that he has more flexibility in his approach to life. Then playfulness can be a charming attribute rather than a prison.

Dilettante Diane

Diane barely scratches the surface of life or of anything that she studies. Separated from any sense of inner purpose, she dabbles in art, literature, science, and motivational seminars. She superficially learns a bit of this and a bit of that and only presents fragments of ideas to others. If she were to write what she knew about each of the topics that she has studied, she would scribble one or two sentences about each. She needs to develop a deeper sense of service to others. Then she could focus more deeply on some of the topics so that she might be able to share her knowledge with others.

Coiled Spring

Coiled Spring contorts his face with tension and tightness. His racing mind controls his life, and he, too, takes on too many projects for him to comfortably handle. He develops nervous tics in response to inner tension. Being around him is like being next to an electrical cord with a short in it—randomly sputtering sparks. He drives too fast, talks too fast, and runs too fast. He runs from himself and has never learned how to relax and allow the mind to rest. His mind clatters day and night until he suffers what is known in popular parlance as a "nervous breakdown." He, too, needs to learn how to direct his mind rather than being at its whim. He needs to find his center. Then his gift of a quick mind can be liberated from bound-up energy and used creatively in the world.

Crafty Fox

Crafty Fox resembles a stereotyped used car salesperson—a person who uses her clever mind and words to manipulate others into buying whatever she has to offer whether that be products, office politics, or social engagements. She adroitly uses humor if it serves her purposes, and her intelligent, witty repartee catches people off guard. She prides herself on her shrewdness and may be disdainful of others' ignorance and lack of savvy. Crafty Fox skillfully uses social skills to get whatever she wants, yet she remains unaware of her true needs. She misuses her Gemini tools, believing that she must use her brilliance against others in order to survive. Her cunning serves her well for awhile but eventually becomes hollow. In order to experience true love, her deepest need, she must learn new methods of relating as equals.

References for Chapter 3

[1]. Huber, 1984, p. 70.
[2]. Rudhyar, 1970, p. 45.
[3]. Huber, 1984, p. 67.
[4]. Huber, 1984, p. 73.
[5]. Burt, 1988, p. 91.
[6]. Oken, 1973, p. 111.
[7]. Rodegast & Stanton, 1985, p. 88.
[8]. Rodegast & Stanton, 1985, p. 88.
[9]. Moore, no date, p. 4.
[10]. Rudhyar, 1970, p. 49.
[11]. Dobyns, 1972, p. 6.
[12]. Dobyns, 1972.
[13]. Rudhyar, 1970, p. 46.
[14]. Hickey, 1970, p. 15.
[15]. Burt, 1988, p. 76.

CANCER

June 22 - July 22

CHAPTER 4

CANCER

Oh, Aunt Em! I'm so glad to be home again! There's no place like home!—Frank Baum, *The Wizard of Oz*

I have penetrated to the source of my Being, to the womb, to the primal source. Here I feel myself to be secure, supported, protected. I can feel the pulse beat of life, I am one with the basis of all life. A deep peace enters me.—Louise Huber[1]

Affiliated House:	4
Ruling Planet:	Moon
Element:	Water
Quality:	Cardinal
Polarity:	Yin
Dates:	June 22 - July 22
Key Words:	I FEEL
Symbol:	Crab
Anatomy:	Breast, stomach, upper lobes of liver

Imagery Experience for Cancer

Become aware of the your breath. ... Imagine that the breath is like gentle ocean waves, and with each breath, the wave gently moves through your body ... cleansing and refreshing you. ... Feel the body relaxing. ... Allow the emotions to calm and to experience the rhythm of the ocean waves. ... Feel the mind at rest. ... Imagine now that you are a crab, encased in your own shell, and that you are safely secluded under a rock. ... Be aware of what you feel and experience as this crab. ... Imagine that you, the crab, now feel safe enough to venture into the sunlit water, and be aware of everything that you experience now. ... Imagine now what it would feel like if you knew that you were infinitely safe. ... When you are ready, express your perceptions about Cancer in whatever form suits you.

Essence End of the Continuum

Spiritually advanced Cancerians sustain themselves by an inner wellspring through which flows an eternal source of healing, nourishing, purifying water. Like the Universal Mother, Cancerians provide boundless nourishment for anyone in need—food for hungry bodies, warm and gracious empathy for hurting emotions, and spiritual sustenance for eager souls. They not only reach out to humanity in need; they also provide a safe haven for anyone. Children splash joyfully, delightfully, in the water knowing they are protected in this Universal Mother's presence. Oken suggests that advanced Cancerians devote their "life to the cohesive networking of men and women of goodwill."[2]

In esoteric readings, Cancer represents the door through which the Soul enters into consciousness for another cycle of lifetimes.[3] At first, the collective unconscious powerfully pulls. This means that individual thought submerges into unconscious beliefs and fears held by the general populace. If the collective contains deep fears of doom through global war, fear rules individuals who absorb those beliefs. Cancerians need to overcome mass consciousness and to relinquish dependence on the collective. Then they evolve towards Self, receiving inspiration and illumination that accelerates growth. As esoteric ruler of Cancer, Neptune invokes expansion of universal consciousness and love.

The esoteric seed thought for Cancer states, "I build a lighted house and therein dwell."[4] The more a person expresses universal love for others, the more that light will be attracted. With greater light, they provide unlimited nourishment to the world. These advanced Cancerians experience infinite safety and hold that truth for others as well.

Middle of the Continuum

Reversing the trend of expansiveness into new relationships which Gemini started, Cancer focalizes on roots. Cancerians must learn how to be safe in the world, how to meet their own basic needs, and how to become more rooted in their own Being. With that accomplished, nurturance and interdependence top the list of Cancer characteristics.

They also express the following qualities:

- ♦ Sensitive and emotional;
- ♦ Protective and internal;
- ♦ Active and insistent;
- ♦ Domestic and home loving;
- ♦ Nostalgic and attached to the past;
- ♦ Cautious and security-oriented;
- ♦ Absorptive and psychic;
- ♦ Responsive.

Nurturant and interdependent

All human beings have needs, and the most fundamental needs must be met in order for any of the other needs to even be relevant. Maslow's famous hierarchy of needs[5] proves valid for all human beings, and the bottom two rungs especially ring true for the Cancerian experience.

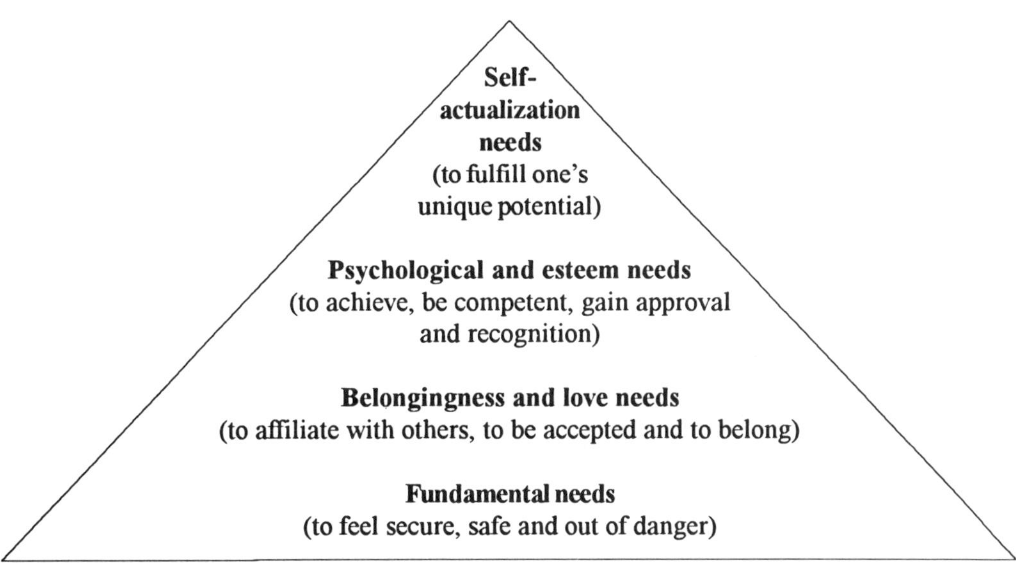

Although Cancer traditionally represents the archetypal mother and child, in today's world this symbol really represents whichever parent provides the most nurturance. On the one hand, Cancerians express as the inner child demanding that its needs be met, indeed requiring that those needs be met in order to remain alive. On the other hand, they represent the nurturing parent. When their own needs remain unmet, they play out the child side more often, and when their cups are full, they possess the capacity to parent the world. Actually, these two sides of the same coin frequently become subpersonalities within the same person—a needy child and a caretaker. Integrated Cancerians both nurture in healthy ways (as parent) <u>and</u> bask in safety and comfort (as inner child). Then the gifts of nurturance and interdependence can be available depending upon the need of the moment.

Integrated Cancerians offer wise guidance, love and warmth to others without depending upon others' responses. Cancerians reassure the insecure, assist the needy, and provide milk, hugs, cookies and lullabies when appropriate. On the other hand, as Burt says, "This nurturing archetype invests emotional energy and expects a return on the investment."[6] The Statue of Liberty, symbol for Cancerian United States, symbolizes protection and comfort. These symbolic national qualities can express in a distorted or healthy fashion, just like for any Cancer person.

While interdependence remains the optimum expression of potential, most Cancerians experience dependence upon others instead. Some battle this side of their personality, demanding independence, while inside deeply yearning for emotional safety, a sense of belonging, and dependence. At other times, each person in the relationship mutually expresses dependence, meets shared needs and desires, and retains a sense of individuality. Huber attests to the difficulty of moving beyond dependence in that the Cancerian has to "swim against the current—and that always requires the dissociation of ourselves from collective dependence, a step outward from the security of our safe nest in order to become an independent individual."[7]

Sensitive and emotional

Like all of the water signs, Cancerians possess a strong feeling nature and often identify with this aspect of their personality. Yet, each of the water signs manifest emotionality differently depending upon the quality—cardinality, fixed or mutable—and upon the inner meaning of each of those signs. Although the manifestation of each depends upon where the person operates on the continuum, basically emotionality in Cancer is characterized by vulnerability, in Scorpio by intensity, and in Pisces by a desire to merge with the Cosmos.

When Cancerians feel rooted in Self, providing an underlying foundation of security, they possess the greatest gift from their feeling nature—empathy. As Zip Dobyns explains, "Water communicates directly and immediately, through actual emotional participation in others. . . It is a very real sharing of feeling and action by those who love each other, whether with or without conscious expression in words."[8] Without the connectedness provided by empathetic feeling, the world would indeed be a dry place in which to live. They exhibit softness and tenderness towards others, feeling what others experience.

On the other hand, when they closely identify as being their emotions, they act hypersensitively and hurt too easily. Then they respond as if every cross word were directed at them and feel sorry for themselves. Sometimes they experience upset stomachs, gastric problems or milk allergies when responding too much to the whims of their emotions. Although hypersensitivity often expresses in Cancerian subpersonalities, this characteristic warrants mention in this middle range since nearly all Cancerians occasionally react too much to others unless they emerged from the womb as miniature Christs or Buddhas.

. . .NEARLY ALL CANCERIANS OCCASIONALLY REACT TOO MUCH TO OTHERS UNLESS THEY EMERGED FROM THE WOMB AS MINIATURE CHRISTS OR BUDDHAS.

Metamorphose for the Cancerian must occur within the context of feelings. All water signs experience the Self through their feeling nature. They may sense the existence of the Self by a heartfelt tear of joy or connection; they may tingle with warm feelings; they may experience an ecstatic mood. Through these contacts with Self, the Cancerian grows and eventually becomes Soul-infused.

PROTECTIVE AND INTERNAL

Cancer, the Crab, carries its dwelling place on its back, protected from the dangers lurking in its environment. Sometimes they act like hermit crabs needing the safety found in reclusiveness, yet they also need the nurturance and comfort provided by close friends and family. Like the crab, Cancerians emerge from under their hiding rocks when they feel safe and then quickly skitter back sideways under the rock whenever danger approaches. They need to connect with their innermost Being where they are free from all external dangers.

Cancerian protectiveness expresses as shyness in the personality, especially for children. Some older Cancerians just learn to better cover timidity with an outer facade; others learn that they are infinitely safe in the universe and transcend shyness. In any sense, Cancerians do not express openly or showily. They often fear that their vulnerabilities may be revealed which would open them for attack. Rather than knowingly present their soft underbelly, they quietly hold back unless they trust implicitly.

> CANCERIAN PROTECTIVENESS EXPRESSES AS SHYNESS IN THE PERSONALITY, ESPECIALLY FOR CHILDREN.

In relationships with others, Cancerians usually present themselves indirectly and even elusively. They fear being pinned down which might prevent them from easily retreating into protection. Therefore, they often speak in vague subtleties so that if pressed later, they can always say that they meant something else. Oken summarizes Cancerians' protectiveness by saying that the "urge to retreat back into the watery protectiveness of the mother's womb will be as strong, if not stronger than, the urge to be born into the light of individualized self-definition."[9]

ACTIVE AND INSISTENT

In seeming contradiction with the above qualities, this cardinal expression sets Cancer apart from the other water signs. Even though preferring protection and quiet, Cancerians usually tenaciously, even if not overtly, demand that their needs be met. They insist upon response from others in order to receive reassurance of love and nurturance. Rudhyar says that they "can be the most helpless or the most determined in a strange, silent way."[10]

While seemingly passive in external ways, they are very active beneath the surface. Never forget that some bank presidents and heads of corporations possess Cancer as a dominant factor in their charts. They nurture people and projects, needing emotional involvement with their colleagues and workers. They initiate and start things. With their Moon-induced unrest and mobility, Cancerians bring about new life. Huber reminds us that the "individual Will awakens like a germ in the sign Cancer."[11]

Even though they push to keep people moving and responding, they reluctantly express this energy physically. They generally resist exercise as if it were something for beings from another planet. They move very quickly only when frightened, just as the crab moves swiftly when danger approaches. Otherwise, as the crab slowly moves from sand to water or from water to sand or beneath underwater rocks, so, too, moves the Cancerian.

Domestic and home-oriented

The social units of family, clan, or tribe have provided security, safety, warmth, support and a sense of belonging to people since the beginning of time. Certainly these units sometimes exhibit dysfunctional characteristics and do not adequately provide basic needs; nevertheless, they provide the structure from which roots and a foundation are formed. Ultimately, people yearn for rootedness in Being and a connection with a sustaining Source of all Being. The ability to move to that spiritual layer of Being arises out of a matrix of first having needs met in the context of a safe family or surrogate family. Referring to the esoteric seed thought for Cancer, Bailey asks, "Is the house you are building yet lit? Is it a lighted house or a dark prison? If it is a lighted house, you will attract to its light and warmth all who are around you."[12]

Cancerians yearn for a relationship with their childhood, parents, ancestors, community, and homeland. They desire to feel a part of something, to belong. Many Cancerians research the family tree, request family reunions, and look up long lost cousins when they travel to other places. They prefer close family ties, and some Cancerians extend that sense of family to their "spiritual family"—kindred spirits. Cancerians may sign up first for the military to defend their homeland during a time of war, for their patriotism reflects a sense of belonging to a bigger clan.

THEY PREFER CLOSE FAMILY TIES, AND SOME CANCERIANS EXTEND THAT SENSE OF FAMILY TO THEIR "SPIRITUAL FAMILY"—KINDRED SPIRITS.

They almost always want to feel emotionally included in whatever happens even if they choose not to participate. With such a strong need to belong, they feel devastated when excluded. They sometimes feel left out even when that was not the intention of the other person. Desiring an emotional connection with others further leads to feeling lonely in a crowd.

No matter where they travel, they always want a home to return to. They almost never experience wanderlust as a permanent condition, for they love puttering about their home nest. They often enjoy cooking creatively, watering the plants, taking care of household members, and just moving about their treasures dotting the house.

Nostalgic and attached to the past

The items that fill Cancerian homes become treasures because these things remind them of feelings they experienced or connections they felt with someone or something. Some Crabs store their dried prom flowers for years or stash old notes or letters in drawers for decades. A Cancerian woman loves wearing her grandmother's pearls to her wedding and saves her own wedding gown for her daughter's and granddaughter's weddings—just in case. They highly value photograph albums, often with pictures loosely jammed in piles between pages, as a tangible record of family and experience. Cancerians collect souvenirs, mementos, old stories, and memories as an antique dealer lovingly collects antiques. Actually, they love antiques, too. They can almost sense the feelings carried in fine old furniture as if previous owners left indelible impressions in the wood itself.

Some Crabs store their dried prom flowers for years or stash old notes or letters in drawers for decades.

Collecting the past leads to a Cancerian tendency to clutter. They never quite know what to do with their treasures. Certainly they cannot throw away Aunt Sally's letter, the old can opener they used as a bride or groom, or other memorabilia. Piles build, and the attic swells to beyond capacity. Most Cancerians believe that if they release something, the item will be needed within a few days. Some even say that they will need the item within the next hour. Although the crab temporarily sheds its shell at every new cycle, most Cancerians hold onto the outworn shell, storing it in some safe place should they need it again. Even if they do not need it again, they savor the memories attached to it.

Tevya from the musical, "Fiddler on the Roof," certainly must have had Cancerian qualities when he said that a people keep their balance and know their identity through tradition. "Without tradition, our lives would be as shaky as a fiddler on the roof," he said. Cancerians feel safety in the boundaries that tradition provides, being shaped just as a flowing river is shaped by its banks. While retaining the valuable from the past, Cancerians need to learn to live in the present.

Cautious and security-oriented

Cancerians find security in being surrounded by the past, and they also experience caution about the future. What if the job does not work out? What if the benefit package changes? What factors would work against me? What if management changes? Can I extend my leave of absence for another year so that I have a place to return to if this does not work out? If the crab moves from one body of water to another, he wants a guarantee that the other body of water exists and is of good quality. Otherwise, how could he survive? Although caution and a need for security sometime distort into a fearful subpersonality, positive common sense also arises from these qualities. It only becomes a detriment when Cancerians become fear-bound which prevents forward movement.

Absorptive and psychic

Like all of the water signs, Cancerians innately swim in a sea of sensations and absorb impressions beyond what the physical senses provide. This quality is further delineated in Part II, Chapter 5, in the chapter on the element of water. Cancerians slightly vary from the other two water signs in that they enjoy floating in collective unconscious waters just as a fetus floats in amniotic fluid. The mind goes into neutral while this person just becomes one with its environment. They feel especially pulled to mass consciousness because of absorbing impressions and feelings from the collective unconscious. Traditions and conditioning of family and culture, including fears, provide a harbor, and yet, if Cancerians remain unconscious, they experience a lack of choice. Instead, they just respond instinctually.

Cancerians must learn to protect themselves from the onsurges of unconscious material. Finding light in their house, as the esoteric seed thought suggests, provides the safety needed. "So Cancer moves in and out of psychic sea, bringing its alternating rhythms to the earth as she seeks her port of Earthly anchorage."[13]

Responsive

Like the tides that shift in response to the pull of the Moon, so, too, the Cancerian shifts in response to the Moon's phases, to others' moods, to environmental stimuli, and to the pull of the collective. Cancerians reflect their environment just as a lake reflects any images above it. They sometimes respond too quickly, reacting to perceived hurt and rejection. Not only do they respond <u>to</u> their inner and outer world, Cancerians also want emotional response <u>from</u> others. If they make a statement such as, "This is a nice day," they expect others to respond so that they know they were deeply heard.

Cancerians like music that evokes deep feeling and soul-stirring responses. Music such as gospel often evokes deep feelings and an audible response. Other Cancerians prefer listening to Beethoven's Sixth Symphony. Others respond emotionally to a country western song that pulls at the heart.

Subpersonality End of the Continuum

Baby Jane

Although she may have been deeply wounded in childhood by not having her needs met, Baby Jane retains enough spark to keep fighting for her needs. She sees the world as a cold, unfeeling place, and at the same time, she never gives up hope that someday, somehow, someone will mother her. If her spouse leaves on a trip, she cries, "How could you leave me!!!" If a family member fails to remember her birthday or ignores her pleas for special attention, she protests the outrage with a temper tantrum. Feeling bereft of nurturing, she does not know how to gain a more centered perspective. She does not know that many in her presence want as much nurturing from her as she wants from them. Therefore, her demands merely push people further away, for her insistence contains blame that the other person did not do a good enough job in meeting her needs. As she eventually learns to move into her own nurturant nature and to heal the wounded child, she begins to re-parent herself. Paradoxically, as she learns self love, she relaxes and opens. Others then likely also respond in caring ways.

Hypersensitive Harry

Harry does not comprehend the dictum, "Act—don't react," for he so strongly identifies with his emotions that he reacts to everything said and done. If a TV character acts surly, Harry cringes almost feeling that the hostility was directed at him. He possesses little objectivity about any situation that involves himself. If someone inadvertently yells after a bad day, he feels wounded and personalizes the attack. After a time, Harry's few remaining friends walk on eggshells around him trying to prevent him from hurting.

Until Harry's deep insecurities heal and he disidentifies from his emotions, his life remains miserable. As he learns to love himself and develop a sense of self, he detaches more from others' opinions and actions. He begins to determine his own responses rather than being at the mercy of his moods. Then his gift of sensitivity can be restored to its rightful, healthy expression.

Smothering Parent

She reminds her children to wear their mittens and boots in winter lest they catch cold; she tucks in extra cookies in their lunch box just in case they feel a little lonely; and she always remains awake until her adolescents safely return home. She mothers everyone whether they be a six months old baby, her forty-year-old husband, her friends, or her aging parents. She often gains too much weight because of her tendency to nurture herself and others through

> SHE SUFFERS TERRIBLY FROM THE EMPTY NEST SYNDROME WHEN HER CHILDREN LEAVE HOME.

food. Living vicariously through her children, she sacrifices for them. "I can't go back to school until Johnny has graduated from high school. He needs me," she says. She suffers terribly from the empty nest syndrome when her children leave home.

Overly identified with the parenting role, she even calls her husband "Dad," and he likely calls her "Mother." In their bedroom, she prefers to cuddle and tuck her partner under the covers more than having sex.

If not needed as mother, she believes she is useless. While her wonderful gift of nurturance remains available, she also needs to develop other aspects of her identity. She needs to know that her worth surpasses any one role.

Clinger Clancy

Like a clinging vine, Clancy attaches himself to significant others and hangs on for dear life. He prefers to keep close, loved ones in sight, and he always wants someone by his side. He cannot imagine going shopping or to a movie by himself. Like a baby that needs reassurance of its mother's heartbeat, he almost believes that he will cease to exist unless in physical proximity with others. Developmentally, he never successfully separated and individuated from his parents, and his needs likely remained unmet. Therefore, he never developed enough security to launch out on his own. A little boy in a grown up body, he constantly seeks reassurance. He likes to physically touch those around him further giving him a sense of closeness.

In family life, he enmeshes with people, unaware of appropriate boundaries. He feels free to poke through family members' closets and drawers as if they were his own. He opens doors uninvited just as he did when he was a toddler looking for mommy or daddy.

He needs to renegotiate through the adventure of separation and individuation which can only happen when he learns a deep, inner security. Like his cousin, Baby Jane, he can eventually learn how to parent himself and provide self-care and love. Then his gift of joyful tenderness returns.

Moody Mandy

She mopes and feels sorry for herself when her feelings have been hurt. She experiences depression after watching a sad movie or the evening news. She dances for joy upon receiving surprise flowers. Her associates and family never know how to predict her behavior because of her fluctuating moods. Mandy can retain her gift of spontaneity by learning how to disidentify from her emotions so that she can freely choose how and when to respond.

Clutterbug

While most Cancers possess some kind of collection and feel fond of mementos from the past, Clutterbug goes to the extreme and is owned by his clutter. He feels overwhelmed by his piles, never knowing what to do with any of the items. Sometimes in frustration, he boxes up stacks of papers and memorabilia and stashes them in a closet, the attic or storage shed. The next day, he is inundated again by new clutter. What does one do with old *National Geographics*? Certainly he cannot throw them away. Neither can he discard tapes of family conversations, old concert ticket stubs, the photo of Clutterbug and the first fish he caught, recipes for cooking on a rainy day, and sentimental articles about devoted families. Even his walls are covered with name tags from conventions he attended, old election buttons, posters and other collections. He may reluctantly agree to a garage sale, but on the day of the sale, Clutterbug slips half of the merchandise back in the house already feeling the pangs of loss. Too attached to everything, he has forgotten that his true essence transcends his objects.

WHAT DOES ONE DO WITH OLD *NATIONAL GEOGRAPHICS*?

In order to healthily integrate, Clutterbug does not have to relinquish all of his treasures. He needs to identify more deeply with Self so that he lives in the present. Then he can part with items no longer needed and stay in charge of his possessions rather than they of him.

What If

Submerged in fears about the future, What If swims in insecurity. She frowns; she stews; she sometimes panics. She worries about the end before starting. What if the food supplies do not last? She buys another case of green beans, crackers and powdered milk just in case the truckers go on strike. What if her loved ones die? She holds on even more tightly to memories of the times she has had with them as well as her fears. She worries about who will take care of her. What if her friends do not want her at the party? She wants to be accepted while she sets up scenarios in her mind of what might happen if she is not included. Common sense goes out the window while she gives over her life to immobilizing fears.

She believes that life is not predictable, and she flounders, having lost all perspective. She needs to disidentify from being her emotions and to call upon the assistance of her rational mind to help her examine her options more clearly. As she regains a sense of inner security, she can again provide the gift of security for others as well as herself.

Hermit Crab

Filled with fears, this crab isolates rather than risk exposing his vulnerabilities. He believes that the world remains unsafe and probably had plenty of experiences as a child to account for the belief. In spite of his deep loneliness and unconscious yearning for relationship, he believes that he does not need people. When he does interact with others, he carefully does not to reveal his real feelings. He says, "I won't tell you what I think because it might hurt your feelings," and what he really means is that he fears exposing his own vulnerabilities. He would rather isolate and reject than experience someone else's rejection first. Sometimes he just puts his brain in neutral, numbing his loneliness.

The journey to the awareness of ultimate safety takes considerable time as he gradually establishes trust in someone else, perhaps a sensitive, caring therapist. He also needs to learn to trust in his own well being even when others disapprove. Freed to come out of his hiding place, he then experiences more of life. His gift of sensitivity can also be released for use as a healthy expression in the world.

References for Chapter 4

[1]. Huber, 1984, p. 92.
[2]. Oken, 1990, p. 183.
[3]. Bailey, 1951.
[4]. Bailey 1951.
[5]. Maslow, 1968.
[6]. Burt, 1988, p. 123.
[7]. Huber, 1984, p. 86.
[8]. Dobyns, 1972, p. 7.
[9]. Oken, 1990, p. 180.
[10]. Rudhyar, 1970, p. 57.
[11]. Huber, 1984, p. 87.
[12]. Bailey, 1951, p. 343.
[13]. Oken, 1990, p. 179.

LEO

Ann Nunley

July 23 - August 22

CHAPTER 5

LEO

Whether Leo people are constructive or destructive in their approach to life depends on who drives their chariot: self or Self. — Isabel Hickey[1]

Because of its transpersonal qualities, unconditional love opens the heart-center. — Edith Stauffer[2]

Affiliated House:	5
Ruling Planet:	Sun
Element:	Fire
Quality:	Fixed
Polarity:	Yang
Dates:	July 23 - August 22
Key Words:	I WILL
Symbol:	Lion
Anatomy:	Heart, sides, upper back

Imagery Experience for Leo

Become aware of your breath. ... Imagine that each time you breathe you breathe in golden, healing energy from the sun. ... As you breathe the next five breaths, allow this radiant energy to fill every cell of your body. ... Experience the warmth as the rays of the sun melt away any tension. ... Imagine now that you are Leo, the Lion, with a heart that radiates unconditional love ... surveying your kingdom. Allow yourself to fully experience the sensations and emotions of being this lion. ... When you are ready, express your perceptions through writing, art or movement.

Essence End of the Continuum

The expression of Leo in its most whole and spiritual form emanates from the heart chakra, the innermost heart from which unconditional love radiates as molten gold energy. The great love and radiant joy from the Self pours forth from the heart warming and sustaining others just as sunlight sustains life on earth. The creative potential bursting forth from the Leonine person inspires those in its presence. Experiencing no blocks to the outpouring love, Leo recognizes that together we all compose one great heart, unified by love.

Edith Stauffer, author of *Unconditional Love and Forgiveness*, further explains this kind of love:

> "Unconditional love does not mean keeping the object of our love happy and comfortable on a personality level. It means using foresight and wisdom to keep alive those qualities which will stimulate the growth and well-being of our loved ones. Love guards, stimulates, and protects, yet it does not hinder freedom. Unconditional love engenders a sense of personal responsibility."[3]

The esoteric seed thought for Leo, "I am that, and that I am"[4] alludes to the development and awareness of individuality in Leo. Also, this seed thought refers to the Source which infuses the Self which, in turn, permeates the personality. The soul-infused personality realizes the nature of the unfolding Divine Plan. This spiritually evolved person experiences inner power and strength to help transform the outer environment, bringing it into synchronicity with this divine plan. Leo enjoys creatively acting upon the world. From this level of expression, power remains safe to express because spiritually attuned Leos are sensitive to the Self within others as well as to their own Self.

Middle of the Continuum

Leo moves beyond the womb of Cancer by shining forth, dazzling the world with its radiant individuality. With the Sun itself as its planetary ruler and with its connection to the heart, Leo exudes love, generosity and warmth.

In addition, Leo expresses the following qualities:

- Self expressive and creative;
- Confident and risk-taking;
- Royal, majestic and proud;
- Vital and outwardly radiating;
- Powerful and dominating;
- Focused and decided;
- Loyal,
- Steadfast and courageous;
- Entertaining and dramatic.

Loving, generous and warm

The most important task for Leo involves developing a deeper sense of love through opening the heart. Unconditional love opens the heart center and allows goodwill and warmth towards self and others. Leos often give and receive generously. They share gifts with people they like and consider loyal, although they prefer choosing to whom they give rather than being asked. Sometimes, though, Leo's wounded pride and clenched heart prevents both giving and receiving.

INNER TRANSFORMATION BEGINS FOR LEOS WITH OPENING THE HEART.

Unconditional love expresses on several levels: physically as lighter and warmer; emotionally as less defensive and more open; mentally as a non-judgmental attitude; and spiritually as a deep trust and inner knowing of connection with Self and with the Source.[5] Inner transformation begins for Leos with opening the heart.

Opening the heart helps heal Leo's most vulnerable physical organ — the heart. While *Dr. Dean Ornish's Program for Reversing Heart Disease* is intended for everyone, especially people with coronary blockages and problems, Dr. Ornish's message especially relates to the Leo experience. He maintains that most people who suffer coronary difficulties feel isolated. A few chapters with timely advice for Leos are titled, "Opening Your Heart to Your Feelings and to Inner Peace," "Opening Your Heart to Others," and "Opening Your Heart to a Higher Self."[6]

The fifth house, Leo's natural home in the astrological chart, traditionally represents affairs of the heart, courtship, and opening the heart in relationships. They prefer being with a mate so that both a king and queen rules their kingdom. As Leos allow greater intimacy and vulnerability in close love relationships, they break out of the isolation sometimes caused by being too majestic for closeness. Their hearts sing, healing themselves and others.

SELF-EXPRESSIVE AND CREATIVE

Self-expressive refers to the development of genuine self-awareness and a sense of conscious identity. The search for Being and wholeness consecrates in Leo as the individuated self becomes aware of itself and sees glimmers of illumination from its spiritual center, the Self. For the first time in the zodiac, true individuality is born, although this statement should not be construed to mean that people born under the previous signs lack identity. Developmental tasks exist with each sign, and Leo's task is to individuate, first developing an ego or a sense of self. Leos gradually maneuver through the stages of self-determination.

With the development of an individual ego, Leo especially focuses on self-esteem. Leo offers the opportunity to celebrate ourselves and to feel pride in certain areas. One client with a Leo Sun maturely handled her need to be honored by telling her boss whenever she had done a task that she felt deserved applause. Her boss readily acknowledged her accomplishment, and she was satisfied.

A deeply meaningful exercise sometimes done in groups involves having each participant take a turn being in the center of the circle. All of the other participants, one by one, say the name of the person in the center, followed by "I see you and honor you." When celebrated in this way, many people cry. Before the ego can be surrendered to a Self, an ego must exist. The ego must be formulated enough to surrender. As Elmer Green has wisely stated, even when one can listen to the messages from the Self, the ego must be excited and interested enough to participate in the work at hand.[7]

Leos zing with aliveness when involved with artistic and creative activities. They drive to express themselves. Many artists have Leo prominent somewhere in their charts. Leos vitalize any organizational task, and some express their creativity by managing people and projects. Others find a creative outlet in working with children, and Leo qualities can be a great asset to teachers. In addition, the fifth house is associated with one's own children, another expression of the creative urge. One's children can represent actual progeny or figurative "children" of the mind such as creative projects.

Confident and risk-taking

The greater the sense of self, the greater the genuine confidence that exudes from Leos. Even less evolved Leos, only dimly aware of their real essence, confidently assert themselves in the world—perhaps with a braggadocio flair. They confront, direct and talk with everyone from paupers to kings and queens, sure that the recipient will bask in their light.

Deep self confidence allows risk-taking. They cannot imagine failing. Rudhyar states that they enjoy taking risks as much as managing people—no small assertion for a Leo.[8] In the astrological chart, the fifth house has also become identified with gambling and speculation which comes from Leos penchant for believing that they can win with high stakes. Unlike Aries who regularly pit life and limb against danger, Leos more likely chance the stock market or embark on risky ventures that leave the body intact. They may start a new consulting business with no capital, confident that everyone delights in their services.

. . .LEOS MORE LIKELY CHANCE THE STOCK MARKET OR EMBARK ON RISKY VENTURES THAT LEAVE THE BODY INTACT.

The more that Leos sense the presence of the inner Self, the more that inner joy bubbles spontaneously out from their beings. Their self-assurance and joy inspires others to trust Leo's abilities. People often lose their own doubt and fear just by being in the presence of a radiantly confident Leo. These optimistic, forward-looking Leos draw others to them as a lighted candle attracts moths to the flame.

On the contrary, some Leos resemble the Cowardly Lion in the *Wizard of Oz* who must learn courage and confidence. These timid types usually have other planets, such as Saturn or Pluto, afflicting the Sun or have Leo planets placed in water houses squelching their exuberance.

Royal, majestic and proud

Many Leo persons enter a room with regal bearing like a king or queen making a grand entrance. Even highly evolved Leos present themselves majestically which makes people notice them. They carry themselves in a dignified and cultivated manner. As Leos like to lead, often autocratically, they prefer to have followers unlike Aries who gallop ahead often forgetting to notice whether anyone follows. Certainly Leos almost always express strong opinions on what needs to be done. Like royalty, most Leos do not like people to approach too closely unless invited.

MANY STATUS-CONSCIOUS LEOS RELISH MEETING CELEBRITIES FOR PERSONAL SOCIAL AGGRANDIZEMENT, AND THEY DELIGHT IN FESTIVITIES AT WHICH THEY CAN SHINE.

Many status-conscious Leos relish meeting celebrities for personal social aggrandizement, and they delight in festivities at which they can shine. More evolved Leos also enjoy socializing with people, including the rich, royal and famous, because these Leos are comfortable with themselves and confident in expressing themselves no matter who they are with or where they are.

In the beginning of Leos' self-conscious development, they often think that the solar system revolves around them, like their ruler the Sun. They believe that they totally create their own destiny without realizing that energies from Self assist in this task. They become vain, boastful, and arrogant in their lust for honor. Leos defend anything for which they feel pride, and they both fear and abhor being ridiculed. Pride even describes a group of lions, Leo's symbol. As Leos move towards the Self, they develop a greater sense of universality with which comes the sacred awareness of right relationship to others and to the world.

Vital and outwardly-radiating

Leos pour out enormous creative energy—whether promoting, teaching, entertaining, presiding as royalty, or having a sexual orgasm, each of these being represented in the fifth house. They radiate tremendous energy outward and expect a return in terms of applause or appreciation. They are living dynamos whose intense directiveness and energy overwhelm more sensitive types. Some watery types tire just reading the letters of Leos. For more fiery and energetic types, Leos' wealth of sustained energy uplifts, catalyzing inner joy and exuberance. They make effective leaders unless they overrun others with their generating force. Leos' magnetic vitality either attracts or repels, and they are so outwardly-oriented that they seldom realize when they are "too much" for others. Huber asserts that Leo "experiences himself as the motivating and originating Ego around which everything else moves."[9]

They seldom tire, and they remain remarkably vital and high spirited throughout their life. One Leo woman in her seventies can still wrap Christmas presents until three in the morning while her less exuberant children and grandchildren wearily fall asleep much earlier. They need to bask in real sunshine or experience other fiery activities in order to keep their inner fire kindled. Leos represent reflected points of divine light, according to Bailey,[10] and those in touch with that inner radiance express a vivid joy of life. They heal and warm those around them like golden rays of sunshine. Leos less in touch with Self may scorch and burn what they touch, just as relentless rays of Sun also do.

POWERFUL AND DOMINATING

With the will so strong in Leo, the question remains, "What is the Right use of Will?" If Leo's will is imbued with intelligence, goodness, and wisdom, then its expression proves purposeful and meaningful, in service to the higher good. With the higher Will moving through them, they can move mountains. However, If Leos willfully work through the ego, danger lurks in their rule. They misuse and overpower others, sometimes even cruelly.

In either case, the sheer force of Leo's personality brings about dominion over others, one of Leo's hallmarks. Rudhyar explains, "If in the midst of confused and disheartened people, Leo will at once sense his chance and rise to the occasion; power will build him up in an amazing way and he will glow just as an adulated 'young prodigy' usually does."[11] When the ego dominates Leo's quest for power, ruthlessness and intolerance result. They lust for power as did Napoleon and Mussolini. When Leo's expression of power emanates from the Self, then domination transforms into "dominion over their own unsubjugated forces," as Hickey asserts.[12] They learn self mastery. With poised self control, these centered Leos provide leadership with heart.

WITH POISED SELF CONTROL, THESE CENTERED LEOS PROVIDE LEADERSHIP WITH HEART.

As an expression of their power, Leos excel at organization. When directed by inner love and wisdom, they benignly mobilize family, friends and employees into activity and productivity. One Leo grandmother relishes the task of arranging outings, games, entertainment, and educational opportunities for her multi-generational offspring. She marshals her progeny into these activities, assuming that she knows better than they what is good for them. Acting with professional authority can be a stumbling block, for they have trouble delegating. They may delegate authority and then take it back again, never quite trusting others' creative genius as much as their own.

Focused and decided

Leo's intense power and spirit of self- determination expresses as sustained and fixed fire. The unrelenting flames cause Leos to unwaveringly pursue their goals. Once Leos have firmly decided upon a course, they act decisively and do not deviate from the plan. Because of sheer determination and concentrated power, they quite often obtain what they seek. Campaign managers appreciate the fiery zeal and idealism of their Leonine candidates who unflinchingly march toward victory.

The Leo mind holds as tightly to opinions as a bulldog does to anything it grips.

The Leo mind holds as tightly to opinions as a bulldog does to anything it grips. At times their emotions overheat in the focused passion for a person or their indignation regarding a cause. Leo people honestly and forthrightly tell others their views and generally expect, since they believe only one view is possible, that others will quickly see the light and believe as they do. They expect everyone to side with them whether that be views on politics, religion, enemies, or the weather. They remain focused fire.

Loyal, steadfast and courageous

As with all of the fixed signs, Leo possesses steadfast inner strength and courage which permits loyal following of convictions. Leos, especially attuned to heart energy, follow their heart unwaveringly unless betrayed. Betrayal, so glaringly at odds with their values, especially affronts Leos. They expect and demand that others demonstrate as much loyalty as they themselves give. At times, they love possessively.

As leaders, Leos esteem loyal followers, and their courage and loyalty inspire the followers to remain in the group and to experience pride in being part of the whole. As protective as a mother lion of her cubs, Leos fight for their own in times of trouble and proudly acclaim those in their fold in times of peace.

Entertaining and dramatic

No other sign of the zodiac excels at entertainment and drama as much as Leo. Their emotions intensify through stage and screen, natural media for their expression, and they can stir the emotions of crowds. More actors and actresses are born under the sign of Leo—or have Leo prominent in their charts—than any other sign. Even Leo children often daydream of the day when they will be on stage or, at least, in the limelight. These children suggest to their friends putting on a play and turning the living room into a stage with chairs, sheets and old clothing. This gift of entertainment endears adult Leos to children. Unlike Cancerians who woo children through nurturance, warm milk and cookies, Leos delight little ones, capturing their imaginations in play and wonder.

These shining stars motivate and enrich others' lives when they radiate their magnificent energy from Self, or they can suffer others' disdain when they too glaringly aggrandize themselves, creating a billboard of self perpetuation. At the personality level, they need recognition and admiration, and they want the world's feedback and applause for validation.

They carry drama into their regular life, wearing flashy, bright, golden yellows, oranges and reds. As dramatic as their verbal overstatements, their clothing reflects their need to impact the world. They are fond of big, golden jewelry and bold, colorful, sometimes gaudy, clothing. When they walk into a room, others notice. The more Leos center themselves, the more their presence commands attention just by their inner energy. When closer to the end of the continuum with dramatic subpersonalities, the more they strut like peacocks.

Subpersonality End of Continuum

Strutting Peacock

Like a rock singer in glittering outfits, Strutting Peacock dazzles the world with his brilliant colors and distinctive dress and movements. He parades into rooms, expecting his audience to be thrilled with his spectacular presence. Distinctive in the world, he craves adulation and praise and is, therefore, susceptible to flattery. When in bed with his lover, he glances frequently at the mirrors on the ceiling, appreciative of his own performance. Every step, gesture, and word demand, "Look at me."

His Leonine heart pinches shut in his narcissistic search for ego gratification, and his own gift of providing entertainment for others becomes shallow and vain. He desperately needs recognition to bolster his self esteem, even though his performance falsely indicates an over-abundance of self esteem. While recognition from others represents a basic human need, Strutting Peacock forgets that a sense of self worth must first come from within. As he learns to truly love himself, he will rely less on his outer dazzle to win that love and recognition.

> His Leonine heart pinches shut in his narcissistic search for ego gratification. . .

Theatrical Tillie

Tillie lives her life as if she were the heroine in a melodrama tied to the railroad track with a train roaring towards her. Whether in peril or not, she exaggerates her responses to everything—affection, anger, hate, fear. All of life becomes a melodrama. She flings her arms around someone she barely knows feigning long-lost friendship, or she throws a tantrum at the supermarket checkout over a disputed price. Her self-centered drama so absorbs her that she fails to notice that others also have real-life problems and needs. She demands reassurance, praise and approval from others as if she were the center of the universe. Often she spends excessive amounts of time on her appearance, sometimes expressing inappropriate sexual seduction.

Tillie probably failed to receive consistent and appropriate attention when she was a child and now seeks to have that need met in ways that satisfy only in the short run. As she eventually learns to deeply see herself, she will begin to open her Leonine heart and to see others. Then she can use her innate gift of drama, not only for her own pleasure in self expression, but also for the service of others.

Arrogant Arthur

Arrogant Arthur chants "I am the greatest" like his mentor, Muhammad Ali, the former heavyweight boxing champion. He exudes superlatives, and humility and humbleness are absent from his vocabulary and experience of life. Arthur knows it all, and he authoritatively tells his opinions to anyone who listens. If he were running the country, he would do thus and so and be far superior to the current president, he tells you. His escapades during the war were the bravest, his plans for management of the company the best, and his style of leadership the most effective. He swaggers through doorways just as John Wayne did in the movies and condescendingly flaunts his self-believed superiority.

HE SWAGGERS THROUGH DOORWAYS JUST AS JOHN WAYNE DID IN THE MOVIES. . .

Arrogant Arthur meets his need for self esteem by trying to convince both himself and the world of his superiority when in truth he unconsciously feels unworthy and inferior. He defends against this intolerable awareness. In order to grow along his continuum of possibilities, he will eventually have to face his fears and weaknesses which paradoxically will empower him to believe more deeply in himself. Then confidence can move from a grandiose defense to an inwardly radiated quality.

Overwhelming Dynamo

Her display of energy equals that of a mild hurricane steadily propelling itself towards the shore. Caught up in her forceful expression of the life force, Dynamo forgets that anyone else might possibly have a slower rhythm or a need for privacy and space. She plunges through life, demanding that everyone follow her lead. She activates even the weary into activity. Heaven help the shy man in the back row of the PTA meeting if Dynamo decides to appoint him as director of the recycling committee. She takes no "no's" for answers. She singlehandedly organizes the block party, oblivious to any resistance. Her energetic manner bruises the psyches of those lesser spirited folks, and she castigates them for holding back or cajoles them to participate against their will.

Dynamo distorts her gifts simply because she has not learned how to properly channel her vibrant energy or to appreciate that others have a right to self determination. As she learns to connect with the energies of the Self, her heart will open, and she will better be able to see others as they are, not as reflections of herself. Her dynamic energy can then be applied to carrying out a higher Will and creating a better world.

Wounded Willy

Like a fallen king, Wounded Willy plays a tragic role in life. Having fallen from his self-proclaimed pedestal, his pride is wounded. Even in disgrace, Willy vainly tries to maintain his image at all costs. Arrogantly, he blames everyone but himself for his problems—his shrewish (his depiction) ex-wife was blind to his fine qualities; his ex-boss failed to recognize Willy's great talents; the community was too small to appreciate his gifts. In all cases, he expected others to see his brilliant qualities that he so intensely projected over the years. Broken-hearted and lonely, the displaced king petulantly searches for another throne.

Willy mistakenly believes that the image of himself that he projected is his identity. He falsely identifies with his ego. As he learns to take responsibility for his own mistakes and the problems caused by arrogance, Willy develops enough humility to learn that he transcends the ego, and that his Self exists. Then he, the lion, can accept help in removing the thorn from his paw. Only then can he truly ascend his rightful throne.

Prima Donna

Prima Donna looks in mirrors as often as Narcissus looked into the pond to see a self image. She requires profuse admiration from others, constantly seeking compliments and affirmation. She reacts excessively to any form of criticism by raging, crying, pouting or stomping. Donna perceives herself as being so unique that she can only be understood by other unique, special people. With a grandiose sense of importance, she demands that she be treated like a queen who has ascended the throne by divine right—not by meritorious service. Feeling entitled to special treatment, she dashes in front of others in lines, demands being seated at the table in front of the window, and tolerates no delay in any kind of service. When not in the queen's role, Donna

SHE REQUIRES PROFUSE ADMIRATION FROM OTHERS, CONSTANTLY SEEKING COMPLIMENTS AND AFFIRMATION.

fantasizes herself on stage receiving dazzling awards and accolades.

Donna may be compensating for a lack of truly "being seen" when she was a child. Whatever the cause, healing for her now involves developing a deeper sense of self independent of the whims of the outer world. She must open her heart and truly "see" and love others, just as she must see and love herself. With greater integration, her gift of showmanship with heart can emerge.

Intolerant Commander

Although he may wear a business suit, blue jeans, or a crisp Army uniform, he appears as if he were a general preparing for battle. In fact, regardless of his profession, he probably secretly desires to command a conquering army, a modern-day Genghis Khan in disguise. You can almost hear him bark, "Hup, one, two, march," as he imperiously parades around his domain—whether that be home, office, industrial plant, or street corner. At times, he can be cruel and ruthless as he maintains his oppressive position of power. As a father, he marshals his children into cleaning the backyard or going to bed in military style. As the boss in any situation, he allows no questions about his commands, permits no back talk, and demands full obedience. As lord and boss of his domain, he remains unflinchingly dogmatic no matter what the cost to his "subjects." He staunchly believes that democracy and openness to feelings belong to the weak.

HE LACKS THE ABILITY TO GIVE OR RECEIVE LOVE; YET HIS HEALING COMES FROM EVENTUALLY OPENING HIS HEART TO THIS VERY LOVE.

He fears being powerless and, therefore, overpowers others. With a heart hardened to the pain and suffering of those in his command, he remains unaware of his own inner pain caused from having cut off his connection to love from his deepest Self and the universal life force and from others. He lacks the ability to give or receive love; yet his healing comes from eventually opening his heart to this very love. As he moves up the continuum to a more centered position, he then can reclaim his capacity for loving leadership.

Gaudy Maudy

Gaudy Maudy could play herself in a television situation comedy, wearing tights with leopard-printed spots, flamboyant hair tied with colorful ribbons, and spiked heels. She just loves decoration. She bedecks herself with flashy ornamentation, including glasses studded with fake jewels. Long after the holidays have faded, she cannot bear to take down the sparkling tinsel that adorns her doorways because of her love of bright and showy things. Unlike her narcissistic cousin, Strutting Peacock who does not allow others to know how he truly feels, Maudy wears her heart on her sleeve and gushes over those she loves calling many "Dearie" and "Honey."

Harming no one, her distortion comes not from over decorating herself or her environment but in not realizing that her true identity goes beyond surface glitz and glitter.

References for Chapter 5

[1]. Hickey, 1970, p. 18.
[2]. Stauffer, 1987, p. 92.
[3]. Stauffer, 1987, p. 94.
[4]. Bailey, 1951.
[5]. Stauffer, 1987.
[6]. Ornish, 1990.
[7]. E. Green, 1980.
[8]. Rudhyar, 1970.
[9]. Huber, 1984, p. 100.
[10]. Bailey, 1951.
[11]. Rudhyar, 1970, p. 62.
[12]. Hickey, 1970, p. 18.

VIRGO

Ann Nunley

August 23 - September 22

CHAPTER 6

VIRGO

Life is led as an act of love. Devotion to the universality of humankind is at the core of her being, and that core is now enlivened and enlightened by the radiance of the Soul.—Alan Oken[1]

He must make everything that has been damaged whole or clean again. The law that dwells within him demands it. At the present time this is one of the most important qualities which can make our world whole again.—Louise Huber[2]

Affiliated House:	6
Ruling Planet:	Mercury
Element:	Earth
Quality:	Mutable
Polarity:	Yin
Dates:	August 23 - September 22
Key Words:	I ANALYZE
Symbol:	Virgin with sheaves of wheat
Anatomy:	Intestines, liver, pancreas, gall bladder, lower plexus, upper bowel

Imagery Experience for Virgo

Allow your awareness to focus on the inward and outward movement of your breath. ... Experience the peace and quiet as you move to your deepest center, to that place within where devotion resides. ... Allow each breath to soothe away any tensions so that only quiet remains. ... Imagine now that you are pure and cleansed from your innermost being enabling you are to provide joyful service ... preparing matter for divine spirit. ... Allow yourself to fully experience this Virgo expression. ... Returning your full awareness to your surroundings, begin to draw, write or express in movement your understandings of Virgo.

Essence End of the Continuum

With work consecrated to the Greater Whole and sense of purpose aligned with Self, Virgo devotes her life to serving others. She realizes that service to the collective purpose transcends any one person's ego and that she exists as a purposeful cog in the cosmic wheel. By her humble and quiet example, she inspires others to service. Mother Teresa's life outwardly expresses strong Virgo qualities.

From the spiritual level of experience, Virgo receives impressions of the divine through her Self and translates them into practical form. She possesses the patience to wait and the willingness to mature as she fine-tunes her abilities. Unlike her Leonine predecessor, she willingly sacrifices her ego to become a neophyte in training. She carefully hones her skills and learns discernment which allow her to be an even more effective spiritual disciple for the Highest Good. She heals the broken places, slowly and carefully working for wholeness. Our world desperately needs this healing in order to become whole and sane again.

The esoteric seed thought for Virgo, "I am the Mother and the Child. I, God, I Matter am,"[3] provides awareness that Virgo represents a cosmic mother. While Virgo patiently waits through the long gestation period, her esoteric ruler, the Moon—Mother of Form, assists in the birthing of her creation. Oken, writing of the esoteric meaning of Virgo, declares that "Matter and Creator are but one continuous line of cosmic expression."[4] Virgo prepares matter for the divine spirit, protecting, nurturing and finally revealing the spiritual reality.

THE ESOTERIC SEED THOUGHT FOR VIRGO, "I AM THE MOTHER AND THE CHILD. I, GOD, I MATTER AM,"[3] PROVIDES AWARENESS THAT VIRGO REPRESENTS A COSMIC MOTHER.

Middle of the Continuum

Reacting to the excesses of its predecessor—as does each zodiacal sign, Virgo is imbued with humility and modesty and reacts against Leo's flamboyance by living with quiet and reserve.

The Virgo also possesses the following characteristics:

- Perfection-oriented and pure;
- Precise and efficient;
- Detail-oriented;
- Analytical and discerning;
- Service-oriented and nurturant;
- Productive and industrious;
- Health conscious.

Humble and modest

Free from arrogance and self-righteousness, Virgos prefer to live simply and unpretentiously. Eschewing flamboyance and preferring quiet humbleness, they feel disgusted when others sound trumpets for their own victories. Modest by nature, Virgos do not embellish anything, preferring the unadorned, matter-of-fact, simply stated truth. They unassumingly present themselves without airs.

Humility can be found all along the continuum of Virgo possibilities. The closer to the center or Self, the more they express respect for the other person through service without seeing themselves as less. They can wash another's feet while maintaining an attitude of equality and self dignity. In the most spiritual sense, they enact the meaning of the Sanskrit word "namaste" which loosely translated means, "I salute the divinity which is in you and which is in me. When you and I meet at that place, we are one." The closer to the subpersonality end of the continuum, the more that humility distorts into self depreciation. At that end, Virgos self-deprecate so extensively that they figuratively beat themselves bloody. In any case, they generally err on the side of underestimation rather than overstatement when evaluating themselves or their assets.

Quiet and reserved

With Autumn-like qualities, Virgos quietly withdraw and reflect, repelled by their noisier and more ostentatious cousins. They do not rush into superficial relationships; they prefer taking more time. Due to their gentle nature, they often have many friendships which have quietly developed over time. They can clearly articulate their analysis of a situation or project, but they have difficulty communicating their innermost feelings which sometimes remain submerged beneath the business of life. In their reserved way, Virgos usually remain unobtrusive, preferring to serve in the background. Some are shy, others just quiet. In any case, they are self-restrained and rarely overly assertive. Although they do not display sensitivity on their sleeves as do Pisces, they remain deeply aware of others and take care that no one gets hurt, a quality that emerges in their work with others. The Sanskrit word "ahimsa"—meaning non-injury, non-violence and an attitude of love for all creatures—applies to Virgos, especially those who are more aware of their spiritual essence. Among other things, the Sixth House represents small animals and pets, so compatible with Virgo's gentle qualities.

Perfection-oriented and pure

The virgin holding a sheaf of grain, which represents purity and perfection, symbolizes Virgo. The asteroid Vesta, named for a virgin goddess, closely affiliates with Virgo. People often misunderstand Virgo's inner urge to perfection, for the distorted end of the continuum—represented by pickiness and excessive criticalness—unfortunately receives most of the press.

More spiritually evolved Virgos realize that in order to birth the divine impulses from the Self into form, personal hindrances such as nervousness and fear must

> "BLESSED ARE THE PURE IN HEART, FOR THEY SHALL SEE GOD."

be eliminated. Rudhyar gives an analogy of a gasoline tank that runs most efficiently when impurities are absent.[5] As Virgos prepare to receive and express their inner light, they cleanse themselves of impurities that block awareness of the Self. Therefore, they constantly adjust and heal their attitudes on the path to purification. The sixth beatitude from the New Testament of the Bible applies to Virgos' yearning for purity: "Blessed are the pure in heart, for they shall see God."

The house that contains the sign of Virgo indicates in what areas of life one desires perfection. If Virgo rests on the seventh house cusp, for example, the native prefers a perfect mate; in the fifth house, perfect children; in the sixth, perfect employees or to be a perfect worker. One woman with Virgo planets in her fourth house cleans house until it sparkles after her husband and children have gone to bed and then drinks tea—with the teacup on a little coaster—relishing her tidy house. Another woman with fourth-house Virgo complained of her "messy" home when the most visible offending item was a coffee cup on the counter. Exacting standards may be applied wherever Virgo resides in the chart. The more centered Virgos are, the more they understand the underlying purpose of perfection. They can accept themselves and others along the path of evolution rather than demanding instant perfection.

In relationships with others, Virgos sometimes seem unfeeling and alienate others when they find too much fault. Even then, those Virgos mean well and are attempting to help the other person to do or be the best that they can. They almost always maintain high standards for themselves. Virgo children—and adults, too—may wad up papers in disgust if the writing does not meet their expectations. They need to learn to be more gentle with loved ones, co-workers and themselves.

Because they often demand a great deal of themselves, they dislike criticism from others because they notice their own faults long before anyone else does. Criticism rubs like salt in an open wound. On the other hand, Virgos often cannot easily accept compliments. For example, when Virgo musicians perform superbly and are complemented, they sometimes respond with qualifiers such as, "But I made a mistake in the third bar at the beginning of the second movement." Parents of Virgo children learn that compliments stated as personal preferences which cannot be argued with are more favorably received than purely evaluative statements. That is, "I like this picture" is more readily accepted than "That is a good picture."

PRECISE AND EFFICIENT

From Virgos desire for perfection evolves the great ability to refine and fine tune skills, plans and work. Many Virgos express great satisfaction in working with something until it is "just right." One woman with Sun, Mercury, Venus and Mars in the Sixth

House who works as an educational consultant talks about the pleasure she experiences when she has fine-tuned a workshop by repeating it several times. Then she knows precisely how much time is needed for sitting and how much for moving; how many "right-brained" and how many "left-brained" activities are required for optimum learning; and exactly how many materials are needed and in what order. Her perfectly orchestrated workshop results from her mutable desire to correct, adjust, and fine tune.

Similarly, a woman with six planets in the sign of Virgo, describes her urge to fine tune her foreign language skills to the point that other people would think she were a native speaker. As an exchange student, she listened to and repeated the accent so precisely that no one detected her American accent, much to her satisfaction. In this regard, Rudhyar discusses the value of apprenticeship for the Virgo as a way of learning effective techniques that lead to mastery: "He must become objective to his own ways of behavior. He must analyze them and refuse to be blind to their defects. He must be absolutely honest and un-glamoured in the evaluation of any performance: his and others' also. He must learn to criticize dispassionately and without prejudice."[6]

As Virgos develop quiet efficiency and greater mastery, they satisfy their need to feel effective. They embody the Virgo phrase, "I work competently," coined by Zip Dobyns.[7] They expose wastefulness and inefficiency in the workplace—both as apprentices and later as master teachers or trainers. The first person to suggest a recycling bin for the office might likely be a Virgo.

The sense of precision carries beyond the workplace. Most Virgos prefer things to be precise and orderly in some area of their life. One woman with Venus in Virgo triple folds her underwear and places them in color-coded piles in her dresser drawer. Many non-Virgos feel lucky if all of the underwear even reaches the proper drawer. Other Virgos describe how they clip coupons and file them into proper categories. Burt attests, "Virgo loves to tidy up the cosmos, patch up the world mentally, physically or spiritually."[8]

". . .VIRGO LOVES TO TIDY UP THE COSMOS, PATCH UP THE WORLD MENTALLY, PHYSICALLY OR SPIRITUALLY."[8]

Most Virgos excel at tasks requiring precise, fine-motor coordination, and their hands never seem to rest. Many baseball pitchers' charts prominently display Virgo in their charts. Virgos often enjoy playing the piano or other musical instruments. Others unite form and function into crafts such as needlepoint projects which often require patience for minute detail. Undoubtedly the artist who paints pictures on grains of rice has an abundance of Virgo planets.

Detail-oriented

Virgos can fine tune because of their capacity to pay attention to detail. When in charge of organizing a conference, they leave nothing unnoticed. Anyone who has ever organized any event knows that the most minute details can make the difference between success and disaster. By paying attention to each distinct part and every cog in the wheel, Virgos assure the efficient functioning of the whole. Clear and sharp-eyed, they combine their capacity for detail with routine, allowing the time to further fine-tune the details through repetition. These skills prove invaluable in fields such as science, research, accounting, bookkeeping, computer programming, library science, graphic design, and medical fields. A hospital patient prefers a nurse or doctor who knows—and notices—the difference between a microgram and a kilogram.

The challenge for Virgos remains to be aware of the bigger vision while attending to the particulars. They often miss the forest for the trees. One student complained that her Virgo linguistics professor not only missed the forest but the entire tree, he so intently studied the individual leaves, the minutia of language. Bothered by a shifting world, Virgos need to feel effective. Robert Hand notes, "Thus in an effort to achieve control by letting nothing escape its notice, it tends to concentrate on details."[9]

Virgos' memory seems to be housed in vast quantities of computerlike storage files in their brain which can be retrieved almost at will: phone numbers of a friend from third-grade whom they have not seen for twenty years; every street address they have ever lived on even if their father was in the Army and they moved every year; the name of every teacher they ever had, the color of the table cloth at the restaurant where they ate last year. Virgo astrologers remember most details about planet placements and house cusps for clients they have met only once. One man with a Virgo Sun who worked in an auto parts store memorized every part and its number and knew exactly where each item was stored.

VIRGOS' MEMORY SEEMS TO BE HOUSED IN VAST QUANTITIES OF COMPUTERLIKE STORAGE FILES IN THEIR BRAIN WHICH CAN BE RETRIEVED ALMOST AT WILL:

Virgos tend to fall into two seemingly paradoxical camps: scattered or fastidious. The tidy types meticulously insist that every cup be in place in the cupboards, or that their pencils be sharpened exactly right and placed in the correct niche of their desk, or that their closets be cleaned every few weeks. Imagine the horror of one careful Virgo when she learned that her fiance believed that kitchen utensils would rise to the surface from crowded cabinet drawers when needed. Others may have just one area of their life where they demand perfection regarding certain details, such as towels folded in thirds; the bath mat always laid over the tub side; clothing placed by category in the closet; or soap bubbles cleaned from the kitchen sink before the job can be considered complete.

More cluttery types may have thirteen filing cabinets in their living room stuffed with papers, or the shelves lining their walls may be crammed with old journals, books and projects. Their desk may be a mess. Even so, they usually insist on order within the chaos. For example, one three-year-old child with six planets in the sign of Virgo was disconcerted when her mother cleaned her room because now she did not know where to find the book that was placed third in a stack at the bottom of her bed. Sometimes Virgo clutter results from the inability to decide what is important. Oken explains, "As the fear of introspection predominates to such a large extent, there is the tendency for Virgo to exteriorize a protective wall of materiality and excessive attention to outer details. In this way, Virgo can protect herself from yet another deep anxiety—that other people may also perceive her lack of cohesion and the apparent void at her center. Yet it is within this very void that she may find her salvation and peace."[10]

Analytical and discerning

The gift of analysis assists Virgos in deciding what is important and making sense of the morass of details they have accumulated. They constantly use their minds, honing the art of analysis of data and knowledge. They sift through storehouses of facts, looking for clues to solve their current puzzle. Blessed with exceptional reasoning powers, the capacity to analyze and consider consequences, and a search for order, they are born researchers and scientists. Dobyns attests that in Virgo we come "closest to ... Western Science, with its goal of knowledge and control of the physical realm, though final control is to be deferred to the last earth sign—Capricorn."[11] Professionals such as librarians and teachers prize these qualities along with a love of learning and a desire to further knowledge, also Virgo characteristics.

If Virgos stopped with just sorting data, they would miss the crucial ingredient in their personal and spiritual evolution: discernment. By analyzing information, they can discriminate between what is false and what is true, between what is important and what is not. They move to the core. When they respond with intelligence and discernment, they wisely choose what remains essential for their own lives, work, and service. Discernment translates into common sense in maneuvering through everyday decisions and into spiritual wisdom in evolving towards the center.

Service-oriented and nurturant

The urge to serve in Virgo is embedded deeply in ancient symbolism: the goddesses Isis, Eve, Ceres, and Mary all represent the World Mother working through matter. Bailey asserts that "Virgo is called the womb of time in which the seeds of great values are planted, shielded, nourished and revealed."[12] Virgos continue to learn and

> "VIRGO IS CALLED THE WOMB OF TIME IN WHICH THE SEEDS OF GREAT VALUES ARE PLANTED, SHIELDED, NOURISHED AND REVEALED."[12]

grow so that they may fulfill what they consider their true purpose—work and service. Leo Tolstoy, with several planets and the Sun in Virgo, states his Virgo-colored view of life as if it were true for all people: "The vocation of every man and woman is in serving other people."[13] At any rate, Virgos competently serve, working quietly in response to a noble purpose.

Virgos deeply desire to contribute to the welfare of others and to help others with less resources. With such a strong urge to serve, they often forgo higher salaries in more lucrative professions in order to help heal others and to provide better living conditions. Professions such as social work, education (especially special education), physical therapy, occupational therapy, x-ray technology, nursing and other health-related fields will always attract people with Virgo prominent in their charts. Virgo responds as an earth sign by improving conditions for people and ministering to their needs rather than being so attuned to the world of nature as does Taurus. Although they possess the patience of Job in waiting for results, they may eventually experience disillusionment and think that all of their work is for nothing if improvement does not occur.

Virgos abhor being called "selfish"—the greatest insult. In their concern for others, they deeply identify with being unselfish. Evolved Virgos realize that they must take care of their own needs and inner world even though that means occasionally saying "no" to others. They realize that they must replenish themselves in order to serve most fully and capably. Other Virgos, who make a life style of self denial, feel selfish when they begin to take care of their own needs. These overextended ones always volunteer to clean the tables and wash dishes after a community dinner; they teach Sunday school after working in their own classroom all week; they stay in long-ago defunct marriages to take care of their spouses' children from a former marriage. In the last few years, a spate of books on co-dependency have been written about these folks.

PRODUCTIVE AND INDUSTRIOUS

Like industrious ants in a colony, Virgos work diligently, tirelessly, all doing their part for the good of the whole. They do not scramble for power, and they do not lust after the Queen's role. Instead each persistently, dependably, and efficiently works at its assigned tasks. Virgos experience an inner urge to engage in purposeful, productive activity. Employment and work issues are Sixth House matters. From a spiritual perspective, Virgo and the Sixth House deal with Right Livelihood, that is, finding work in harmony with the soul.

Zip Dobyns, who has helped the astrology community become more aware of the importance of asteroids, has lectured extensively on Vesta as a ruler of Virgo. Certainly this work-related asteroid enhances any astrological reading regarding employment. As workers, Virgos often remain calm, self-reliant and resourceful. With their pragmatic ability to maneuver through obstacles, they create order out of chaos, finding satisfaction in doing and helping. The Virgin carries her harvested sheaves of wheat to those in need just as Isis allegedly scattered wheat across the sky creating the Milky Way to light the way for others.

Health conscious

With their inner urge for purification and movement towards wholeness, they care about the purity of the food and water that they consume or the air they breathe. Their interest in hygiene and cleanliness serves them well in medical fields. One Virgo even fell in love with her boyfriend when she found him cleaning her stove. When they move further away from their center and operate from fear, some become overly fastidious and exacting about their health choices. They make sure that they exercise aerobically the right number of times and minutes per week, that they consume no more than the maximum recommended fat grams per day, and that they drink enough wheat grass juice. Others approach health more flexibly, welcoming the opportunity to fine tune their bodies as they do their work, aware of the advantages of living holistically. In a more spiritual vein, they gather in the proper nutrients—from wholesome food to positive thoughts—to nurture their growth so that blocks to a fuller expression of the Self may be removed. The Virgo gift of discernment provides the key to sorting out what the essential from the non-essential on the journey to health and wholeness.

Many Virgos worry too much and become high strung. Excessive worry and negativity can impact health, another Sixth House matter. If relatives or friends have not arrived yet, some Virgos assume that their loved ones have had an accident and are lying in a ditch somewhere. If their cholesterol level reaches 180, they know they will soon be hospitalized with a coronary. As they learn to relax, they begin to cultivate inner calm. Laughter—with compassion for themselves and others—heals, and they gradually learn to not take themselves and their tasks so seriously. They eventually realize that others can also share responsibility for saving the world.

LAUGHTER—WITH COMPASSION FOR THEMSELVES AND OTHERS—HEALS, AND THEY GRADUALLY LEARN TO NOT TAKE THEMSELVES AND THEIR TASKS SO SERIOUSLY.

Subpersonality End of Continuum

Paralyzed Priscilla

Priscilla suffers from the PPP syndrome otherwise known as Perfectionism-Procrastination-Paralysis. She at first merely demands of herself a flawless, saintly performance. In the beginning, she even manages to function fairly well in the world, although with a lot of anxiety, sweaty palms and nail biting. Her term papers get written, her bills paid, and her jobs completed. As she demands more and more of herself, she begins to put off finishing the paper for fear that it will not measure up to her standards. The fear—"What if it isn't good enough?"—awakens her in the night. What if she cannot perfectly accomplish the task the boss gave her? Finally, with nagging fears gnawing at her insides, she procrastinates going to the library or delays taking the first step on her boss' project. She vaguely reasons that maybe later she will be able to do the task better. While dawdling and stalling, greater fears of failure plague her, yet she seems immobilized. What if she is not good enough? If the paper is four weeks past due, if the boss is about to fire her, how can she now start the project? The task overwhelms, and she suspends all activity, paralyzed from action. She experiences intense discomfort at even the thought of leaving her house, a prisoner of her own fears, a captive of perfectionism.

SHE EXPERIENCES INTENSE DISCOMFORT AT EVEN THE THOUGHT OF LEAVING HER HOUSE, A PRISONER OF HER OWN FEARS, A CAPTIVE OF PERFECTIONISM.

All human beings need to be gentle with themselves as they sojourn their evolutionary paths, and Priscilla even more desperately needs this gift of compassion. Eventually she learns not to catastrophize what might happen if she performs imperfectly—that is, if she is human. Accepting herself as a human being who makes mistakes <u>and</u> who learns and grows from these mistakes and goes on with life, she learns that her worth transcends how she performs. Then she knows of her intrinsic worth as a spiritual being.

Critical Carl

When he criticizes his wife for driving too fast, when he chides his son for sloppy handwriting, when he reproves his secretary for not having the letters out in the evening mail, Carl's tone of voice sounds suspiciously like one of his own parents. Seldom aware of the similarity, Carl believes—as did his own parent—that he merely makes things right and that, without his "help," disaster would surely result. He looks for faults and points out defects, fully believing that if he does not offer criticism that he fails in his own duty. He believes the other person would remain unaware of his or her errors. "Stand up straight!" "No, feed the baby this way!" "Don't invest money in that kind of house!" Each sentence carries a sharp edge as if to say, "You dummy."

Closely paired with Carl is a wounded child subpersonality who cringes each time Carl picks at another flaw. Both the wounded child and Carl exist within the same person. The wounded child first formed in response to Carl's own parent who criticized, and then later Carl formed, resembling the parent. These pairs—critical parent and wounded child—repeat generation after generation unless someone along the way breaks the pattern through healing. Only when Carl finds a deep inner acceptance can his natural gift of discernment be released. What has been distorted into painful criticism—which perpetuates wounding—can be transmuted into the ability to discern between important and non-important, when to act and when to remain still. Then Carl lives in the best of all worlds.

Worry Wart

Worry Wart fidgets each time the phone rings afraid that someone is calling to report that a disaster has happened to someone in her family. While ringing her hands and sighing, "Oh dear, oh dear," thoughts of her own troubles and those of her family and the world interweave through her angst. Although she does not expect to solve these problems, she worries as if they were her sole responsibility. Wavy lines caused from fretting etch into her brow. Unwholesome, false, and morbid thoughts and feelings deepen her misery. She seldom encounters peace, and even when the most intensely anxious times have subsided, she experiences vague, uneasy feelings of discomfort. Excessive worry about the future or "what might happen if" robs Worry Wart of her enjoyment of the present. Riddled by doubt and fear, she has learned not to trust that good can come in her life. Her gift of diligence and responsibility can be liberated only when she learns to deeply trust herself and eventually to let the light of the Self into her everyday awareness. Then she can trust that things as are they should be. She will understand the wisdom of the serenity prayer which includes letting go of the things that cannot be changed.

Nitpicker

If Nitpicker works as a teacher, he notices if any i dots or t bars are missing from the handwriting of his pupils, and he says that for their own good, he must point out these details. If he serves as a member of the board of directors, he quibbles about whether $100 or $150 should be eliminated from the one million dollar budget. While on morning coffee

NITPICKER'S GIFT OF PAYING ATTENTION TO AND PERFECTING DETAIL HAS SUNK IN THE QUAGMIRE OF INCONSEQUENTIAL TRIVIA.

break, he may pick lint from his colleague's sleeve. Once he wrote Ann Landers complaining of irritation with people who use the incorrect usage of "ir-regardless" rather than the correct "regardless." Nitpicker's gift of paying attention to and perfecting detail has sunk in the quagmire of inconsequential trivia. He compulsively focuses his attention outwardly on endless detail rather than facing the pain within that ultimately yearns for healing (perfecting). As long as he avoids the underlying causes of nitpicking, he remains irritated and irritating. As he faces his inner fears, he liberates his gift of discernment.

Martyr

Not the only martyr of the zodiac, the Virgo Martyr has a Pisces counterpart. According to some researchers, a high percentage of our population possesses traits of co-dependency. If true, co-dependency must include more people than Pisces and Virgos. However, martyrdom classically relates to Virgo and Pisces. Virgo Martyr always makes herself available to take care of others and to support them, but she rarely knows anyone who wants to take care of her, and she never asks. Because she lacks respect for herself, others seldom respect her as a whole human being either, further perpetuating her sense of victim-ness. People may praise her for "putting up with so much," and occasionally others call her a "saint," but these gratuities only reinforce her role.

She works her fingers to the bone. Often left behind, she does the dishes while the rest of the family goes to the zoo or an amusement park. "Mom will take care of it," they say. She silently suffers, neglecting her own pain and needs. She may have only one dress and take on two extra part-time jobs to pay for her teenage daughter's wardrobe or her husband's gambling, unaware of other choices. She tiptoes around everyone's feelings afraid that someone might get hurt. Her motto reads, "If someone's feelings must be hurt, they might as well be mine." She believes that her only worthiness comes through sacrifice, and sacrifice covers up her own fear of emptiness and inner suffering.

Martyr's great gift of humble service can only be released in its pure form when it emanates from a loving center that provides as much love for the giver as much as the receiver. Thus, the inner pain heals, and she learns new methods of survival and more self respecting ways of meeting her needs. She learns that she can serve and have a multi-dimensional life worth celebrating.

Hypochondriac

Hypo, sharing Cousin Martyr's belief that he does not deserve many of life's goodies, internalizes his suffering, especially angry and hurt feelings. A Virgo by birth, Hypo suffers illnesses related to the intestinal system, pancreas, liver or gall bladder. Illness remains the only legitimate reason that Hypo knows how to take a rest, never having learned that he deserves purely pleasurable rest and relaxation from time to time. Even so, in the first throes of nausea or vomiting, Hypo still goes to work until someone sends him home. Being so duty bound, he does not need to worry about suddenly becoming lazy—therefore worthless in his own eyes—if he takes an occasional day off from work.

When Hypochondriac does not suffer from an illness, he often obsesses about whether or not the vegetable soup contains peas to which he is deathly allergic or whether he took enough Vitamin C today to prevent the flu. He signs up for the first shot to prevent the latest disease and is the first to suffer from an adverse reaction.

Hypo's healing begins with the realization that his worth transcends his output as a worker and that he deserves a well-balanced life. His natural concern for health can be converted into satisfying holistic practices, and he can even share his awareness with others as a means of service if he chooses.

Prim and Proper

If little hair buns drawn tautly at the back of the head were popular today, Prim would enjoy that style. More Victorian Era than Aquarian Age, she wears white blouses that button up to her neck fastened by little brooches. In earlier times, she would have been called an "old maid." Now people call her "single," but her life-style resembles a woman living in a convent. She took the Virgo symbol of the virgin quite literally and lives a straitlaced, puritan life. If lucky, she owns a cat or other pet so that she does not remain totally touch-deprived.

She expresses fastidiousness in all matters of hygiene. She carefully controls and measures her life—as predictably as she can manage. Yet, sometimes she even fantasizes reading a hot and steamy Harlequin novel if she could sneak it out of the library incognito. Inside, fears of what life would be like if she ever lets go plague her. Her gift of purity has become distorted into a rigid prison in which to hide that squelches growth and true purification emanating from spirit. She needs to know that she can safely be herself in the world without tightly controlled patterns. She needs to know that she does not have to do it alone anymore, and that, like a guardian angel, her Self guides and protects her. Then her gift of purity can be freed to more productive uses.

SHE NEEDS TO KNOW THAT SHE DOES NOT HAVE TO DO IT ALONE ANYMORE, AND THAT, LIKE A GUARDIAN ANGEL, HER SELF GUIDES AND PROTECTS HER.

Casper Milktoast

No matter what Casper's actual physical size, he always appears to be a shrunken waif cowering in the corner. Mouselike, he whispers through life, apologizing for taking up too much space or for getting in the way. Bowed down with an inferiority complex that borders on pathological, Casper takes the position in life of "You're okay; I'm not okay." His motto reads, "You feast while I eat leftovers." He quickly accepts responsibility for mistakes made by him or anyone in his surroundings. Actually, he has learned that his subservient behavior lessens criticism, for others feel guilty for attacking anyone so downtrodden.

Casper twists the gift of humility into reverse arrogance and has lost—if he ever realized it—his sense of self worth and dignity which always accompanies true humility. Being subservient protected him from greater onslaughts when he was a child, and he mistakenly believes that he continues to be protected by this posture. As he gradually learns to trust himself and to believe in his own equality with all of life, his gifts will be released, and he will quietly radiate a sense of peace.

References for Chapter 6

[1]. Oken, 1990, p. 198.
[2]. Huber, 1984, p. 118.
[3]. Bailey, 1951.
[4]. Oken, 1990, p. 199.
[5]. Rudhyar, 1974.
[6]. Rudhyar, 1970, p. 67.
[7]. Dobyns, 1972.
[8]. Burt, 1988, p. 197.
[9]. Hand, 1981, p. 223.
[10]. Oken, 1990, p. 196.
[11]. Dobyns, 1972, p. 12.
[12]. Bailey, 1951, p. 259.
[13]. Jocelyn, 1966, p. 84.

LIBRA

Ann Nunley

September 23 - October 23

CHAPTER 7

LIBRA

For the Libran the love streaming out of his own center of Being is the dynamic point of balance which unites all the extremes of life and joins him in harmony with others.—Louise Huber[1]

He who would find the beauty of love and achieve peace, must realize the light which leads to union through the cooperative wholeness of the sign Libra.—John Jocelyn[2]

Affiliated House:	7
Ruling Planet:	Venus
Element:	Air
Quality:	Cardinal
Polarity:	Yang
Dates:	September 23 - October 23
Key Words:	I BALANCE
Symbol:	Scales
Anatomy:	Kidneys, bladder, urinary tract, lower back, adrenal glands

Imagery Experience for Libra

Allow your breath to return you to your center, to that place where you are perfectly balanced. ... As you breathe in and out, allow any tensions or worries to calm and subside. ... Imagine now that you are standing in the light, fully connected with your innermost Being. ... Imagine that you are a beautifully fashioned balance scales and that now your awareness shifts to one side being much heavier ... Now move your awareness to the other side that is much lighter — each out of balance with the other. ... Now imagine being the fulcrum in the center and the feeling of having both sides being in dynamic balance. ... Allow yourself to fully experience the sense of being scales. ... As you return your awareness to your surroundings, begin to draw, write or express in movement the awareness you have gained.

Essence End of the Continuum

In its most spiritual form, the Libran path balances between the personality and the Self, the internal life and external world, and masculine and feminine energies. The esoteric seed thought states, "I choose the way that leads between the two great lines of force."[3] The knife-edged path demands vigilance in maintaining this dynamic, ever-changing balance. As Librans traverse this spiritual path, they liberate themselves from extreme contrasts and from being pulled off center by the desire to please others that often dominates at the personality level. They weigh and evaluate both sides in order to maintain an equilibrium that emanates with clarity from a balanced center.

"I CHOOSE THE WAY THAT LEADS BETWEEN THE TWO GREAT LINES OF FORCE."

With Uranus as the esoteric ruler of Libra, the search for love, beauty, truth and value becomes not only personal but universal. Librans find Right Relationship with themselves, with their groups, and with the entire universe. The "me" or personal self has been so thoroughly integrated that Librans can safely identify with the "we" in partnership and in humanity as a whole, a complex unity. Rudhyar reminds us that the first three signs of autumn—Libra, Scorpio, and Sagittarius—symbolize "steps in the growth of society and of the social consciousness"[4] just as the first three signs of spring—Aries, Taurus and Gemini—represent development of individual consciousness. True serenity emerges from Librans' ability to remain creatively balanced between personal needs and the urge to consecrate themselves to humanity, to the whole, in united action with others.

Middle of the Continuum

Yearning to be as light, beautiful and peaceful as sunlight glistening on a lake, Librans desire to overcome the self-criticism of Virgo and yet retain their discernment. Relationship from the most personal and intimate to the most global dominates Librans' attention.

Libra embodies the following qualities:

- ♦ Partnership or significant-other oriented;
- ♦ Friend/colleague-oriented and cooperative;
- ♦ Group-oriented and social;
- ♦ Gracious and diplomatic;
- ♦ Peace loving,
- ♦ Harmonious and serene;
- ♦ Balanced;
- ♦ Just and indecisive;
- ♦ Aesthetic and beauty-loving;
- ♦ Knowledgeable and objective.

Partnership or significant-other oriented

Libran children often fantasize about growing up and finding their true love. Teenagers and older people sometimes flirt recklessly as they beckon "the other" to them. Prince and Princess Charming stories warm their hearts with recognition, for Librans can never imagine permanently being without a partner—not just any partner, but the right one. Burt says that Libra represents the search for the soul mate.[5] Venus, the exoteric ruler of Libra, yearns for love and connection, suspecting that aloneness is a fate worse than hell. They want genuinely equal relationships, preferring companionship over Cancer-like nurture and comfort. The asteroids of Pallas and Juno, both often associated with Libra, provide clues to Libra's marriage of equals. In mythology both heroic goddesses, for whom the above asteroids were named, wanted equally strong partners. Neither were seen cleaning the hearth or nursing babies.

Librans, consciously or unconsciously, seek the projection of their other half—their own anima or animus—in their partner. They feel more balanced and whole with their complement by their side. The more integrated they are, the more likely that they will be truly enhanced by the partnership rather than just compensating for any personal inadequacy.

Relationships do not always provide Librans with the ease or harmony they so deeply crave. Hickey labeled Libran relationships as "the purifiers of the consciousness,"[6] and Huber insists that "Love can hurl him into the highest happiness, but also into the deepest suffering."[7] Sometimes they place their lovers on pedestals and experience devastation when these lofty images crumble. At other times, they depend too mightily upon their partner and give up too much of themselves, forgetting Pallas and Juno's assertiveness. When problems become too taxing in the relationship, some Librans develop kidney or urinary tract problems due to the retention of toxicity. In any case, partnership remains the arena for Librans to learn the crucial life lesson of successfully maintaining a sense of self while still relating to others.

Friend/colleague-oriented and cooperative

Libran relationships extend beyond the significant other to include important adult relationships whether they be friends, counselors, or social colleagues. Thriving on interaction with peers, Librans seldom live in isolation. They shine when they are reflected by others and become animated and stimulated when intermingling. They hone the fine art of human relations, and embody, in the most spiritual sense, the Buddhist principle of Right Relationship which calls upon the finest within each participant. A few Libran nuns and priests choose to marry God rather than a human partner. However, even they learn significant lessons from relationships with their colleagues within the religious community. Virgos extend a helping hand out of a sense of service; Librans reach out from a deep desire to be connected to others.

In all of their relationships, Librans seek to live in harmony and to cooperate as

"OPEN ENEMIES" RESULT WHEN LIBRANS PROJECT THEIR DISOWNED AND UNCONSCIOUS QUALITIES ONTO OTHERS WHO FIGHT BACK.

equals. As they create and share experiences, they learn to see others as they are. The seventh house in traditional astrology is designated as the house of "open enemies," a title arising out of the experience of Librans who have not fully learned the art of cooperation. "Open enemies" result when Librans project their disowned and unconscious qualities onto others who fight back. The sweet, charming, and very nice woman may attract an angry man who expresses the hostility she represses. They fight, she reluctantly only in "self defense." Neither understand the dynamic ruling their relationship.

Librans' cooperative urge generally supersedes any need to compete and dominate, though they sometimes struggle to maintain a sense of their own needs. Whereas Aries people represent the necessary acknowledgment of "me" in the zodiac, Librans see everything as "we." They say, "We went shopping;" "We got excited about the trip;" "Our friends like pasta." An Aries, even if shopping with a friend, would likely say, "I went to the mall."

Group-oriented and social

A third Libran quality focuses on the organizational dimension of life: the group or society. Quickly sensing form and pattern within organizations and groups, Librans manage group activities with aplomb. With their gift of harmonizing and integrating diverse people together into coordinated units, Librans excel as group organizers. They eagerly seek opportunities to express their natural qualities of gregariousness and sociability. They like to organize everything from the neighborhood block party to the fund-raiser for the art museum to the World Peace Day Celebration.

Twinges of idealism often inspire them to seek the perfect society or group. Ghandi, with a Libran Sun and Ascendant, certainly gave his allegiance to nonviolence and to his dream of a liberated India. Rudhyar attests that the entire purpose of surging, socializing forces within the Libran "is that of making more valid, more actual, more tangible the reality of human interchange, the reality of the community, the reality of living together within an organic, stable, permanent structure of communal behavior."[8] For the first time in the evolution of the zodiacal signs, community and social organization beyond family and work environment becomes paramount.

Gracious and diplomatic

The gifts of grace and diplomacy allow Librans to sojourn with finesse through the world of people and relationships. They possess the people-skills that oil social machinery everywhere and make the world an inhabitable place for humans. Some

Librans seem to have velvet tongues, so exquisitely do they communicate. They can tell someone to "go to hell" with such a sweet smile that the other person thinks, "What a wonderful person that Libran is!" Only later does the other person realize the full import of the message. Politicians would do well to pray that some of these gifts rub off on them or that they be blessed with a few planets in the sign or house of Libra. Knowing the right thing to say at the right moment has saved many a life. Librans could have even charmed the Inquisitors into providing leniency. While tact rates high as a social skill, when distorted, that quality sometimes emerges as superficiality and insincerity.

Being the most even-tempered of the zodiacal signs, Librans restrain themselves from almost all outbursts, often not even recognizing their own symptoms of irritation. Even when clenching their teeth, they maintain self control and deny the underlying anger. "Perfect lady" and "perfect gentleman," while perhaps being outmoded concepts, nevertheless describe many Librans who exhibit exquisite poise and gentility.

Peace-loving, harmonious and serene

No one hates conflict more than Librans, for they deeply prefer harmony and tranquility. They are often appalled by their Aries opposites who thrive on competition and an occasional good fight or by their Capricorn friends who may scramble over others to get to the top. Librans, in true cooperative spirit, look for similarities and ways to get along with others, shunning anything divisive or war-like. Undoubtedly, many Librans involve themselves in the peace movement, although some activist tactics, such as civil disobedience, would frighten, or at the very least, disconcert most Librans. Rudhyar concurs, "Libra dreams, evaluates, reaches toward and radiates the love which should eventually build the new group and the new society; but he does so as an artist rather than a politician—even though he may be a splendid manager."[9]

> LIBRANS, IN TRUE COOPERATIVE SPIRIT, LOOK FOR SIMILARITIES AND WAYS TO GET ALONG WITH OTHERS, SHUNNING ANYTHING DIVISIVE OR WAR-LIKE.

As superb diplomats, Librans learn the fine art of compromise and accommodation. Yet, the fear of alienating others often overrides their sense of balance. They may settle for peace at any price and over-accommodate in the process. They try too hard to please, smile too often, and give up their own sense of self for the sake of not rocking the boat. Rarely will a Libran make a decision that hurts others, even when logic calls for a different response. These Librans hate to take a stand on an issue even though they may have a keen sense of what is right inwardly. They avoid anything grim or unpleasant, preferring sweetness and light.

Librans yearn for tranquility. Before they have learned true inner peace, they camouflage inner turmoil or anger through great composure so that other people may not even realize their inner discomfort. The Libran journey to peace involves the dynamic balance between incorporating knowledge of what is needed for the self and blending that into cooperative peacemaking with others. When that has occurred, their true serenity shines forth as a beacon to others on the path to peace. Others more ruffled and scattered feel soothed by their equanimity.

Balanced

The symmetry of two pans with weights perfectly balanced on either side of a scale symbolically represents Libra. The scales of Libra, unlike all of the other signs of the zodiac which have people or animals as symbols, represent the balancing point between the personal "me" of Aries and the collaborative "we" of Libra, between personal and social consciousness. Libra begins the second half of the zodiac. The first day of Libra occurs at the equinox when daylight and darkness equalize, a balance point between the heat and light of summer and the cold and darkness of winter. Jocelyn adds, "Just as the scales ever strive toward equilibrium, so do Libra-lighted souls always long for and cherish the attainment of inner balance. They know that such a state of poised power effected by equilibrium, would free them from all anxiety."[10]

At the fulcrum of the scales is embedded the will, the power to use the intentionality that emanates from the Self. Through the use of this dynamic gift, Libra creates balance, not as a static condition but as an interplay between ever-changing forces. Libra, as a cardinal sign, energetically and continuously moves forward although constantly seeking equilibrium along the way. Librans must learn to be at peace during the moments of disequilibrium which inevitably occur in the process.

LIBRA, AS A CARDINAL SIGN, ENERGETICALLY AND CONTINUOUSLY MOVES FORWARD ALTHOUGH CONSTANTLY SEEKING EQUILIBRIUM ALONG THE WAY.

In that sense, Librans moderate between the pushes and pulls of life and seek a resolution of opposites. More than any other sign, Libra represents the balancing of polarities, within and without. They stabilize between spirit and matter, building bridges between conflicting parts. Bailey asserts that Libra, above all other signs, is associated with sex because of the balancing of masculine and feminine polarities.[11] Of course, even without a sex partner, Librans seek balance between those two dimensions of their own being. They actually express androgynously, for they carry both the feminine quality of relating and the masculine quality of thinking.

Just and indecisive

Arising out of their ability to weigh and balance, Librans express impartiality. They possess the capacity to see both sides of an issue, and therefore, the bigger picture. A wise old saying speaks to this truth: "The more people know, the less they judge others." Librans are interested in the universal principles of divine law and justice, and they know that growth unfolds in an orderly way. With their intuitive knowledge of justice, many people with a strong Libran influence choose professions that involve the judicial system, arbitration and mediation. The meaning of the seventh house includes litigation. Just solutions arise from the ability to be objective about both sides of an issue and from respect for the individuals involved.

> "THE MORE PEOPLE KNOW, THE LESS THEY JUDGE OTHERS."

However, seeing both sides of an issue sometimes creates difficulties in decision-making. A cartoon humorously addresses this dilemma: "My decision is maybe, and that's final!" Seeing both the positive and negative qualities of their lovers, Librans have a most difficult time in leaving relationships. They may eventually decide to end a destructive relationship only because of their inability to tolerate ongoing conflict. As parents, Librans often delay making any kind of decisions regarding discipline until they are sure that all of the facts are known which may take many hours or days. They bend over backwards to be fair. Indecisiveness arises from relational kinds of decisions such as "what should I say to so and so about this conflict?"—not about what color the sofa will be. Librans know instantly what colors and design they prefer, unless, of course, those preferences clash with those of their significant other.

Aesthetic and beauty loving

Venus, the ruling planet of Libra, finds full expression in Librans' appreciation of beauty, color, and design. They notice line, form and the way that space is utilized and have a keen sense of the aesthetically pleasing integration of elements. Even physically, Librans rarely look unattractive, somehow often being blessed with pleasing and balanced features. Whereas Taureans, who share Venus as a ruler, desire beauty as a sensual experience, Librans appreciate abstract, intellectualized beauty. Many even see beauty in mathematics. Most interior designers have Libra somewhere prominent in their charts or Venus in the sixth or tenth houses. With civilized good taste, they often reel at some of Leo's gaudy choices or by Virgo or Capricorn's frugal purchases. Librans usually prefer expensive clothing, art, and home furnishings—not because the items cost more, but because their eyes enjoy elegance which usually costs more. They drink in color and design.

Robert Hand asserts that "Libra does not necessarily indicate artistic ability, but Libra persons seem to need art more than others."[12] They receive pleasure from seeing anything graceful and in balance, whether that be a fine ballet or a beautiful Japanese flower arrangement. They even appreciate artistic touches on food such as the sprig of parsley on the omelette or the cherry in the middle of the grapefruit. Some Librans become physically ill if they live in an ugly environment. They do not have to be rich to survive, however, for even Librans with little money find artistic ways of sprucing up their surroundings. Sheets can be made into tasteful curtains; a little flower pot filled with growing herbs provides a dash of color—an artistic imagination goes far in creating beauty.

Above all, Librans hate anything resembling filth of any kind, whether emotional or physical. While they yearn for beautiful flowers to fill their lives, and may even secretly harbor a desire to open a florist shop, they hate digging in the mud to produce the flowers, unlike their Taurean cousins who do not mind a little earth beneath the fingernails.

Knowledgeable and objective

As an air sign, Libra represents the higher powers of the mind which is symbolized in the upper bar of Libra's glyph. Librans express great wisdom, often born out of their own suffering and experience. They access intuition and harmoniously blend together ideas which they then communicate with others. Possessing the gift of objectivity from air, Librans excel at conceptualizing what they know into philosophical and understandable terms.

Yet, they evaluate as shown in their ability to see both sides of an issue and to make clear judgments when needed in mediation. King Solomon must have been a Libran! They remain impartially detached in most things except issues surrounding romance. Therefore, they learn the not-so-easy task of balancing head and heart. Burt, who writes of the archetypes related to the signs, says that Aphrodite (Venus) "belongs to both the air and the ocean. She can be objective at work and subjective in relationship. ... Aphrodite is the Libra rising beauty who is warm some days and other days aloof, some days passionate and other days too spiritual to care about the body or sex at all."[13]

Subpersonality End of the Continuum

Mr. Indecisive

Indecisive becomes immobilized when asked to unequivocally make decisions. Sometimes he sees so many options and so many sides of the situation, each of which have merit, that he just cannot bring himself to say that he prefers one over the other. At other times, he waffles back and forth between choices, not making a commitment to either, fearing that either decision will certainly upset or alienate someone. "On the one hand, but on the other hand...on the one hand, but on the other hand..." becomes his mantra and his stock answer when confronted with decisions.

As a boss, he rarely fires someone because he sees too many reasons for and against the termination. Besides, he cannot bear for the employee to be angry with him. As a teacher, grading papers frustrates him for hours as he struggles to decide what the appropriate, fair grades should be. If he ever proceeds far enough in politics to actually win a legislative seat, he may abstain in voting. He takes forever to commit to a relationship, seeing both the reasons for being in and out of the relationship. Once he has committed, he cannot decide to leave the relationship even if his wife runs away with his best friend. He will see their side as well as his own, once again being caught in the middle of the seesaw. His journey to wholeness requires that he remember deep within his being that the will is at the fulcrum of his scales. As he gains in his ability to recognize inner truth emanating from his Self, he will then be able to utilize the gift of evaluative thinking and make a decision. He then can exercise his will in making the right decision, overcoming his fear of hurting others or of being unfair.

HE TAKES FOREVER TO COMMIT TO A RELATIONSHIP, SEEING BOTH THE REASONS FOR BEING IN AND OUT OF THE RELATIONSHIP.

Gracious Hostess

Grace greets her guests at the door with a smile, escorts them to the sitting room, and offers appropriate refreshments. She always knows exactly the right thing to say at the right moment whether talking to king or pauper. If Miss Manners ever goes on vacation, Grace could easily write a substitute etiquette column for her. Although Grace may or may not have money, others are sometimes jealous because they think that she has everything—charm, poise, and a full social life. So what is the problem? Little do others realize that Grace feels empty inside and tosses and turns at night because she feels disconnected from others and from her innermost Self. She just goes through the motions, saying all of the right words, feeling hollow. Her distortion from her center, from her Truth, lies in superficiality and insincerity. Only when she reconnects with her Self will she be able to make genuine, heart to heart, connections with others and her true grace will emerge.

Accommodating Ambrose

Ambrose sees himself as a "nice guy," and so do most people he meets. He never intentionally hurts anyone or upsets any apple carts. If, after years of being too busy, his doctor orders him to leave one evening per week free just for himself, and if his wife asks if he could shop for the new kitchen table that evening, he quickly agrees to go with her. Ambrose should attend assertiveness classes which teach the art of saying "no."

When Ambrose makes social plans with a friend or lover, he always asks, "What do you want to do?" He casually responds to anyone asking what he wants to do by saying, "Whatever you want." Yet, Ambrose possesses some Libran strength in spite of his accommodating behavior which becomes distorted into passive aggressive tactics. He goes along with whatever people want, and he occasionally accidentally slams the door. Always being nice becomes an annoying burden, even though Ambrose carefully hides this fact even from himself. Until Ambrose learns that he can be accepted as a person with preferences—and that he has a right to have preferences and to state them—he remains untrue to himself. As he overcomes his fears of rejection for being assertive, his gift of getting along with others becomes freed up to express more authentically. Then he lives in the best of both worlds: being with people in a cooperative manner and being true to himself.

Politician Paula

Although she can truly see both sides like her cousin, Indecisive, Politician Paula often possesses a keen sense of what the most appropriate decision or action would be in a given situation. Like her brother, Accommodating Arthur, she has trouble clearly stating her preferences—even when she knows them—because she worries about others' opinions. Paula adroitly manipulates language so that she seems to agree with whomever she talks. One evening she might speak to a pro-life group and the next to a pro-choice group, each group thinking that she walks on their side. Big problems occur when both groups sit in the same audience. She does not necessarily intentionally express dishonesty, because she can see merit in both viewpoints. Paula sacrifices the truth when she fails to act when needed. She fears being out of favor, so she sacrifices her own power in the quest to retain approval. In the end, she loses approval, power, and her sense of Self. Only when she frees herself from dependence upon others' opinions can Paula begin to live her life more fully and truthfully.

SHE FEARS BEING OUT OF FAVOR, SO SHE SACRIFICES HER OWN POWER IN THE QUEST TO RETAIN APPROVAL.

Legalistic Larry

Larry's mind thinks in legalistic terms whether or not he has graduated from law school. In order to defend against encountering his feelings in relationships, Larry experiences life primarily through his mind. Although he inwardly quakes when conflict surges or becomes too loud, he thinks, "What would be fair in this situation?" He carefully thinks out a solution, overriding any feelings that might erupt into his own consciousness. He offers his judicial point of view as a way of objectively mediating the conflict and avoiding his own inner fear. "We agreed to do it this way," he says to his wife. "The regulations clearly state that this task must be done this way," he tells his employees. As long as he can arbitrate, he feels in control of himself and the situation. His fear of feelings distorts his gift of objectivity into rigid thinking. His path to healing includes re-owning his feelings and becoming the master of his mind rather than slave to the rational.

Addicted Addy

Many books have been written about Addicted Addy in the last several years. She cannot conceive of being whole without a partner. While still a child—and even as an adult, she loved stories about Prince and Princess Charming who always live happily ever after in their little cottage with the white picket fence. As she yearns for this ideal, visions dance in her head of Mr. and Ms. Charming kissing passionately while watching the sunset together; walking on the beach whispering sweet, adoring words in each others' ears.

More than anything, she fears loneliness; she never learned the difference between aloneness and loneliness. Fears for her very survival reverberate through her being when she feels threatened by abandonment.

Thoughts of her partner and their relationship absorb her consciousness to the extent that almost no moments remain to become aware of her own pain, wants or needs. She does anything to keep the relationship going, wanting desperately to please. If he prefers her to wear slinky, black lace underwear or if he needs her to be hostess for his friends who drop in at a moment's notice, she accommodates no matter what she wants for herself.

Addy has lost herself in the process of trying to become the perfect mate, the perfect partner. The first step in her journey to wholeness involves learning who she is again. She must reconnect with her own needs and learn to assert those in the context of the relationship. In some cases, she may need to be alone for a period of time in order to recapture her own essence before she can be a whole self and be in relationship.

Placater Perry

Perry hates conflict of any kind, and when his adult siblings start to argue, Perry soothes, "We must all get along and not let little, petty things get in the way." Even as a child, he attempted to be the family peacemaker to avoid conflict. Sometimes he diverted their attention; sometimes he tried to keep the peace by being an extra good boy. He fears being caught in the cross fire. Before even admitting the extent of his anger, he offers forgiveness—not a genuine releasing of expectations and anger but a quick, premature forgetting of anger. He mollifies out of fear rather than from a deep inner conviction in the rightness of pacifism.

Like other members of his Libran family, Placater Perry must find new ways to be at peace in which he deeply experiences a sense of his Self. Healed from the fear of conflict, his gift for reconciliation can be released in a more pure form, motivated from deep belief in cooperation. Then he stands strong and firm, the iron fist in the velvet glove, seeking resolution of conflict without sacrificing integrity.

Sweetness and Light

S & L tiptoes through life with an almost prepubescent innocence, untouched by the shadow-side of life. Like Persephone before being drug into the underworld by Pluto, she runs through meadows with a garland of flowers on her head, oblivious to suffering. Her own fears and sorrows are tucked neatly into some hidden closet away from view, away from feeling. She glibly chirrups to her friends that she has the "perfect marriage," not noticing her husband's behind-the-scenes escapades. She smiles until her face aches from holding the pose. From the time she was three, people exclaimed, "Isn't she sweet!" Fortified by denial and avoidance of the muck of life, S & L relies more and more upon a phony facade to get her through life. She cons even herself into believing that all is sweetness and light, forgetting that real beauty comes from holding both darkness and light.

In order to become whole, she must learn that she can walk amongst the shadows and pain and still live. In fact, she only becomes a woman and comes of age by expressing the gift of light-heartedness and working through human heartaches.

References for Chapter 7

[1]. Huber, 1984, p. 136.
[2]. Jocelyn, 1966, p. 98.
[3]. Bailey, 1951.
[4]. Rudhyar, 1970, p. 79.
[5]. Burt, 1988.
[6]. Hickey, 1970, p. 21.
[7]. Huber, 1984, p. 134.
[8]. Rudhyar, 1970, p. 74.
[9]. Rudhyar, 1970, p. 78.
[10]. Jocelyn, 1966, p. 95.
[11]. Bailey, 1951.
[12]. Hand, 1981, p. 225.
[13]. Burt, 1988, p. 235.

SCORPIO

Ann Nunley

October 24 - November 22

CHAPTER 8

SCORPIO

In Scorpio the desire to be a separate individual is being overwhelmed with dramatic intensity by the need to be more than oneself; by the urge to flow into others, as little streams merge into great rivers and rivers into the sea.—Dane Rudhyar[1]

Scorpios are truly powerful when they do not seek power for self, but seek to be used by the power to heal and bless others. Their goals are reached by service, purity, compassion and humility.—Isabel Hickey[2]

Affiliated House:	8
Ruling Planet:	Pluto
Element:	Water
Quality:	Fixed
Polarity:	Yin
Dates:	October 24 - November 22
Key Words:	I DESIRE
Symbols:	Scorpion, Eagle, Phoenix
Anatomy:	Genitals, bladder, rectum, reproductive organs

Imagery Experience for Scorpio

Allow your breath to return you to your center deep within your being. ... Experience your innermost rhythm as you continue to deepen your awareness beneath the surface, deeper ... deeper into your being. ... Imagine that you are a caterpillar crawling on the ground ... and that deep within you is the primordial awareness that someday you will be different. Sense what that is like. ... You begin to fashion a chrysalis ... until you are completely encased. You wait inside the darkness gradually experiencing changes yet not consciously knowing the outcome. ... Metamorphic changes occur — wings have emerged in the moist darkness that cling to your sides. ... As you begin to slowly move, the chrysalis cracks open ... and you tenderly and slowly emerge from the darkness. ... You sit for a long time on the stem which held your home of transformation. ... Gradually, your wings dry, and you gently flutter the wings, taking off in flight. ... Take as much time as you need to complete this experience, and then when you are ready, write or draw or dance your experience and your awareness.

Essence End of the Continuum

From this end of the continuum, spiritual warriors and warrioresses have already won a great victory. As the esoteric seed thought suggests: "Warrior I am, and from the battle, I emerge triumphant."[3] These Scorpios have fearlessly battled their own physical, emotional, and mental desires and limitations. Even when fear surfaced, they accepted the challenges and plowed forward in spite of the fear. They relied upon their own resources, conquering personality pride and desire to control, allowing the higher Will from the Self to flow through the personality.

"Warrior I am, and from the battle, I emerge triumphant."

In the drive for purification, spiritual Scorpios conquer and transcend destructive impulses such as fear, greed, and control. The personality self becomes the instrument for the spiritual Self, allowing the light of the Self to shine into the world. St. Francis' beautiful prayer contains this truth, "It is in dying (to self) that we are born to eternal life." Destructive qualities transmute to fearlessness, joy, selflessness, humility, and harmlessness. Oken describes the transformation: "The Disciple emerges and the Eagle is transformed into the Phoenix who, rising out of the ashes of the desires of the personality, bursts forth aflame with inner radiance and abundant healing and magnetic powers. The essential unity of the lower and Higher selves has been achieved. He is now ready to do battle for the Plan and fight for humanity as a whole."[4] More than any other sign, Scorpio seeks out the challenges that ultimately lead to total transformation.

Middle of the Continuum

After Libra's lightness and airiness, Scorpio feels impelled to go beneath the surface, deeply plumbing the depths of psyches and relationship. Through the depths, Scorpios experience the urge to transform.

The sign of Scorpio also represents the following qualities:

- Retentive versus flowing;
- Investigative and interested in hidden knowledge;
- Deep and private;
- Strong-willed and powerful;
- Partnership-oriented and sexual;
- Strategic and combative;
- Intense and emotional;
- Self-masterful and adept.

Transformative: Death and Rebirth-Driven

Whatever harmony and balance that were achieved in Libra soon give way to the forces of destruction and change in Scorpio in order that new forms may be born. When Scorpios resist change too strongly, their clutched security is ripped from them. Even though Scorpios fear the inevitable insecurity that accompanies great change and real or perceived loss, they paradoxically yearn, even if unconsciously, for transformation. Huber attests, "As soon as we stand still holding on anxiously to old rights or believing that we may relax, we receive a symbolic 'push from behind.'" The Self relentlessly battles to transform the personality.

Traveling the Scorpio path resembles riding a conveyor belt that inexorably moves towards a small doorway, big enough only for the traveler. Accumulated baggage—old habit patterns and beliefs—must either be graciously or reluctantly set aside prior to reaching the doorway. Otherwise, Scorpios experience having the baggage being forcefully scraped away from them when they enter the portal of transformation. In the end, the outcome remains the same: the old has been stripped away, the journeyers mourn their losses and are reborn. The more consciously Scorpios agree to let the old die, the more they experience being participants in the process rather than victims of things seemingly happening to them. Eventually, they must find security in insecurity.

ACCUMULATED BAGGAGE—OLD HABIT PATTERNS AND BELIEFS—MUST EITHER BE GRACIOUSLY OR RELUCTANTLY SET ASIDE PRIOR TO REACHING THE DOORWAY.

Symbolic of Scorpio's transformative urge, the mythological Phoenix bird returns from the wilderness every five hundred years—the amount of time that the planet Pluto takes to revolve twice around the Sun—and builds its own funeral pyre from gums and spices. The Phoenix then lights the fire by beating its wings and is consumed by the flames. From the ashes arises the reborn Phoenix.[5] Limitations and fears are burned allowing birth at a new level. As Scorpios continue the process of death and rebirth, they often feel as if they experience several lifetimes in one body.

Retentive versus Flowing

Scorpio retentiveness often expresses as vindictiveness, resentment, and jealousy. Dobyns graphically describes the holding-on process: "To dwell upon experiences beyond their point of usefulness or to try to possess what was never really ours is to invite psychic constipation, hemorrhoids, and eventually surgery—all of them Scorpio warnings of the failure to learn when to stop and when to let go."[6] Physiologically, Scorpio rules purification and elimination of waste. Spiritually, Scorpio represents the deep need to forgive old wounds and hurts, for retained resentment creates toxicity within the body/mind/spirit. Refusing to forgive blocks transformation. In *Paradise Lost*, Milton said that the human mind can make heaven out of hell and hell out of heaven, a statement powerfully relevant to the Scorpio experience. Addictions of all kinds are born from grasping onto security and believing in scarcity of love, food, safety or something else.

When Scorpios let go, they not only are propelled towards transformation; their gifts can flow outward towards other people. They have learned the lesson of sharing resources rather than hoarding for themselves, which is one of Scorpio's lessons and the meaning of the eighth house. The eighth house includes inheritance, taxes, the government, insurance, alimony and other shared resources. Retentiveness transforms to a flowing willingness to share with others and a yearning to identify with the Greater Whole.

Investigative and interested in hidden knowledge

No other sign probes as deeply into the mysteries of life as Scorpio. Hickey called Scorpio the "mystery sign of the zodiac."[7] Whether searching for new scientific discoveries, evidence of reincarnation, or the meaning of dreams, Scorpios delve deeply. They become absorbed in whatever they delve into, sometimes obsessively so. They excel at careers involving any kind of investigation such as detective work, espionage, scientific research, occultism, and depth psychology. Because of this ability to probe intently and to search for anything hidden beneath the surface, they serve as expert diagnosticians in medical and psychological fields. Scorpios seem to possess x-ray vision into the inner workings of body, emotions, mind and spirit.

> SCORPIOS SEEM TO POSSESS X-RAY VISION INTO THE INNER WORKINGS OF BODY, EMOTIONS, MIND AND SPIRIT.

While Scorpios' research and investigative skills may be practiced in mainstream, traditional fields, they often also have a penchant for exploring hidden knowledge, another name for the occult—even if this remains merely an avocation. Frequently books on psychic phenomena, alchemy, Hermetic traditions, life after death, and ancient initiation practices populate their library shelves. One man, who dearly loved his father, was disappointed that he was unable to learn more about the process of dying during his father's death. Missing out on that knowledge angered the man more than the death itself. The tuft of feathers at the back of the Phoenix's head, the mythological bird symbolizing the highest level of Scorpio development, represented the pineal gland or the third eye according to ancient Egyptian mystery schools.[8] In many yogic and other traditions, the pineal gland is considered the opening to hidden wisdom. Scorpios possess an incredible urge to understand the mysteries of life at deeper and deeper levels.

Deep and private

The person who says, "You won't guess my sign" generally possesses Scorpio qualities, for they prefer presenting themselves as mysterious rather than public and open. While they yearn for closeness and intimacy, they cherish privacy and solitude. They almost always keep their secrets intact and appear silent and withdrawn rather than superficial in any way. They have no comprehension of how anyone—such as Geminis or others—could chatter about their inner life as if talking about tea and cookies. They consider their psyche an extremely private, serious matter and will divulge only small portions of its contents to a very select, trusted few. Their secretive, non-talkative nature endears them to supervisors in fields as diverse as psychotherapy and detective work which both demand confidentiality. Without a few Scorpio qualities, CIA agents would likely fail at their jobs. Some Scorpios live their entire life without ever revealing inner fears, desires and secrets to another human being. Others learn that being selectively open better meets intimacy needs.

Huber speaks to Scorpios' need for deep experience: "There are dramatic moments in our lives when we recognize that we can never find real satisfaction in the external things of this life, but that we can only react correctly in unity with the innermost motivations of life."[9] Whether penetrating the depths of their psyches or morbidly introspecting, Scorpios descend into the "underworld" of consciousness and are stripped of their innocence. In Sumerian mythology, Inanna descends in Scorpio style to the underworld, going to the darkest part of her psyche, stripped naked and dying in the process. When she eventually returns above ground, she never again naively flits through the meadows oblivious of the depths. Each descent allows Scorpios to loosen old rigidities and defenses, preparing for inevitable transformation.

Jung urged people to face their shadows or be dominated by this aspect of themselves. Scorpios sense, more than most people, the power of the unconscious, and they both probe its depths and repress the feared contents. When they refuse to face their own shadow, they become dominated by fears of the unknown which can manifest as projection onto others—seeing their own less than desirable characteristics in others—or in paranoia about what others might do to them. They have the capacity to psychically sense the shadow which exists to some extent in everyone. Due to their great willpower, they can also repress consciousness of their own shadow. However, feelings and desires cannot be pushed down with safety since the repressed material gnaws away at them through fears, resentments, jealousies and possessiveness. When they face and conquer their

> When they face and conquer their deepest, darkest parts, they can become gifted psychotherapists, hypnotherapists or shamans

deepest, darkest parts, they can become gifted psychotherapists, hypnotherapists or shamans, depending upon their cultural background. Instinctual knowledge of the inner worlds assists their healing practices. If they practice these professions before dealing with their own shadow, they may misuse power, controlling and manipulating.

Strong willed and powerful

Like all fixed signs, Scorpios possess a strong will which can be a tremendous gift of strength and courage to do whatever needs to be done or can be misused against other people in a battle of wills which destroys relationships. Oken says that a Scorpio may ruthlessly achieve its ends or be "relentless in the pursuit of its desires, even if such desires are for the well-being of others and not just for personal gain."[10] Most psychotherapists have Scorpio or Pluto aspects prominent in their charts somewhere, and they must monitor their desire to "make others get better" and learn instead how to provide quiet strength that leaves the other's self determination intact.

Because of their quietly exuded charisma and strength, Scorpios magnetize people. Although they often command respect from outsiders, Scorpios have to earn respect from their own family members and close friends who may not be so eager to have a Scorpio will imposed upon them. Eventually the path to wholeness calls for Scorpios to transform their urge to control others into self-mastery. Power over others changes to empowerment of self, which allows true volition from the Self to flow through the personality. Then Scorpios become like powerful warrior men or women so in tune with their inner truth that they embody the Serenity Prayer. When things need to be changed, they possess the inner strength and courage to do so. When things should not or cannot be changed by them, they let go of trying to control. And, they are blessed with the wisdom to know the difference.

. . .Scorpios become like powerful warrior men or women so in tune with their inner truth that they embody the Serenity Prayer.

Partnership-oriented and sexual

Rudhyar tells how Scorpio goes beyond the mating urge found in Taurus to an "urge in the individual to merge in absolute union with other individuals in order to constitute together a greater organic whole."[11] The deep desire to be bonded and blended together at physical, emotional, mental and spiritual levels propels Scorpios into both terror of losing self and yearning for this type of incredible intimacy. Those Scorpios who still lack a deep sense of self respond to this urge in a variety of ways. Some back away entirely and isolate from relationship which leaves them feeling desperately lonely even though preserving some sense of self. One Scorpio woman became celibate for seven years to avoid another experience of feeling like she was dying (losing self) in the midst of a sexual experience. Others become consumed in addictive relationships in which they confuse deep intimacy with being so bonded to the partner that they blend their own identity into that of their lover. Then they try to control every move of their partner. Still others experience merging only from the waist down and confuse lust and genital contact with intimacy.

For those Scorpios who experience a greater sense of self and wholeness, intimacy becomes an opportunity to learn to relate in a lasting, deep way. In speaking just of the sexual aspect, Rudhyar claims that the "individual becomes more than himself."[12] The experience of being mirrored in relationship, working through defenses that stand in the way of intimacy, and of taking full responsibility for personal actions and attitudes provide Scorpios regenerative experiences. Profound relationship allows for balancing of the anima and animus—feminine and masculine—within the relationship and for integration within the individual. Thus, deep relationship becomes a tool for transformation for two, equally strong people. As Scorpios transform their own inner natures, their conflicted relationships finally become deeply meaningful vehicles for further growth as well as self-transcendence.

Strategic and combative

Like Army generals, Scorpios innately know how to plan strategically, outwitting opponents more often than hitting them head-on. They maneuver to defend their position or seek retaliation rather than just looking for a "good fight" as an Aries might do. Like the Scorpion which sits in its dark corner and stings only out of self-protection or revenge, Scorpios attack defensively. They often "poison" with sarcasm. Generally, even though they fight with no holds barred, they battle indirectly and hurt their opponents in subtle ways to "get even." The use of black magic exemplifies extreme Scorpio tactics. Mozart's untimely death has been attributed to Scorpio-like influences. Salieri, a noted composer of Mozart's day, resented such a young, impudent upstart receiving more acclaim than he. According to legend, Salieri plotted Mozart's early death by getting Mozart to accept desperately needed money in return for writing a funeral mass (which turned out to be Mozart's own requiem mass). Salieri maintained secrecy by wearing a death mask during his dealings with Mozart. Secrecy, revenge, and intrigue characterize one side of Scorpio.

THE USE OF BLACK MAGIC EXEMPLIFIES EXTREME SCORPIO TACTICS.

Unlike other water signs, Cancer and Pisces, once Scorpios have decided to battle, they fight fiercely with determined effort, enjoying the fight and the victory. They may be intolerant and unyielding with a chip on their shoulder, or they may bravely enter into battle for what they strongly believe. Oken says that "Mars on this level works as the defender of the faith and enforcer of just ideals."[13]

Intense and Emotional

Scorpios cannot choose whether or not they express intensity—only how they do so. They will never hum along as a five on a ten point scale, even though some resist growth for fear that life will be boring when the intense roller coaster has subsided. Their fears are unfounded, for even the most spiritually advanced Scorpios experience intensity. For those who realize the Self emanates through them, intensity becomes passion for life. They possess the gift of being totally present whether watching a sunset, listening to a client's darkest hour, gazing intently into their lover's eyes, or composing a symphony. Oken says that Scorpio possesses the "ability for focused direction of purpose unequaled by any other." He goes on to say, "Once desire is brought to the forefront of consciousness (and this can be the desire for spiritual enlightenment and human betterment), Scorpio loses not one atom of energy through diffusion: the Path is clear and he goes for it!"[14] Scorpio clients coming for astrological consultations prefer an intense experience that may focus on only a few, deep points which may bring a tear or two to the surface than to be presented with a lot of information about many things.

> . . .SOME RESIST GROWTH FOR FEAR THAT LIFE WILL BE BORING WHEN THE INTENSE ROLLER COASTER HAS SUBSIDED.

For those persons who experience life more at the subpersonality end of the continuum, intensity translates into emotional melodrama and moodiness. Nothing seems lukewarm; they live by the "all or nothing" credo. No ecstasy seems more exquisite than their peaks, no pain more poignant than their valleys. They often are addicted to their emotions, for they would rather feel intensely bad and know they are alive than to feel nothing. Crisis becomes a way of life—if not crises within their own life, crises within their friends' and relatives' lives. They must face and conquer their primitive and primordial instincts in order to transform. Even transformed, many of their deep passions remain beyond logic and reside in the deep, emotional nature.

No matter whether Scorpios experience life on the most spiritual or most distorted end of the continuum, their eyes intensely pierce into the souls of others, and they pride themselves on not allowing their calm exterior to be ruffled by any emotion. Yet, those still addicted to emotional roller coasters churn tempestuously inside. Brooding, turbulent emotions surge like volcanos erupting through the ocean waters, for rage and despair seem to be the precursors to transformation. Prior to transformation, Scorpio's key word, "I desire," reverberates through many Scorpios who insist incessantly that pleasures, appetites, possession, and sensuality be satisfied.

Self-masterful and adept

For others on the transformative path, "I desire" becomes a call for self-mastery. Zip Dobyns has written and spoken extensively about Scorpio's task of learning self mastery. She states, "The Scorpio who has learned the lessons of his sign is the Adept, symbolized by the eagle. The black magician uses similar powers to seek to control others—the scorpion with hidden poison in his tail."[15] In order to become Adepts, Scorpios must develop self knowledge about all levels of their being—physical, emotional, mental and spiritual, and then apply that knowledge. This urge for self-mastery evokes the desire for challenges. One Scorpio foreign exchange student chose to leave home, country, and friends—including girlfriend, more to see if he could master the emotional challenge than to learn about another culture as a Sagittarian would have. Shifting attitudes and eliminating old, limiting beliefs empowers Scorpios to accomplish what they formerly deemed impossible.

They must develop moderation with all of their desires from expressing sexuality to eating to controlling others; they must overcome addictions and over-attachments, whether that be to turbulent emotions, relationships, fear, or a myriad of other things. They learn self-mastery, not by suppression or compensation, but by "realizing that the life in us is eternal movement and change and that we must become permeable for the finer emissions of the soul."[16]

In the process of becoming masterful, Scorpios learn that they can always choose how to respond to situations and that they are responsible for their own actions—hallmarks of healthy adulthood. They no longer need react defensively to situations. With the awareness of choice, Scorpios can let go of their roles of victim/persecutor, whether subtle or extreme, and experience greater freedom. They choose life rather than a living hell. Scorpio's self-mastery prepares the way for the universal, zodiac signs which follow.

> Scorpios learn that they can always choose how to respond to situations. . .

Subpersonality End of the Continuum

Resentful Rosa

Rosa walks around with a chip on her shoulder, inwardly snarling at the world. She is angry that other people at work seem to be assigned easier jobs than she, and she silently seethes inside each time she hears them discussing job assignments. She jabs sarcastic comments through a clenched smile. Inwardly she seethes, though the exterior remains controlled. Never forgetting an insult dealt to her, grudges simmer in her boiling pot most of the time. Without realizing that others perceive her anger, she wonders why people stay away from her and then resents them for liking others better. She also does not realize that her resentment defends against her own feelings of inadequacy. If she can project blame onto others for her plight, she never has to probe into her own underlying fears.

While wanting connection, Rosa unwittingly created chasms between herself and others. Gifted with intense feelings, her distortion lies in getting stuck in anger—holding onto it. Learning how to appropriately express anger and then let it go provides a way out of Rosa's dilemma. Then she can experience the other side of anger: loving connection. In the process of letting go of old, seething hurts and resentments, Rosa reconnects with more spontaneous, flowing feelings. Loving, she heals her own fears as well as her relationships with others.

Jealous Jack

Even though Jack has been married for thirty years to a woman who has remained faithful, he worries when another man pays attention to her. Perhaps her staff meeting lasts longer than he expects, and he wonders if she's having an affair; perhaps the minister focused his eyes on her too long. She speaks with her high school sweetheart at her 35th high school reunion. Jack replays these scenes over and over in his mind like a movie on a continuous loop. Although Jack has mellowed a little with age, he still obsesses with jealous thoughts. He nearly destroyed his marriage in the early years by constantly accusing his wife of seeing someone else or of wanting to spend more time with others than she did with him. He would hardly let her out of his sight, and eventually she succumbed to the pressure, acquiescing to a limited social life.

Jack has distorted Scorpio's tendency to hold on too tightly into a consuming addiction. Although he might not admit this, he believes that he possesses his wife and that he has a right to control her. Fears of his own insecurity, dependency, and intimacy unconsciously drive him. Like Resentful Rosa, as long as he focuses on the possible wrongdoing of the other, he avoids looking into his own motivations. Freed from jealousy, Jack's desire for deep intimacy is also freed to find fuller expression. As long as he hammers accusations at his wife, true intimacy fails to materialize, so he is protected from those fears while at the same time possessing her. Only as he allows the energies of the Self to emanate through him, healing his old wounds and fears, will Jack be able to find his true gift of intimacy.

ALTHOUGH HE MIGHT NOT ADMIT THIS, HE BELIEVES THAT HE POSSESSES HIS WIFE AND THAT HE HAS A RIGHT TO CONTROL HER.

Peaks and Valleys

P & V has surged between ten's and zero's on a ten-point-scale since she was a small child. Very likely she suffered significant emotional losses and crises while still very young, so she perceives these roller coasters as "normal." Adrenaline rushes during intense crises and emotions crash to rock bottom time and again with each new disaster. She seems to have more than her share of predicaments. Her boyfriend suddenly abandons her; she is mugged on her first subway ride; her friend attempts suicide; significant others die; as the only one available, she rushes an injured relative to the hospital emergency room. If she is not undergoing personal crises, people around her seem to need her for their crises. As long as her life shakes, she feels alive—even if stressed. She fears boredom should life be without inner earthquakes. Besides, as long as she is consumed by the current upheaval, she does not have to focus on her inner fears or her need to grieve some of the losses she has experienced. Each one remains frozen inside, overshadowed by the present experience.

IF SHE IS NOT UNDERGOING PERSONAL CRISES, PEOPLE AROUND HER SEEM TO NEED HER FOR THEIR CRISES.

P & V's gift of passionate presence remains distorted in addiction to emotion until she learns that she can still experience intensity in other ways. For example, she might work as a substance abuse counselor, an emergency room technician, or a hospice volunteer. She can learn the joy of being totally present while smelling roses or being absorbed in a deep conversation with a friend. First, she will have to heal her inner wounds and connect more with her inner purpose.

Lusty Loins

In esoteric language, Lusty's libidinous longings are translated as the "lower desire nature." Lusty seems to have a board through his midsection which prevents any connection between his heart and genitals. Therefore, this Lothario seduces whomever he pleases, perhaps priding himself on technique and stamina. He puts little slogans like "Lusty Loins" on his office desk so that everyone who enters the room will realize, if they did not already from his manner, that he is first and foremost a sexual man. He both fears and wants intimacy, yet the board in his middle—a psychological and energetic block—prevents awareness of either his fear or desire. He cons himself into believing that the sexual act alone is intimacy, so he avoids his fears.

Unconsciously, Lusty yearns for merger at all levels—physical, emotional, mental and spiritual—which requires an integrated sense of self and a deep connection with his own heart. He, too, needs to heal his inner fears and disconnection in order to experience this level of intimacy. Only then does he become a true lover, a lover who deeply values the other and himself. Then he can choose to express sexuality as a way of sharing with his significant other, and he develops his identity around his whole being—not just his groin.

Rebellious Victim

Unlike other people who give away their power in relationships and feel that others abuse them, Rebellious Victim fights against her aggressor. She may even violently strike at the other person. She certainly yells. Yet, she maintains the belief that she is an innocent victim while the other person is the "bad guy." She protests, complains and blames; she certainly does not passively decide that she must have done something wrong to deserve this treatment as her Virgo cousin might.

Out of her belief in being powerless as a victim, she distorts power. While railing against the other person, she does not comprehend her full range of choices that would truly empower her, for she attaches too strongly to the role of victim. If she gave up that role, she unconsciously fears, "Who would I be?" She would have to assume responsibility for her own choices and happiness and could no longer blame everything on her sparring partner. She would have to find virtue in other ways of being, an initially scary task. Yet, she can transform once she finds other ways to meet her needs. The gift of inner power over her own life releases, and she is empowered to be her real self in the world.

Morbid Max

Often barely able to move, Max silently broods in the midst of a huge, black cloud. Even though he exists in his own netherworld, being around him is like being sucked into a black hole, he so strongly expresses negativity. No wonder that people avoid him as much as possible. If his thoughts could be penetrated, one would find that he sluggishly obsesses on gloomy scenes and feelings. Darkness permeates his whole physical-emotional-mental being, and he has completely lost touch with a connection to Self or spirit. Having isolated himself, he has even lost touch with his inner yearning for the light that precedes transformation. He almost savors the depression and darkness.

EVEN THOUGH HE EXISTS IN HIS OWN NETHERWORLD, BEING AROUND HIM IS LIKE BEING SUCKED INTO A BLACK HOLE, HE SO STRONGLY EXPRESSES NEGATIVITY.

In the process of transformation, the caterpillar needs to be encased in darkness within the chrysalis in order to change. Morbid Max distorts this process by cutting off from his inner transformative urge and his Self, thus remaining a caterpillar stuck in a useless form. He must reconnect with the light and let go of his defense of separation in order to become a whole person again.

Controlling Coretta

Coretta shrewdly manipulates situations so that she gets her own way without ever having to directly order someone to do what she wants. She inspires guilt in her children: if they do not visit her, they feel guilty—she might die tomorrow; if they experience anger towards her, they feel guilty. Her controlling ploys entangle them in a sticky web without their ever realizing how they have been manipulated.

Coretta prides herself on not allowing emotions to ruffle her surface. With clenched jaw, she asserts her intolerant opinions about others' behavior and threatens to cut them off emotionally—or out of her will—if they disregard her wishes. If others leave to avoid her, she stubbornly refuses to initiate contact with them. She may go to her grave still believing she was wronged and, therefore, justified in her separative behavior.

She desperately needs to forgive others when they do not meet her expectations which then frees unconditional love to flow through her heart. Gradually, she learns that her tremendous inner strength and willpower provide tools for her own self-mastery which brings deep satisfaction once accomplished. Only then will she be able to relate in deeply meaningful ways to others from a heart-level and to allow them to follow their own path.

Retentive Ralph

Ralph has been constipated all of his life, literally and metaphorically. When he was six, Cousin Martha told his mother of a misdeed he committed. Sixty years later, he retains the memory of her betrayal as freshly as if it happened yesterday, and he has not forgiven her. In his mind, even though Martha passed through puberty, adolescence, early and middle adulthood, he assumes that she remains as terrible as she was on that day when they were six years old.

Ralph not only retains memories of past injustices; he possessively holds onto anything that he thinks belongs to him. Believing in scarcity, he holds onto his financial wealth like a Scrooge. He tries to control who will receive his things after his death, although he prefers to take these things with him. Erroneously believing that he must hold onto everything in order to survive, he misses out on the joys of life. Only as he lets go does his true spirit begin to flow again. Only then will his squeezed shut system begin to open so that the profoundly meaningful emanations from the Self find expression within his personality. With his old fears of scarcity healed, Ralph transforms.

NOTES:

References for Chapter 8

[1]. Rudhyar, 1970, p. 81.
[2]. Hickey, 1970, p. 23.
[3]. Bailey, 1951.
[4]. Oken, 1990, p. 214.
[5]. Eichler, 1984.
[6]. Dobyns, 1972, p. 16.
[7]. Hickey, 1970, p. 22.
[8]. Eichler, 1984.
[9]. Huber, 1984, p. 154.
[10]. Oken, 1990, p. 213.
[11]. Rudhyar, 1970, p. 81.
[12]. Rudhyar, 1970, p. 82.
[13]. Oken, 1990, p. 211.
[14]. Oken, 1990, p. 208.
[15]. Dobyns, 1972, p. 16.
[16]. Huber, 1984, p. 156.

SAGITTARIUS

Ann Nunley

November 23 - December 21

CHAPTER 9

SAGITTARIUS

He is interpreter, reader of omens and "signs of the times," planner, prophet and seer. But what he "sees" is what there is a social need for him to see. He is the servant of the community.—Dane Rudhyar[1]

He is always searching for new goals, for a new truth; he is never satisfied with what he has achieved; he is incessantly striving for greater realization.—Louise Huber[2]

Affiliated House:	9
Ruling Planet:	Jupiter
Element:	Fire
Quality:	Mutable
Polarity:	Yang
Dates:	November 23 - December 21
Key Words:	I UNDERSTAND
Symbol:	Archer's arrow
Anatomy:	Hips, thighs, upper leg

Imagery Experience for Sagittarius

Become aware of the rhythm of the breath ... in ... and out. ... Imagine the sunlight shining down upon you ... and that with each breath, you breathe in this healing light. ... With each exhalation, allow the light to permeate every cell of your body with its healing energy. ... Imagine that you are an exquisite archer holding your bow and arrow, ready to shoot. ... All of a sudden, bow, arrow, target and you become one. ... Arrow is released. ... Zap into the target. ... Another target comes into view. ... Repeat the process. ... Take a few moments to integrate the experience, and then write, dance or draw your Sagittarian impressions.

Essence End of the Continuum

Sagittarians living at the spiritual end of the continuum shoot arrows of Truth and Wisdom. As Oken says, "The arrow is, in actuality, a clear shaft of light released by the Higher Mind of a developed human being in order to bring expanded awareness into the lives of the people of the world."[3] They are intuitively enlightened, free and independent from ego and the pull of mass consciousness. As visionaries, they inspire others to raise their aspirations and ideals. Constantly urging others and themselves to become all that they can be, they embody the esoteric seed thought, "I see the goal. I reach that goal and then I see another."[4] Their visions and experiences unfold like the opening of a thousand-petaled lotus.

Their awareness expands beyond the mundane to the universal, and they remain far more interested in the whole than the parts. Sagittarians identify with the energies of the entire planet as an organism more than with its smaller components, the Earth being the esoteric ruler of Sagittarius. Mythological centaurs, also symbolic of Sagittarius, were sons of Gaia—the Earth.

Out of the search for vision and wholeness comes wisdom. Burt likens the evolved Sagittarian to Kwan Yin Bodhisattva, the compassionate, wise goddess of China who "rides upon clouds wielding her bow and arrow to make war upon Evil."[5] Burt reminds people that Kwan Yin makes war upon evil, not evildoers, just as Sagittarians fight against untruth and ignorance with shafts of light. They lead the way into the last quadrant of the zodiac, the signs concerned with universalities and society as a whole.

. . .JUST AS SAGITTARIANS FIGHT AGAINST UNTRUTH AND IGNORANCE WITH SHAFTS OF LIGHT.

Middle of the Continuum

After deep and sometimes dark introspection in Scorpio, Sagittarius bursts forward, transcending the darkness and finding the purpose of all life, not just individual psyches.

Sagittarians exhibit these qualities:

- ♦ Visionary and expansive;
- ♦ Truthful and direct;
- ♦ Trusting and generous;
- ♦ Optimistic and inspirational;
- ♦ Philosophical and eager to learn;
- ♦ Ethical and socially-principled;
- ♦ Holistic and synthetic;
- ♦ Wise and perceptive;
- ♦ Free-spirited.

Visionary and expansive

The creative fire soars for Sagittarians who constantly expand into new territory never to be contained. They move about incessantly, following the fire which leads them through a brilliantly varied life. Even Sagittarians whose primary interest lies in spiritual wisdom and meditation seem to have minds with broad sweeping ideas shooting in many directions. They require change in order to grow, so expansion becomes a way of life. Sagittarian teachers can never rest on last semester's plans, for even though greater work is required, no self-respecting Sagittarian could ever do the same thing in the same way twice.

They also have a propensity for being involved in many things at once—having too many irons in the fire. By the time they have undertaken a new project, seven others have sprung into consciousness ready for action. Even with sterling intentions to finish every project, this tendency can lead to lapsed deadlines and procrastination because Sagittarians sometimes do not know where to start. When they have exceeded their own internal speed limit—which is relatively faster than non-fiery persons—their sciatica, hips or thighs may clang painful warnings that reflection time and rest are needed. Whether vices or virtues, everything seems big with Sagittarians.

Propelled into the future by their expansive spirits, Sagittarians seldom have time to hold grudges or to ruminate on the past. Instead, they perceive and move towards the goal. Oken says, "One of the fundamental purposes of an incarnation with the Sun or rising sign in Sagittarius is for the individual to orient himself to some lofty objective—one which will unfold a higher goal and a conscious direction in life."[6] They yearn for the unfolding of potential and deeply believe that everyone should become all that they can be. One Sagittarian youth worker so clearly saw the promise in her charges that she almost forgot that middle steps were needed before that raw potential could be manifested in the physical world. Ultimately, Sagittarians seek the awakened soul or unfolding Self. Many experience an urgency along the path leading to the true Self. Others gallop along seeking answers, only dimly aware of the underlying spiritual motivation. Although perceiving the goal, or at least the next greener hilltop, seems natural to Sagittarians, they need to expend energy on developing methods and disciplines to accomplish their visions—a less easy task.

Truthful and direct

No other sign concerns itself with truth as much as Sagittarius. Sagittarians instinctively know that Truth, indeed, sets people free. They prefer being on that cutting edge whether they are three or ninety-three years old. From the time they are very small, they think and inquire about the Big Questions of life. Although the actual questions vary from person to person, most Sagittarian adults still remember the queries that intrigued them as children: "How big is the universe? It must have edges, but if it has edges, what's on the other side? What is God? Who is God? Does God have a form? What is the purpose of life? Why are we here? What is time? If now is now, then it can never be now again. What did cave people think about, and what did they believe?" Rabbis, priests, ministers, and theologians of various faiths throughout the centuries have expressed the Sagittarian yearning for understanding of these questions.

Huber attests that "The Sagittarian loves and cherishes his visions, ideas and ideals until an opinion, a philosophy, a usable structure of thought arises out of them, which he can pass on full of conviction."[7] Unfortunately, sometimes Sagittarians become so enamored with their own truth that they believe they know the Whole Truth for everyone. They can arrogantly argue dogma, offending others with diverging points of view. Other Sagittarians more in tune with the energies of the Self realize the wisdom of not blabbing all of their opinions and not trying to convince others. In ancient times, Sagittarius was called the sign of silence[8] because of the need to learn restraint of speech through control of thought. In that way, true wisdom was shared only with those ready to hear.

In everyday life, the celebration of truth emerges as directness and straightforwardness. Sagittarians, more than any other sign, hate lies. Their words, like arrows, zing straight to the target. If they were in the unlikely occupation of espionage, they might share secret information rather than deceive. At best, they would blurt out that they were not allowed to divulge that information. Sincere and honest, they seldom harbor any malicious intent even when their arrows wound. Usually they remain oblivious to the fact that a comment such as, "You've gained twenty pounds!" may cause pain to the receiver. Sagittarius became known as the "foot-in-mouth" sign for this reason. Even when they exaggerate, as they are prone to do—"I've told you a million times!" "There must have been a trillion cars in that parking lot!"—they intend to stress a point, not to deceive. Sagittarians continue to live with truth as their credo.

Trusting and generous

Faith in something bigger than themselves surfaces time and again as a Sagittarian issue. The more that meaningful faith is fully embedded into Sagittarians' experience, the greater their happiness. In looking for life direction and purpose, they seek that which can be trusted. Dobyns warns that "if our faith has been placed in something less than universals—in a person or a possession or too much self-will to the disregard of the needs and rights of others—then sooner or later we will have that less-worthy object of worship and security taken from us, to enable us to learn a larger faith."[9]

Their own mind—both a gift and a hindrance—challenges Sagittarians' faith. When faith becomes only intellectualized rather than embodied, it lacks depth. One Sagittarian woman reports that she has always known and trusted God. Yet, until she was faced with a life

> WHEN FAITH BECOMES ONLY INTELLECTUALIZED RATHER THAN EMBODIED, IT LACKS DEPTH.

threatening illness, she did not realize that her prior faith was a mental understanding rather than an implicit faith. Both seem to be important. Understanding at the mental level underlies how Sagittarians direct their lives, so it remains a necessary component of their experience. Burt distinguishes the ninth house, the house naturally affiliated with Sagittarius, as the "House of the Way of Life" rather than of religion as it is usually dubbed. The "Way of Life" is based upon an instinct for truth whether spiritual or religious."[10]

Out of Sagittarians' trust of life arises their generous—and sometimes extravagant—nature. Believing in abundance, they feel free to share their "wealth," whether that be ideas, time, hard work or financial support for charitable causes. They especially enjoy giving generously to causes that promise to optimize potential for people. Benevolent and amiable by nature, Sagittarians open their homes to people from various cultural backgrounds. Their giving, expansive nature remains rooted in an optimistic, ebullient trust.

Optimistic and inspirational

No other sign fits the "cockeyed optimist" description found in a song from the musical, *South Pacific*, as well as Sagittarius. They are also noted for joviality and humor. Old astrology books contained references to Sagittarians being lucky. Their luck, however, does not arise from genes or stars but rather from their belief that good things happen to people, including them. Positive thinking contains its own rewards. With a perennial view that the glass is half full, not half empty, they exude confidence in themselves and in life. Fired by joy, they enthusiastically progress toward the goal, rarely doubting that they will reach it. Upon meeting that goal, they promptly set their sights upon another one.

POSITIVE THINKING CONTAINS ITS OWN REWARDS.

Liz Greene, Jungian analyst and astrologer, notes the flip side of this quality, which she attributes to Chiron, a wounded healer, teacher and prophet from Greek mythology and now the name of an asteroid associated with Sagittarius. "Sadness and woundedness are an integral part of Sagittarius and form a kind of depression or despair beneath the bright optimistic surface of the sign. I believe this is why Sagittarians can be so manic in their strenuous efforts to be happy and entertaining."[11]

Whatever the motivation, Sagittarians inspire and motivate others—and themselves—to do the impossible and to see the invisible. By perceiving potential and believing that everyone possesses more possibilities than they realize, Sagittarians fire up people to accept greater challenges. They uplift and warm the hearts of others with their infinite hope and trust in the human capacity. Even though not emotional by nature, they may dab away tears while reading stories about incredible challenges and faith. Learning about others who have gone beyond the norm motivates them to even greater heights in responding to their own inspirational call. Mountain climbers who survive, against all odds, after falling off an icy cliff, sustained only by belief in themselves and a greater purpose definitely inspire the Sagittatian. People riddled with cancer who still manage to inspire and encourage others to be all that they can be and all of the Helen Kellers of the world are their heros. They affirm life itself through their expression of hope and faith. They love life.

Philosophical and eager to learn

Like their polarity, Gemini, Sagittarians perpetually learn, often just for the sake of learning. One Sagittarian story, purportedly true, concerns a 104-year-old woman. Upon discovering that the woman was learning Hebrew on her death bed, a surprised nurse asked her why she was undertaking such a task. She responded that she wanted to meet her Maker in His native tongue. Not every Sagittarian chooses the same learning goals, but their shared philosophy remains: "Learn until the dying breath." Whether through formal education—accumulating several graduate degrees along the way—or through life's experiences and by exploring ideas with people, they constantly seek to understand. Their vast and inspirational minds delve into philosophy, religion, cross cultural perspectives, anthropology, and education. Huber adds, "For the developed Sagittarian, the capacity for thought is the most important tool for acting effectively in the world."[12] In writing of esoteric astrology, Bailey says that while initiation occurs in Capricorn, the prerequisite education occurs in Sagittarius.[13] Thus, Sagittarius represents the initiate.

> . . .THE WOMAN WAS LEARNING HEBREW ON HER DEATH BED. . .

Most Sagittarians teach in one way or another. Many choose education as a profession; others teach wherever they go. One Sagittarian psychotherapist keeps wall charts and chalkboards available so that he can explain principles of the psyche and theories he is using in therapy. Another Sagittarian, a business person, says that she loves to train new employees, sharing ideas and information. Only a rare Sagittarian would still be teaching the same subject twenty years after beginning unless new courses and materials were constantly being added. They thrive on learning new ideas, theories and methods from seminars and workshops to add to their variety. Mostly, Sagittarians teach because they incorporate that which they teach into their own understanding. As they share, they integrate the knowledge into their own awareness, so they prefer teaching what they are currently exploring. The old adage, "We teach what we need to learn," especially resounds as truth for Sagittarians. By the time they really know the material, they become bored and zoom onto new subjects. When not busy teaching, they write, advertise and publish about their many interests.

Sagittarians believe that life resembles a cosmic school in which everything that happens provides learning experiences. An episode with cancer, a broken leg or marriage, a trek in the Himalayas—all provide grist for the mill of learning. This view is so ingrained into the Sagittarian mentality that they have to be careful not to ask friends, clients, students, and others who have had accidents what they have learned from that experience before the plaster has dried on their body casts. Perhaps with age, Sagittarians learn a bit of tact so that they can more sensitively ask such questions.

Ethical and socially-principled

Interested in the principles and patterns of society, Sagittarians ponder ethical belief systems and the nature of morality. Naturally, some pursue the study of sociology and theology. Although some Sagittarians become quite pedantic, most are not so much concerned with dogma or creed as with spiritual and ethical principles applied to the social order beyond home and personal life. They see the broad issues of society and seek to unite people with a larger philosophy and deity. Concerned with the practical application of ethics, "Nothing has more significance to the higher type of Sagittarian than the 'need of the times,' the need of the community to which he belongs," says Rudhyar.[14]

Social workers at heart, they crusade for justice, bringing their zesty fire to the battle. In their efforts to maximize everyone's potential, they champion the cause of the weak and downtrodden, calling for greater opportunities for all. They accept the status quo only if rightness and truth remain uncompromised. One of the meanings of the ninth house concerns law, an outgrowth of the desire for a social order based on fairness. They take their Libran cousins' pursuit of fairness a step further by extending it from personal and social relationships to the whole social order. At best, Sagittarians transcend the personal ego when pursuing these campaigns. At worst, they become ego-identified as great crusaders.

Holistic and synthetic

Holistic beliefs and practices pervade Sagittarian thinking. They perceive and think universally and globally, often glossing over details that would make a Virgo cringe. A Sagittarian teacher, preoccupied with a classroom full of students as a whole picture, might not notice an individual student's new hairstyle, even if semi-outlandish. They often intersperse conversations with comments such as, "I forget the specifics, but the gist of the message is ..." Generally, they hate anything to do with statistics, numbers or "minor details," as they call most things less than the global picture. They do not fare well at games such as *Trivial Pursuit*. When pondering God, how can they be concerned with or care whether tomatoes are fruits or vegetables, or what size of shoes their children wear, or who starred in a 1930's movie? Oken states that a Sagittarian "can glide over the minor annoyances of life, for he is only concerned with large issues and will not become confined by petty details."[15]

Seeing the interconnectedness of all life and looking for commonalities in diverse religious, cultural or philosophical views, they formulate generalizations based upon these observations. Like Ghandi, they might see themselves as simultaneously being Jewish, Christian, Muslim and Hindu. Sagittarian mystics might see similarities in all religious beliefs and not care if that which is called "Holy Spirit" in one religion is named something else in another. Fundamentalists from any religion might be appalled and offended to know that they are all often lumped together, in the Sagittarian's view, with others with seemingly disparate points of view.

Rudhyar reminds us that Sagittarians synthesize more than they idealize. He says that a Sagittarian likes finding "all possible connections between every part of the whole and by seeing them operate properly. He is interpreter, rather than inventor of new goals. . . . He finds new meanings, new dimensions of thinking. . . . He pierces through veil after veil."[16] They prefer interpreting the gestalt rather than examining its parts.

Wise and perceptive

A key phrase for Sagittarius reads, "I perceive." Out of the ability to see the whole arises wisdom. Oken says that "Sagittarius gains the 'wisdom of the ages'—the philosophy of life—in order to comprehend and teach the common links between all people, thus serving as a vehicle for planetary love and unification."[17] Gurus, sages, yogis, oracles, and philosophers through the ages have undoubtedly been well endowed with Sagittarius or Jupiterian qualities. On a more everyday scale, counselors, personnel directors, ministers, and guides of many kinds benefit from Sagittarian perceptiveness and good judgment. Sagittarians especially enjoy mentoring others.

GURUS, SAGES, YOGIS, ORACLES, AND PHILOSOPHERS THROUGH THE AGES HAVE UNDOUBTEDLY BEEN WELL ENDOWED WITH SAGITTARIUS. . .QUALITIES.

Sagittarians do not emerge from the womb as baby Buddhas, however. Animal nature binds the centaur's soul. In spite of the incessant urge to transcend, they struggle with their own nature in the search for understanding. Wisdom ripens with years of seeking out experience after experience, learning after learning, enabling them to see the bigger picture and to more deeply comprehend the meaning of life. Being mutable, they adjust to changing circumstances and constantly incorporate new perceptions. Occasionally, they wax pedantic about their current knowledge—only to have it change and expand again and again. Especially during the second half of their lives, their horizons turn inward and upward opening to greater wisdom.

FREE-SPIRITED

An old cowboy song, "Don't Fence Me In," could be the motto for most Sagittarians. They hate confinement of any kind: closed-in spaces; a routine, nine-to-five job; stuffy, conservative clothing; and protocol or other formalities. As teachers, they enjoy beginning fresh and new each semester, and they count the months until the next sabbatical. As seekers in the universe, they want to freely pursue the Holy Grail in their own fashion—unfettered. Foreign service workers, pilots, and travel agents (those not confined to a computer in an office) possess some Sagittarian energies, for Sagittarians are the wanderers and gypsies of the zodiac, always longing for the far and wide.

. . . SAGITTARIANS ARE THE WANDERERS AND GYPSIES OF THE ZODIAC, ALWAYS LONGING FOR THE FAR AND WIDE.

They forgo relationships which interfere with their pursuits. Spouses who would have the audacity to say, "No, Honey, I don't want you to go to the seminar in New Guinea," might find themselves without a partner, the Sagittarian having chosen freedom over closeness. Burt says that "their spouses often complain to the astrologer that this dedication to larger goals keeps them away from the family for a good deal of time or that they uproot the family and take it along on one of their crusades."[18]

In the pursuit of freedom, Sagittarians soak up nature's spaciousness in the great out of doors. Some avidly jog, cross country ski, swim and play softball. They enjoy being in the fresh air and energizing their bodies more than competing. Other Sagittarians just look at the trees and sky while reading a stack of books.

SUBPERSONALITY END OF THE CONTINUUM

Unquenchable Quester

Quester seeks purpose and meaning in his life through trips to the far ends of the earth and seminars on every human potential topic known. He has walked amidst the ruins of ancient civilizations in Mexico, lain in a sarcophagus in the pyramids of Egypt, trekked up Peruvian mountains, and conversed with a Masai chieftain in Africa—all in the hopes that now he will finally be enlightened. He has written in journal classes, breathed in holotropic breath workshops, and drummed with the men. No experience ever fully satisfies his longing. He fails to realize that what he really seeks is the Self which has always resided within him, enhanced by outer experiences but not created by them. Until he connects with the Self within, he will continue to fear his own emptiness and gallop from experience to experience.

Maximal Millie

Millie has at least seventeen projects going at once. She was elected president of the local environmental group seeking to eliminate toxic wastes in her city, teaches four courses at the local university, oversees the foreign exchange program for professors; has three manuscripts for books in the works, participates in a women's spirituality group, and runs for the school board. Millie usually arrives fifteen minutes late to her meetings because of unforeseen complications with her other projects, and she has now accumulated twelve speeding tickets. She apologizes when reports continue to be late, phone calls are not returned, and papers are not graded for many weeks, saying her intentions are good. Each time an exciting, challenging opportunity arises, she has a hard time saying "no" because each one provides such interesting potential for learning. Besides, she is addicted to experience for the sake of experience. She distorts the Sagittarian gift of expansiveness and exuberance to the point that even her usual smile and gusto have become frazzled and strained.

Like Quester, she has lost touch with her Self and with the inner purpose for involvement. Although her natural pace may always be relatively faster than many others, and she may be able to accomplish more tasks than the average person, she needs to slow down so that she realizes her true inner rhythm. Only then can she consciously choose the experiences that optimize her own growth and learning rather than running like a hamster on a wheel.

The Coach

The Coach shows people how to do things whether barking instructions from the sideline of a football field or assisting a doctoral candidate on a dissertation in comparative religion. He cajoles the reluctant, bolsters the meek, refuses to accept an "I can't" from anyone, and instructs everyone. Well intentioned and extroverted, he remains oblivious to annoyance on the part of those who do not wish to be coached.

His distortion remains being so identified as The Coach that he loses sight of other dimensions of his personality and being. He also rides roughshod over the preferences and tender feelings of some of his coachees, believing that he knows the best way to do things. The Coach meets his own esteem needs by acting as someone who knows best. His gift of mentoring can be more worthwhile once The Coach realizes that his true value transcends any role he plays.

Pollyanna

Pollyanna gushes her favorite phrase, "Oh, isn't that wonderful!" several times a day. No matter what befalls her or anyone around her, Pollyanna speaks positive words. Her best friend fell down the stairs and bruised her whole body. Pollyanna says, "Oh, it could have been so much worse—you could have broken your back." Her grandmother dies, and she tells her grandfather, "It's so much better for her now. Aren't you glad that she didn't suffer!" Her marriage of fifteen years ends when her husband leaves with another woman, and she assures others that "Everything is going to be just fine." The budget is cut thirteen-fold for her school district, and she glibly says, "This is such a wonderful opportunity for us to be creative!"

Looking on the bright side certainly has advantages. Pollyanna's gift of optimism has been distorted, though, through her denial of the existence of any shadow-like experience. She denies pain and grief, prematurely transcending them and missing the rich growth that comes when these experiences are integrated and healed in a meaningful way. Therefore, the human emotions of anger, sadness, and grief gnaw away at her through unconscious processes. As she becomes depressed—which she also denies and overrides, she tries even harder to act high spirited. Eventually, her facade crumbles into despair simply because she fails to acknowledge and come to terms with her humanness. Only as she confronts and vanquishes her fears of the dark side will her gift of positive thinking be revealed in its true form of inspiration.

Foot-in-Mouth

Foot-in-Mouth prides himself on being a "straight-shooter," someone who can always be counted on for the truth. Without hesitating, he confidently tells his new girlfriend—as if presenting her with pearls, "You are the third most pretty woman at this party." After a friend agrees to go to the movies with him, he says, "I'm so glad you can go. The first ten people I called couldn't." In examining a new ceramic bowl on the coffee table which Foot-in-Mouth does not realize was hand made and cherished by his friend, he blurts, "Where did you get this ugly thing?" His water-type friends shrink in his presence, and he remains oblivious. He missed out on the lesson of "thinking before talking" and certainly never heard of Sagittarius being the sign of silence as the ancients called it. Although not malicious by nature, his arrows wound. He needs to develop sensitivity and tact that can only be truly learned through tapping into his inner wisdom and experiencing feeling connections between himself and others. He needs to learn that truth can be expressed in more constructive ways and that he does not need to blurt out every thought that enters his head. Only then can his gift of truthfulness and directness be utilized in healing and insightful ways.

> "YOU ARE THE THIRD MOST PRETTY WOMAN AT THIS PARTY."

Grandiose Gladys

Gladys dreams and envisions on a big scale, and she carries her plans into action with sweeping bursts of gusto and energy. The city needs a new school for ghetto students that challenges them as no other school ever has. Like a whirlwind, she assembles volunteers, hires teachers, and rents a building without carefully considering either curriculum or financial base. She just assumes that the money will somehow appear. Her fiery nature energizes her into action whizzing past the dreary, preliminary planning stages. Impatient to get on with the grand plan, she avoids all details which bore her—nearly all of them. So strong is the urge to fling herself into movement and to ignore any sense of her inner core that if she were a planet, she would be flung out of orbit beyond the stabilizing force of gravity.

Her great gift of creativity and energy have become distorted so that she is driven by them rather than expressing them as an outgrowth of the unfolding Self. They own her rather than she being their master. She must take time to slow down so that she can be in harmony with the inner messages of what is needed in the outer world. She may still choose to accomplish big projects, but they will be based on deeper, inner motivation rather than a passionate whim.

Crusader Charlie

Charlie always lends his energy to some cause, fighting for right, whatever he perceives that to be. Throughout the ages, holy wars have been fueled on both sides by the beliefs of people like Charlie who "know" The Truth and feel honor bound to fight for it. Although he generally crusades for big causes, Charlie even sparks family feuds because he zealously fights for "right," overriding any compassion for differing needs. He fights to save whales and marshlands; he campaigns to get drugs out of the schools; and he sometimes espouses his religious beliefs from a TV pulpit.

Charlie meets inner needs by seeing himself as a modern-day Prince Valiant and feels empty when not campaigning for or against something. Having built an identification around crusading, he misses other opportunities. If he meets his esteem needs in new ways and connects with his Self, he will be free to crusade or not crusade; to rest or be active; to be light-hearted or serious.

Professor Penelope

Penelope teaches wherever she goes. Like her cousin, The Coach, she never misses an opportunity to share her knowledge. Almost robot-like, if someone presses her "on" button, she launches into explanations about why Rome fell, why holistic medical practices excel over traditional procedures, and how politics affect her university. She seems to know something about everything. When not teaching others, she absorbs herself in stacks of books, research projects, half written manuscripts, and piles of partially read professional journals. She never completes them all.

Questing for her own spiritual knowledge and growth has become overshadowed with scholarly burdens—most of her own making. She has forgotten the underlying gift that inspired her to be a professor in the beginning. Like so many of her Sagittarian cousins, she needs to reconnect with her inner Self for deeper motivation and to learn additional ways of being in the world so that she is not stuck just playing one role.

References for Chapter 9

[1]. Rudhyar, 1970, p. 91
[2]. Huber, 1984, p. 166.
[3]. Oken, 1990, p. 216.
[4]. Bailey, 1951.
[5]. Burt, 1988, p. 327.
[6]. Oken, 1990, pp. 215-216.
[7]. Huber, 1984, p. 171.
[8]. Saradarian, 1980.
[9]. Dobyns, 1972, p. 22.
[10]. Burt, 1988, p. 341.
[11]. Greene, 1984, p. 240.
[12]. Huber, 1984, p. 172.
[13]. Bailey, 1951.
[14]. Rudhyar, 1970, p. 89.
[15]. Oken, 1973, p. 188.
[16]. Rudhyar, 1970, p. 89.
[17]. Oken, 1990, p. 217.
[18]. Burt, 1988, p. 335.

CAPRICORN

Ann Nunley

December 22-January 20

CHAPTER 10

CAPRICORN

"How can I use this?" differs from "how can this be of use to others?" These attitudes show the difference between the unevolved and the evolved soul born in Capricorn.—Isabel M. Hickey[1]

The Saturnine Capricorn force draws everything to itself, concentrating, centralizing, collecting and conserving what has already been established, molding a firm structure which is hard and resistant, forming essences. It is therefore capable of achieving with these concentrated energies of unity and Will incisive and profound results.—Louise Huber[2]

Affiliated House:	10
Ruling Planet:	Saturn
Element:	Earth
Quality:	Cardinal
Polarity:	Yin
Dates:	December 22-January 20
Key Words:	I USE
Symbol:	Mountain goat and unicorn
Anatomy:	Knees, bones, teeth and skin

Imagery Experience for Capricorn

Imagine being on the side of a mountain. ... Breathe in the crisp mountain air and fragrance from the trees. ... You are climbing a little path up to the top of the mountain. Notice what the path is like — narrow or wide? ... open or obstructed? ... smooth or rocky? ... straight or winding? ... As you near the top of the mountain, be aware of your feelings about having nearly completed the climb. ... As you reach the summit, experience light radiating down upon you. ... Take a few moments to savor the experience of being on the mountain top in the light. ... And then return to the valley at the foot of the mountain. ... Take some time to record or contemplate your experiences.

Essence End of the Continuum

Capricorns on the more fully integrated end of the continuum have already developed a healthy and integrated self at the personality level and acquired a sense of inner authority that transcends the need to seek approval from the outer world. They properly use power which comes from a deeply secure personality rather than from an insecure one which misuses authority over others in self-interests. With a keen awareness of the energies emanating from the Self, Capricorns are aware of their own purpose as it fits in with the greater divine Plan. At this end of the continuum, the Unicorn symbolizes Capricorn who, like the mountain goat, purportedly climbs safely along treacherous trails high in the mountains. The Unicorn has only one horn, symbolic of its one-pointedness in pursuing the Plan. The key to successfully pursuing the goal one-pointedly involves the right use of will which comes from the Self rather than subpersonalities.

. . .THE UNICORN SYMBOLIZES CAPRICORN WHO, LIKE THE MOUNTAIN GOAT, PURPORTEDLY CLIMBS SAFELY ALONG TREACHEROUS TRAILS HIGH IN THE MOUNTAINS.

Capricorn represents the sign of initiation in esoteric circles. Huber adds that Capricorn can pass through the "gateway of initiation" only when he or she "has learned to kneel in all humility and, with his knee on the rocky mountain summit, to dedicate his heart and his life to the Soul and to the service of humanity."[3] While still on the mountain peak, Capricorns bask in "light supernal," as stated in the esoteric seed thought[4], but then they return to the valley in the service of others. The actual esoteric seed thought states, "Lost am I in light supernal, yet on that light, I turn my back."[5] In keeping with this plan, a spiritual prophesy states that in the next century, elected officials will only be those who have been transformed and are committed to genuine service rather than greed and exploitation.[6]

Thus, the Capricorn spiritual path involves first healing and integrating the personality and then finding: 1) Right motivation for life (inner rather than outer directed); 2) the Right use of will (inner authority rather than outer authority); and 3) Right service (according to the spiritual Plan).

Middle of the Continuum

Whatever excesses may have existed in Sagittarian's expansiveness screech to a halt in the much more down-to-earth sign of Capricorn. Rudhyar says that the "Perceivers of the beyond are superseded by organizers of empire."[7] Capricorn may safely build the empire by being grounded in the sense of justice, truth and universality learned in Sagittarius.

Capricorn's qualities include:

- ♦ Goal-oriented and ambitious;
- ♦ Aware of consequences and limitations;
- ♦ Hard-working and self-disciplined;
- ♦ Practical and pragmatic;
- ♦ Powerful and authoritarian;
- ♦ Proficient and professional;
- ♦ Responsible and mature;
- ♦ Traditional and conservative;
- ♦ Security-oriented and cautious.

Goal-oriented and ambitious

In no other sign do goals carry such significance as in Capricorn, for reaching the top of the mountain motivates almost all Capricorns. Those who are closer to the most integrated end of the continuum intently follow the Path of the Heart or their Dharma, as this path is known in some Eastern religions. Head and heart align with their deepest sense of purpose which emanates from the Self. They know the divine plan for their life as surely as an acorn "knows" that it will become an oak tree. These Capricorns define success as following this inner plan and allowing the entelechy to unfold. From this perspective, life direction and purpose in the world honor a deeper meaning for the tenth house than just career, although career is usually included.

Other Capricorns who are closer to the subpersonality end of the continuum push too hard, climbing over others in the process of scrambling to the top of the heap. Their key word could be "I misuse" rather than "I use." These Capricorns define success in outer-world terms whether that be titles, positions, degrees, accumulated material goods and money, or standing in the community. Developmentally, the thrust of life in the twenties and sometimes thirties is to "make it in the world," so these goals seem appropriate and fulfilling at these stages. For many, self-esteem and worth are born from seeking and achieving these goals. However, they begin to ask, "Is this all there is?" and to feel empty if they perpetually only seek goals that provide approval from the world rather than listening to their inner heart.

In any case, Capricorns have a gift of being able to set priorities and to follow them. They approach life as a series of tasks to be completed and objectives to be reached. Dedication and commitment are required for the climb to the mountain summit—the completion of their goals. Hickey says that a Capricorn "faces calculated risks in that climb, but nothing is going to stop him before he attains his objectives."[8]

CAPRICORNS HAVE A GIFT OF BEING ABLE TO SET PRIORITIES AND TO FOLLOW THEM

Aware of consequences and limits

A child who sticks his finger in a flame learns that fire burns. If someone whizzes down the highway at ninety miles per hour, he may crash into a bridge and die. A sky diver who jumps out of an airplane without a parachute will most likely splat onto the ground. People who seethe hostility whenever encountering others generally have few friends. From personal to international, people are governed by rules and laws which limit their actions enabling a system—whether family, community, nation, the world—to function. Natural laws such as time and gravity operate allowing some predictability. Capricorn represents the principle of karma which essentially means that people reap what they sow and that all actions, whether internally or externally directed, produce effects.

Authority figures such as parents, administrators, judges, and police abound in the world of form to ensure that rules are abided by and to provide consequences when they are not. Almost all cultures have had a governing body or a lawgiver, such as Moses for the Hebrews, present the rules. Unless the psyche is so battered that it does not internalize "should's" as happens with sociopaths, people soak up the familial and cultural rules. When violating their own consciences, they experience anxiety or other psychological consequences. Ideally, as people evolve into more highly conscious beings, outer mandates will no longer be needed. Individuals will be so in tune with what is required for the highest good of all that they will abide by that inner law.

The limitations of living in a world of time and space—an earthly reality—also concerns Capricorn. Even though the journey of the Soul spans lifetimes and even though, at the spiritual level, everyone is united, human beings live one lifetime at a time with individual lessons and struggles. People are born, and they die—a physical beginning and an end. Therefore, Saturn, the ruling planet of Capricorn, represents Father Time and the Grim Reaper. Saturn reminds people that "Things Take Time" and that processes cannot be rushed beyond their natural order. Capricorn's principle of limitation also stands for boundaries, for what belongs to whom, and for where one person ends and another begins. These boundaries provide an essential lesson in how to live in ways that move from unhealthy co-dependence to healthy interdependence.

> EVEN THOUGH THE JOURNEY OF THE SOUL SPANS LIFETIMES AND EVEN THOUGH, AT THE SPIRITUAL LEVEL, EVERYONE IS UNITED, HUMAN BEINGS LIVE ONE LIFETIME AT A TIME WITH INDIVIDUAL LESSONS AND STRUGGLES.

At some level, everyone makes a commitment to accomplish certain tasks and to learn specific lessons during the lifetime. Capricorn especially relates to these cycles, for their life path concerns learning these lessons. Periodically, corresponding with Saturn cycles, people receive "cosmic report cards" letting them know their progress. Approximately every seven years, we all have the opportunity to evaluate the choices we have made during the preceding cycle and to see what needs to be improved and eliminated before moving into the next cycle. We also can affirm and acknowledge excellence. Most people experience these cyclic times as profound and somber. Sometimes we doubt ourselves, occasionally despairing, and we often require time to deeply reflect on their life purpose and direction. If we ignore these signals, we eventually rigidify, and the next Saturn cycle hits us even harder. Saturn returns, occurring every twenty-eight to twenty-nine years, provide even greater opportunities to examine whether our little boats on the sea of life still point in the right direction for the harbor and what needs to be done to correct its course. Are we accomplishing our life purpose? Are we doing what they need to do at a spiritual level? Does our life have deep meaning? Saturn cycles can crush when people's choices have been inappropriate for their own good, or they can be a time of affirmation and renewal when choices correspond with Self. Capricorns who have made "bad" choices are humbled and brought to their knees. Then they have the opportunity to correct their ways and to get on the right path again.

. . .PEOPLE RECEIVE "COSMIC REPORT CARDS" LETTING THEM KNOW THEIR PROGRESS. . . APPROXIMATELY EVERY SEVEN YEARS. . .

HARD-WORKING AND SELF-DISCIPLINED

More than any other sign, Capricorns patiently and unrelentingly persist at completing their goals. If a Capricorn man desires to buy a business which requires saving for ten years, a decade later he hands over a check for the new business. A Capricorn mother who decides that she will singlehandedly put all five of her children through college does just that, regardless of the difficulty of the task or the sacrifices required. They can be merciless in their self-discipline to reach the top. Definitely Capricorns can be called "survivors" because of their ability to muster all of their strength in the indefatigable pursuit of an objective. Huber says that "obstacles spur him on to greater achievements,"[9] and the rewards can be great. When applied to spiritual endeavors, the gift of tenacity moves from self-discipline to Discipleship along whatever path they choose.

Most Capricorns believe that anything worth having must be earned, whether that be respect, material advantage or skills. They pride themselves on climbing to the top through sheer effort, and if they were offered a job solely because of family connections or if they won the lottery and could instantaneously finance a long-struggled-for project, they would be disappointed and not value whatever was given to them. Half of the satisfaction in reaching the goal lies in the awareness of the hard work that was required. This belief sometimes makes the Capricorn path a lonely one, for they also often believe that they have to do it alone.

Most Capricorns truly enjoy performing work that is in alignment with the Self, and they can work without stopping when pursuing their own interests. Confucius reportedly said, "Choose a job you love, and you will never have to work a day in your life." Having the capacity to work hard presents, like most qualities, both a gift and a disability, depending upon which part of the continuum it is experienced. At one end, Capricorns work joyfully, aware of inner purpose and meaning for their endeavors. At another place on the continuum, they work hard to compensate for other lacks, or they become so mired in obligation and responsibility that they lose sight of everything else in life including humor and warmth. They take on responsibilities beyond those required, denying themselves pleasure and vision. Wherever on the continuum, they work hard and discipline themselves one-pointedly.

Practical and pragmatic

Unlike idealistic Sagittarians, Capricorns plant their feet firmly on the earth and work with things that have an established usefulness—not just theoretical possibilities. They are more interested in implementing concrete principles than in pondering their meaning. Therefore, they pay far more attention to truths validated in the "real world" rather than inner, subjective intuitions which they do not trust. Even Capricorns who have several planets in Pisces (in which reality is non-material and intuitive) still demand proof in the outer world. Truth is tested by practical consequences: Does it work? Is it functional? Can it be used reliably? They build sensible forms and masterfully manifest what is needed through hard work. The key words for Capricorn, "I use" apply to the ability to know what can be used in creating earthly realities.

> THE KEY WORDS FOR CAPRICORN, "I USE". . .

Pragmatic questions precede almost any Capricorn enterprise. A Capricorn in love may delay marriage because, "I need to first establish myself financially and to finish the business degree." In response to an ecstatic spouse who has discovered the "perfect" sofa for their living room, the Capricorn demands, "How much does it cost? How long will it last? Wouldn't it make more sense to recover the old one while the children are young?" Capricorn bosses institute tests of cost-effectiveness for everything. Above all else, Capricorns ask, "Does this fit into my priorities at this time?" If not, even though pleasurable, they usually push aside whatever does not fit and pride themselves on their common sense. They embody realism and practicality.

Powerful and Authoritarian

The tenth house includes authority figures such as father or mother (depending on which provided the most discipline and boundaries), politicians and statesmen, administrators and managers, heads of clans or tribes, police, business leaders, and others in positions of responsibility. Capricorn energy will certainly appear in the charts of most people who choose any of these professions. While royal Leos often seem to think their rule comes by divine right, Capricorns rule by authority delegated into certain roles. They yearn for power, and if they still are trying to prove their acceptability to the world, they want hierarchical command over others to aggrandize their ego. Some desire to accumulate money and material goods because of the power these carry in the world. Those who have already developed a healthy, secure identity can separate personal will from universal law and use their positions of authority, including wealth, for the betterment of humanity.

> CAPRICORNS YEARN FOR POWER. . .THEY WANT HIERARCHICAL COMMAND OVER OTHERS TO AGGRANDIZE THEIR EGO.

When Capricorns experience insecurity or a fear of being controlled, they cover it up by controlling others too much. They then sometimes wield authority with dictums like, "Do it because I said so!" A national president may conceal illegal attempts to squelch his enemies. Yet, if they overstep their bounds and defy rules or laws in an attempt to maintain authority, they seem to inexorably be brought to their knees so that they can once again learn limits and humility. Only then can they use authority appropriately and wisely.

In order to maintain their positions, many Capricorns subjugate relationships to their role, sometimes by choice and sometimes by the choice of those under their authority. A fine professor who becomes chairman of his department may find that peers relate differently to him when he administrates than they did when he was just a colleague. Corporate America has long frowned upon upper echelon executives fraternizing with the workers. Sometimes authorities believe that they need to be hard and unfeeling in order to accomplish the tasks that need to be done, and occasionally this unsympathetic attitude carries over into the home. Hickey says that some Capricorns are "street angels" and "house devils."[10] By nature, Capricorns must deal with authority issues. However, they can choose how to express power.

PROFICIENT AND PROFESSIONAL

No other sign excels at organization better than Capricorn. They instinctively know how much and what kind of effort is required at the precise time to most efficiently and effectively accomplish any goal. They can instantaneously list their tasks for the day and which ones have top priority and will, therefore, be completed first unlike the mutable signs which prefer doing things randomly. A Capricorn surely must have invented time-management books which have places for appointments, priorities, tasks and project plans carried around by so many professionals. At least, these devices delight Capricorn types. Undaunted by chaos, they assemble all of the pieces into a pattern and create order.

> NO OTHER SIGN EXCELS AT ORGANIZATION BETTER THAN CAPRICORN.

With shrewd minds and a desire for structure, they make excellent strategists in any field. Their efficiency and ability to organize provide needed gifts to any supervisor, manager or executive. Both cardinal and earth, they also excel at getting projects started and running, and their tenacity allows them to spend however many years are required to complete the enterprise—even a lifetime if needed.

The tenth house rules status, public image, profession or career, and even broader, the outer life direction. Capricorns want that public image to include credibility, trustworthiness, excellence, solidity and professionalism. They would rather receive respect and admiration from others for these qualities than warmth. They strive to present themselves in the best possible light to the world, proving their acceptability to themselves and others. They often believe that prestige and success come to those who have impeccable credentials, and Capricorns celebrate every new initial representing certifications, diplomas and degrees that follows their name. These verifications seem to say, "See, I am really good at what I do, because other professionals agree."

RESPONSIBLE AND MATURE

Huber called the Capricorn an "Iron Man of Duty."[11] Assuming responsibility seems as natural as breathing, so much so that they feel bereft without it. Serious and dependable, they do not fear burdens and obligations. "Yes," the daughter says with determination, "Even though I am only twenty-one, I will carry on my dying father's job as head of the family company because that's what's needed." A teenager unflinchingly takes on the role of breadwinner, going to school full time and working three part-time jobs, in order to support a family hit by tragedy. Someone has to do the job, and Capricorns reason it might as well be them. Other Capricorns not required to carry such a heavy load still take on early responsibility. Most neighborhoods have one entrepreneurial ten-year-old who is envied by his siblings and peers and admired by adults because he has already accumulated a CD player, a video machine, a computer and saved enough money for college from his lawn-mowing and minor repair service.

Sometimes people remark that the infant Capricorn already looks grown-up. Although they often learn to play by middle age or later, Capricorns frequently mention that they were born old and that they can never remember being a child. Integrity and confidence often emerge from such early competence; sometimes just weak knees result from bending under such heavy burdens. In any case, Capricorns respect and value elders for their experience-wisdom, and they often gravitate to the company of older friends and associates. Old while still young and young when old, Capricorns excel with responsibility.

. . . CAPRICORNS FREQUENTLY MENTION THEY WERE BORN OLD AND THEY CAN NEVER REMEMBER BEING A CHILD.

TRADITIONAL AND CONSERVATIVE

Saturn, the ruling planet of Capricorn, represents the principle of contraction and crystallization. Interestingly, many Native Americans and others who work with crystals and other stones or minerals from the earth possess ample Capricorn energy. If they become too stuck in their habit patterns, they may suffer from arthritis or other such ailments. Even their wonderfully witty, dry humor is contained—tongue in cheek—evoking smiles rather than guffaws.

Capricorns focalize and concentrate energy, thus creating form. Thrifty and economical, they know how to make the most from the least. They can manifest that to which they aspire, although they often become prisoners to that very form. Form and structure must develop in order for the ego or personality self to cohere into an identity. Hickey adds that "Saturn builds walls around the self until it is strong enough to stand without them. It is a constricting, contracting influence until the soul is strong enough to break down the selfishness and separateness in him and go free."[12] At the spiritual end of the continuum, Capricorns teach people how to co-create form rather than being captive to it.

Traditional and conventional by nature, they prefer continuity to change and formality and custom to spontaneity. Capricorns generally spark conservation movements, saving the environment from deterioration. They savor the past, often becoming history and antique buffs. Capricorns of every generation and culture complain that eroding tradition makes life feel unstable. They feel more secure while conserving the familiar and known and safeguarding tradition.

Security-oriented and cautious

Capricorns generate feelings of security from a known material life, a life that includes family and possessions. They hate letting go of anything that might ever be useful, often hoarding out of their fear of dearth and poverty. Why throw away Aunt Matilda's canning jars when they could very well be used again, never mind that Capricorn now lives three hundred miles from the nearest tomato plant and one-thousand miles from the closest peach tree. They endure marriages beyond the point of repair, the Capricorn hanging on years longer than most people to empty, outworn shells of relationships. A vague sense of loneliness seems to gnaw at them, and they fear being without mate or family. Having predictable and familiar relationships and things, even when not entirely functional, provides security.

They approach life with caution, both a gift and a problem. This quality gifts them with common sense, an attribute dearly needed in this world. Capricorns naturally find a replacement job before leaving other employment. They pay the mortgage payment and other bills before tackling new, expensive projects. They abstain or use birth control when they do not want to produce a child. When backpacking across the desert, they carry sufficient water to sustain life. However, problems occur with this gift when caution consumes, paralyzing people into inaction. They may become so restrained that they fear taking any risks and become mired in fear and doubt. Possessing both common sense and a need for security, Capricorns provide a stable structure in which people can exist on the earth without constant upheaval.

Subpersonality End of Continuum

Ambitious Alta

Alta drives herself to acquire the most prestige, authority, and success, no matter the cost. She covets large bank accounts and other symbols of success in the outer world, for she believes that her worth directly relates to such acquisitions. She scrambles to arrange the best deals for herself even if others become hurt in the process. If she owns a business, she occasionally omits a few pertinent details that, if known to her customers, would prevent the transaction. If a position opens that represents a promotion for her, Alta makes sure that her name appears at the top of the list and does not hesitate to deviously pass on damaging information about anyone else in line for the job. Her philosophy reads, "What others don't know doesn't hurt them." She only cares about reaching the pinnacle to assure her own image of success.

> SHE COVETS LARGE BANK ACCOUNTS AND OTHER SYMBOLS OF SUCCESS IN THE OUTER WORLD. . .

Her gifts of tenacity and the ability to accomplish have been distorted into grasping exploitation. Her path to wholeness includes realizing the true meaning of success, a success that can be experienced in the world but that emanates from an inner sense of purpose and cause. As energies from her Self touch her awareness, integrity emerges so that she no longer uses others for her own gain.

No-risk Ned

Ned is riddled with fears and doubts for the future, so he stays paralyzed in a rut. Generally, Ned exhibits a gloomy pessimism and seems to be chronically depressed. If he were to even consider jumping into a pool of water, he would first ascertain depth, temperature and whether any rocks or sharks lurk at the bottom. He abhors change because of the uncertainties that emerge in considering the unknown. He believes in the scarcity principle that says that resources are limited and that some remain empty-handed. He worries that the new store down the street will take away his business, that he will run out of money, and that his children will not be able to afford college.

IF HE WERE TO EVEN CONSIDER JUMPING INTO A POOL OF WATER, HE WOULD FIRST ASCERTAIN DEPTH, TEMPERATURE AND WHETHER ANY ROCKS OR SHARKS LURK AT THE BOTTOM.

His gift of common sense and practical caution drains into a puddle of fear, stripping him of vitality. He lacks faith in himself and trust in the universe to provide. He must heal his insecurities and reconnect with his Self which provides an awareness of how to tap into any needed resources.

Workaholic Wanda

Wanda not only made the work ethic her credo; she fashioned her entire identity around it. From dawn till long past dusk, Wanda works, works, works. She beams with pride when people say, "Wanda, I just don't know how you accomplish so much!" Her efforts have brought successes, but each time she completes a major assignment or an enormous project, she experiences depression because of a lull in work. However, she quickly replaces whatever took fifteen hours a day with another goal that requires eighteen hours a day. If her husband insists they take a vacation, she carts along briefcases of work to slave over in their room while everyone else enjoys the cruise. She only sees her children for thirty minutes before leaving for work in the morning.

Wanda does not realize that she works to cover up self-doubt and the fear that she is not good enough. Instead, she tells herself and others, "These things just have to be done." In order to release her gift of perseverance into a healthy expression that includes a balance between work and play and between work and relationships, Wanda must face and conquer her fears. She must listen to the still, small voice within that provides awareness of what is truly important and what is not.

Rigid Rodney

Rodney invents rules if none exist and grimly enforces those already in place. "Employees can only spend fifteen minutes on a coffee break. The children are not allowed any snacks between mealtimes. Even when grandparents visit, children must be in bed by seven o'clock." Every day he brushes his teeth, jogs thirty minutes, showers, eats oatmeal and bananas for breakfast, drives the same route to the office, works, quits at six o'clock, drives home the same highway, reads the paper, eats dinner, watches television and goes to bed. Any variance in his schedule makes him nervous. He quotes Bible verses that support his beliefs and feels most comfortable when surrounded by dogma. Rodney craves structure to make him feel safe and in control, yet he creates straight jackets for his employees, family, and his one or two—if any—friends.

EVERY DAY HE BRUSHES HIS TEETH, JOGS THIRTY MINUTES, SHOWERS, EATS OATMEAL AND BANANAS FOR BREAKFAST, DRIVES THE SAME ROUTE TO THE OFFICE, WORKS, QUITS AT SIX O'CLOCK. . .

He has made structure his religion and way of life, shutting himself off from the creative life force. Whatever wounds that resulted in such rigidity must first be healed before he can feel comfortable with a looser lifestyle. As he feels safer in the world, he can have both routine and freedom.

Hoarder Hanna

Although much more organized than her Cancer cousin, Clutterbug, Hanna also cannot stand for anything to be thrown away. Clutterbug keeps things for nostalgic reasons whereas Hanna hoards because she is afraid that she may need these items in a time of scarcity. Periodically, Hanna purchases huge quantities of canned goods in case a famine comes. She has even stashed cash in her mattress just in case the banks fail. Always afraid she will not have enough—food, money, material goods—Hanna parsimoniously avoids giving away anything. Even if she knew her neighbors were hungry, she would find it difficult to give them anything from her cache. Some call her stingy.

Hanna fears that if she does not stockpile, no one will take care of her and that she will die. Whether or not true, she feels isolated and alone and clings to whatever material security she can acquire. As she connects with her Self and the Source, she may realize that abundance exists in the universe and that she is safe. At least, she may lose some of her fear and apply her skills to conserving with common sense rather than hoarding.

Dictator Daniel

Daniel may head a small nation, a company, or a family. No matter which role he plays, he dictates policies, rules, standards and metes out quick judgment and punishment when these are not met. He acquires a sense of importance through authority and prefers the resulting power over having warm connections with people. Daniel unconsciously or secretly does not believe in himself and so depends upon his role for credibility in the world.

If his sense of self worth increased and he experienced a greater wholeness through expressing many dimensions of his personality rather than just authoritarianism, Daniel could still utilize his gift of management. He could then rely upon an inner authority for his validation rather than external power.

Organized Ophelia

Ophelia invented her own time management book and lives by it. She makes lists, categorizes, and prioritizes. Like her brother, Rigid Rodney, she allows structure to dominate her life rather than it being just a tool to enhance effectiveness. At the office, she lives by her law of efficiency. If she read in a book that a productive manager only allows one minute per phone call, she sets a stop watch for each one. As a manager of personnel who allows ten minutes per visit, Ophelia follows this policy to the letter: just ten minutes for the employee who needs a leave because her baby contracts the measles, husband disappears, and mother dies all on the same day.

AS A MANAGER OF PERSONNEL WHO ALLOWS TEN MINUTES PER VISIT, OPHELIA FOLLOWS THIS POLICY TO THE LETTER: JUST TEN MINUTES FOR THE EMPLOYEE WHO NEEDS A LEAVE BECAUSE HER BABY CONTRACTS THE MEASLES, HUSBAND DISAPPEARS, AND MOTHER DIES ALL ON THE SAME DAY.

Like her brother, Ophelia feels unsafe without structure. As she learns to use her gift of organization and time management as a method to be productive at appropriate times and to relax at other times, she finds greater happiness. Becoming more comfortable with herself, she leads a more balanced life that includes both boundaries and spontaneity.

Patriarch Philip

In a past life, Philip probably headed a huge clan in which patriarchal skills were expected and required for the role. Times have changed, and Philip finds talk about equality quite unsettling, for he only knows how to be in charge. He questions his identity if he must interact as equals with people he previously patronized. He desperately tries to reassert the old values in which everyone knew their place. He wonders why his wife of twenty-five years wants a divorce and is angered when younger family members jockey for power within the family business. Philip has over-identified with a role that is crumbling.

Once Philip has embraced an identity that encompasses many facets of his personality rather than the one familiar role, his gift of leadership can be utilized even more effectively. He will then have more options and flexibility in responding to life.

References for Chapter 10

[1]. Hickey, 1970, p. 25.
[2]. Huber, 1984, p. 184.
[3]. Huber, 1984, p. 191.
[4]. Bailey, 1951.
[5]. Bailey, 1951.
[6]. Saradarian, 1980.
[7]. Rudhyar, 1970, p. 94.
[8]. Hickey, 1970, p. 24.
[9]. Huber, 1984, p. 184.
[10]. Hickey, 1970, p. 25.
[11]. Huber, 1984, p. 184.
[12]. Hickey, 1970, p. 34.

AQUARIUS

Ann Nunley

January 21 - February 20

CHAPTER 11

AQUARIUS

Together we become the stewards of the sacred within the individual and throughout the globe. We are not victims of that future but co-creators of its emergence.—Ruth Eichler[1]

Aquarian energy is electrical energy. It is this energy that will help us break our limitations of time, space, matter and develop our higher psychic powers and use our spiritual perception, straight-knowledge and intuition.—Torkom Saradarian[2]

Affiliated House: 11
Ruling Planet: Saturn and Uranus
Element: Air
Quality: Fixed
Polarity: Yang
Dates: January 21 - February 20
Key Words: I KNOW
Symbol: Water bearer
Anatomy: Ankles, circulation of blood

Imagery Experience for Aquarius

Become aware of your breath. ... Imagine a brilliant diamond above your head. ... As you continue to be aware of the breath, begin to take in light that emanates from the diamond through the top of your head. ... Continue this breathing pattern, just being aware of what happens with the light that you continue to take in from the diamond. ... Sense that the knowledge of the universe can come through the diamond into you. ... What do you suddenly become aware of? ... Now imagine that you disseminate this knowledge to others, clearly and objectively, non-attached to the outcome. ... Take as much time as you need for this experience ... and when it is complete, write down your awarenesses.

Essence End of the Continuum

Humanity yearns for a new level of living together on this planet in mutuality while at the same time recognizing the unique potentials of every human being. In spite of divisive conflict and attachment to separation apparent everywhere on the globe, humanity's spirit rises, reaching for a new synthesis. This yearning emanates from a very real collective human spirit, not just a vision. In its most spiritual expression, Aquarius represents this "reaching for a new level of beingness and creativity, a new level of integration with the earth, and a deeper communion with God," as stated by David Spangler.[3]

Aquarians walk to a different drummer, and from the most integrated end of the continuum that drummer calls them to serve humanity through pouring forth "the Water of Life for thirsty" people, as expressed in the esoteric seed thought.[4] They share humanitarian love and knowledge of truth. Love from this perspective does not emote but streams through people from the Source. Therefore, this transpersonal love concerns not just significant other individuals but people everywhere, transcending race, religion or nationality.

> . . .THIS TRANSPERSONAL LOVE CONCERNS NOT JUST SIGNIFICANT OTHER INDIVIDUALS BUT PEOPLE EVERYWHERE, TRANSCENDING RACE, RELIGION OR NATIONALITY.

Tom Yeomans speaks of three metaphors which depict the process of working with the spiritual dimension of groups,[5] each of which is relevant to the Aquarian experience. He blends ideas from David Bohm, the great physicist, about implicate order and coherence, into these metaphors. Yeomans describes Stage I of group development as the "corona" stage in which a circle of stars exists. That is, individuals assemble together but remain, at this stage, very separate entities even though in a non-hierarchical circle. Each star represents a person with unique talents, gifts, functions, and needs.

He calls Stage II the "shooting star" phase in which individual stars start flaring, creating a very bright circle of stars. The Self of the group (just like the Self of an individual) focuses on one or another individual who carries and expresses what is needed for the group. During this stage, intensity builds as needs diversify. As long as the group cooperates with the Self of the group—holding the polarities and the intensity, deeply listening to and honoring each contribution—the group holds together. This image provides a new model for humanity in working together. The more the group can hold the differences, honoring each individual's truth, the more that integrity emerges which leads to Stage III, the "sunburst" phase.

The metaphor for Stage III includes a very bright, laser-like light that zooms through the middle of the circle momentarily creating oneness. In this stage, the group coheres into a whole, and a common mind or consciousness emerges as a context for whatever differences exist. In these moments, deep meaning and learning arise. Bohm called these times of coherence a microculture in which both freedom and connection exist.[6] Then group members must ground what has emerged into daily life. Although these moments come and go, they represent the quintessence of the Aquarian experience, and the process of working towards coherence epitomizes Aquarius' greatest promise. The possibility for this kind of coherence in group effort only now emerges into possibility. Even in 1973, Assagioli said that the time had not yet come for group psychosynthesis since not very much was known about the process.[7] At the threshold of the new age, we are learning together how to birth this new kind of synthesis.

Middle of the Continuum

If Aquarians reach their highest potential, they must incorporate into their being the lessons, learned in Capricorn, of living with laws in which the rights of each person are honored. Having internalized authority, Aquarians then break free, awakening to new possibilities.

Their qualities include:

- Intuitive and futuristic;
- Egalitarian and androgynous;
- Anti-authoritarian and liberated;
- Revolutionary and new;
- Unique and individualistic;
- Thinking and scientific;
- Communicative,
- Non-attached and objective;
- Socially-conscious and cooperative;
- Altruistic and humanitarian.

Intuitive and futuristic

Aquarian students sometimes receive envious comments from colleagues such as, "Why don't you ever have to study?" Unless electrical circuits somehow are damaged in the brain, Aquarians march to their own drummers as inspired geniuses. Perhaps their brilliance can be attributed to the ability to take in universal knowledge intuitively. Aquarians' knowing often comes like flashes of lightening, and no one knows where these ideas originate. This intuitive ability differs from that of water types who seem to absorb feelings and information from the etheric plane. Aquarians comprehend in a flash as they objectively see the designs and true nature of others. Rather than pouring water from his urn, as the "Water Bearer" seems to do, the Aquarian symbol more appropriately reflects the pouring forth of electricity, representative of consciousness itself. Rudhyar further explains that the Aquarian urge to pour from the urn "is a symbol of the mystic seed-bag, releasing the substance of a new humanity."[8]

This new humanity formulates the basis of the New Age, the Age of Aquarius. Roughly every 2,000 years, our solar system enters another Age, the energies of which color life for all things on the planet during that time. Although astrologers do not agree upon the exact year for the transition from the Age of Pisces, which began roughly at the birth of Christ, most generally concede that the human race is now living in the parentheses between ages. Therefore, every quality discussed here about Aquarius has begun to be felt strongly upon the planet and will mark developments over the next 2,000 years.

THIS NEW HUMANITY FORMULATES THE BASIS OF THE NEW AGE, THE AGE OF AQUARIUS.

Aquarians live in the future—not the past—and can be called "futurists," for they have the capacity to grasp trends and to, therefore, predict future possibilities. Certainly people hired to work in think tanks like the Brookings Institute and others must have Aquarius dominant in their beings. They find original solutions to old problems, and they "break new trails where inventive ideas and new procedures are concerned," says Hickey.[9] They shatter old paradigms, breaking open the space for new world views and archetypes. Not all Aquarians have jobs on the leading edge, but almost all possess views considerably ahead of their time. Even Aquarian farmers, whose only information about the world comes from local, small-town newspapers and television, can uncannily predict political situations that others fail to see. Months—and sometimes years—later, their prognostications become the mainstream view. Because they live on the leading edge, Aquarians set trends. However, by the time their view or interest becomes a fad or has been accepted by most others, they have long ago gone on to other ideas and practices. Fired by intuition, they live in the future, at least one step ahead of the rest of the world.

Egalitarian and androgynous

The word "equality" must be emblazoned on the soul of Aquarians. Oken supports this view: "Probably the greatest gift of the Water Bearer is his vision of equality and essential unity."[10] Their credo asserts that everyone has the right to an equal opportunity regardless of race, creed, color or nationality. This view definitely supports a non-hierarchical view of the world. Even though Aquarians appreciate ritual and ceremony, they insist that everyone possesses some of the truth. Therefore, they assert that priests and priestesses no longer have the sole right to know the mystical secrets of the universe, nor can they be the only ones to render priestly functions. Anyone—male or female—who opens themselves to truth can perform ceremonies, and everyone who dares to know can explore the ancient mysteries. Thus, mystery schools and seminaries are now open to the public—to those who deeply desire to know, not just those assigned by the hierarchy and not just men. Books abound which contain secrets that, if revealed at earlier times, could have sent initiates to their death.

In personal relationships, Aquarians also value equality and prefer that any significant relationship—whether husband/wife, employer/employee, even parent/child beyond the age of six or so—be based upon friendship. Aquarians rebuff any partner who passively accepts everything they say, for they abhor dominant/submissive relationships. Therefore, the eleventh house affiliated with Aquarius represents friends and associations. Not only do Aquarians insist upon equality between men and women, they also present themselves androgynously to the world. They value both masculine and feminine traits and move towards an integration of both gender qualities within their own being. They prefer their partners and friends to do the same, again further supporting equal friendship whether with a person of the same or opposite sex. Aquarians pave the way for an egalitarian society.

Anti-Authoritarian and Liberated

Standing firmly for equalitarianism, Aquarians also push against external authority. If they experience life closer to the subpersonality end of the continuum, they may be against authority just for the sake of being against any kind of control over them. These types sometimes create chaos because of their inability to perceive needs and rights of others. More evolved Aquarians have already incorporated responsibility into their lives, being more guided by inner wisdom which takes the rights of others into consideration.

In any case, Aquarians dislike any type of dogma and almost never consider themselves followers, preferring to think out their own beliefs, even those who study with a certain group. They generally criticize those in authority and act as watchdogs so that forceful leaders do not usurp power. Under no circumstances do they condone coercion. Although they like democracy because the people receive more power than in authoritarian governments, they prefer the consensus model. Under this plan, everyone or their representative delegates must agree to decisions rather than being ruled by the majority. This model has proved workable in many Native American and other councils. Although not yet feasible on a large scale, Aquarians hope that someday people will be evolved and liberated enough to effectively practice such a plan. Zip Dobyns concurs that "no single human being has sufficient wisdom to make laws for his fellow-men but that all

. . .Aquarians dislike any type of dogma and almost never consider themselves followers. . .

should share in their own needed regulation for the benefit of all."[11]

Their need for autonomy carries over into personal relationships. Some marry much later than the cultural norm, fearing being trapped. On the contrary, some Aquarians marry very young, even in middle teen years, to escape parental restrictions. Often early marriages do not last long, though, because these young Aquarians fail to realize that the economic responsibilities that come with marriage, especially if a child appears, hamper their freedom of movement even more than parents. More than any other sign, Aquarians want not only to be their own boss in work and family situations but their own authority as well.

. . .AQUARIANS WANT NOT ONLY TO BE THEIR OWN BOSS IN WORK AND FAMILY SITUATIONS BUT THEIR OWN AUTHORITY AS WELL.

REVOLUTIONARY AND NEW

They find plenty to revolt against: the constricted, controlled and outworn. Rising up against the pull of mass consciousness, they urgently attempt to shatter old forms. The Aquarian has long fought against abuses of all kinds, even to the extent that "his vision becomes darkened and that he only sees the abuses by which be becomes overwhelmed,"[12] as Huber says. Sometimes this fight has meant actually overthrowing intolerable governments, sometimes just leaving the familiar. In any case, Aquarians revolt against habitual attitudes and beliefs and rigid mental forms both within the society and within themselves. In order to truly most effectively combat what no longer serves a purpose, they must first confront their own Saturn-inspired, rigid thought forms and habit patterns. (Saturn has traditionally co-ruled Aquarius with Uranus.) Some who are less thoughtful and self-aware simply rebel for the sake of rebelling. Their changes appear erratic, unpredictable and chaotic. On a personal level, these types perpetuate adolescence long beyond its appropriateness. On larger fronts, they seethe with volcanic unrest and incite anarchy—just fighting against without ever considering what they are moving towards.

Others much more purposefully break free in order to awaken and renew, as if leaving a cabin after a long winter. They may also unexpectedly and suddenly experience changes, and they often cannot predict what the new form will be when the urgency to newness calls. However, they trust their instincts that a new dawn breaks for a reason. Out of the yearning for the unfamiliar arise fresh opportunities, transformation, and spiritual rebirth. On a planetary level, Rudhyar says that "Aquarius represents civilization expanding or reforming itself through its inventors, seers and revolutionists."[13] Those closest to the spiritual end of the continuum break free in order to both change purposefully and to consciously cooperate with the innermost cycles and rhythms of life.

Unique and individualistic

"To thine own self be true" represents the Aquarian archetype. Thoreau spoke to the Aquarian call of individuality when he said that if one's companions were out of step, they were probably hearing a different drummer. The urge to uniqueness takes many forms. Scientists and seers may espouse highly unique and unorthodox views that differ from their peers. They possess an originality and genius that allows them to see beyond the solidified world view of the moment. They experiment, finding new ways to do things. Others, whose conservative parents may despair, eschew traditional careers and degrees. Instead, they choose to learn from a variety of life experiences, unfettered by conventionality. Some like to be different for the sake of being different and grow beards when unpopular and shave them off when in vogue. They avoid, if at all possible, doing anything faddish, for being called conformist or average offends and insults most Aquarians. Some choose the odd and bizarre, arrogantly thumbing their nose at society.

Regardless of the form their uniqueness takes, many experience life as loners—as strangers on earth, never quite finding their place. Most cultures throughout history have birthed unique individuals, although some societies have forced their Bohemians to pay an extremely high price—occasionally death—for expressing the unorthodox.

While both Sagittarians and Aquarians value the whole, each focuses on a different aspect: Sagittarians honor the similarities amidst diversity and Aquarians celebrate individual differences. Aquarians view life on this planet as a wonderfully rich tapestry composed of brilliantly varied colors, each color representing a different and unique culture or individual.

Thinking and scientific

As an air sign, Aquarians approach life through the intellect and mind. The gift of objectivity from the element of air provides the ability to differentiate the real from illusion and glamour. With rational and logical minds, they see clearly. However, Jocelyn clarifies that thinking does not just mean observing and tabulating but also "living." "Living thinking" implies a formulated, concentrated, one-pointed, fixed, intense force in ideation.[14]

As a fixed air sign, Aquarians hate indecisiveness about ideas and prefer making their thoughts concrete. Some become quite attached to their inflexible opinions, while others retain the ability to laugh at themselves, not just identifying with their mental formulations. Those who can be more objective realize, as Assagioli's "disidentification exercise"[15] states, that "I have a mind, but I am not my mind." They know that the Self remains the locus for their real identity.

Ruled by both Saturn and Uranus, Aquarians bring the daringly original into practical and concrete terms. Jupiter, the esoteric ruler of Aquarius, helps to synthesize these polarities. Therefore, Aquarian scientists pioneer new territory. In earlier times, Aquarians such as Swedenborg, Darwin, Copernicus and Galileo—often even at great risk to themselves—set the stage for the emergence of new paradigms of their eras. They probe into the laws of nature with eyes that see beyond what is currently accepted or known. Inventors such as Thomas Edison have also paved the way for changing the social order.

In more recent times, brilliant Aquarian biologists explored the causes of global warming long before other scientists became interested in the phenomena. Courageous Aquarian physicists currently are breaking the ground for new paradigms of reality, sometimes shocking and annoying their more conservative colleagues. They investigate the possibilities of a holographic universe, putting forth a new science for a new age. The new science will emerge as a synthesis of art, religion and science. It has been said that the mystics of yesterday will become the scientists of tomorrow. Astrology—both art and science—is emerging into popularity once again as a symbolic language with the dawning of the new age. Bailey says that "The new astrology will deal with significance and meanings, and not so much with . . . the outer happenings such as events and mundane activities."[16] As thinkers and scientists, they fit the key words for Aquarius, "I know."

Communicative, non-attached, objective

As a thinking, air sign, Aquarians disseminate knowledge whether by mouth, computer, television, a host of other electronic devices, or even by telepathy. Some innovatively teach and train others as a result of their gift of communication. The beginning of the Age of Aquarius corresponds with the explosion onto the planet of the Information Age and the reign of high technology.

> . . .THE AGE OF AQUARIUS CORRESPONDS WITH THE EXPLOSION ONTO THE PLANET OF THE INFORMATION AGE AND THE REIGN OF HIGH TECHNOLOGY.

Many Aquarians gregariously and confidently communicate with others, although they generally remain impersonally friendly. Aquarians can talk loquaciously, therefore, seeming quite open, but they seldom discuss feelings. The realm of emotions remains alien to most Aquarians—at least until they pass into the second half of life. The mid-life crisis for Aquarians sometimes means being shocked by the disruptive emergence of feelings which have been submerged in the unconscious.

Those Aquarians closer to the most integrated end of the continuum embody the highest form of the Buddhist principle of non-attachment. That is, they can care deeply for suffering individuals whether they be the starving children of Ethiopia or their neighbor, <u>and</u> they can be non-attached to the outcome. They remain centered, do what they can do, and let go of the results. Those closer to the subpersonality end exhibit detachment in which they cut off from any real sensitivity to the human plight of others even though they may rant and rave about the conditions of the world. Such persons often receive the label of cold and aloof.

Although impersonality can be a great gift when in the form of non-attachment, many lovers and friends of Aquarians resent being considered in the same vein as unknown children on the other side of the globe. However, the truly spiritual Aquarian views love not as sentiment, emotion or desire. Rather, as Huber says, "Love is the working of a transcendental power and a transcendental process in us. Love does not begin in us, neither does it end in those we love. It has a cosmic source; it streams through us and at length continues on its way."[17]

Socially-conscious and cooperative

That transpersonal love carries over into a social conscience and a realization that people must voluntarily cooperate for the common good. In order for the planet to survive, people must realize that everyone shares the same space. A nuclear explosion in one part of the world carries fallout to every other area. The devastation of war in one country impacts all. Not just spiritually, but ecologically, economically, socially, and politically, everyone on the planet is linked into an interdependent web. Aquarians trumpet the call, "Cooperate or die; voluntary community or chaos."

> "Cooperate or die; voluntary community or chaos."

On a personal level, Aquarians are group-oriented but not group-identified, for they resist anything that implies a loss of individuality. Even an Aquarian organizer of a Tibetan educational center refuses to be categorized as "Buddhist." As long as Aquarians remain label-free, they consent to being part of a whole, part of a universal family, linked not by blood but by humanity itself.

The urge to community emerges from the awareness that individuals, while unique, cannot survive alone. They need to be united in a common spirit, loyal to a common purpose—whether survival of the planet or a commitment to sustainable culture or just a celebration of community. As the New Age dawns, the knowledge of how to create a coherence that honors both individuals and the group remains in the infancy stage. Like David Bohm, who committed his later years to sharing ideas about this work, and Tom Yeomans who has initiated training groups for people who are learning to work with the Self of groups, others around the globe have dedicated themselves to exploring a new kind of community. Only as people learn how to hold the polarities of both dark and light and to honor differences can groups be safe places for the individual. Otherwise, group norms tyrannize. The shadow side becomes submerged into the group unconscious which then erupts unexpectedly, harming both individuals and the group. Training for community with integrity can be one of the most important steps into the new age.

Altruistic and humanitarian

Each year since 1987, the Institute of Noetic Sciences has issued the Temple Awards for Creative Altruism. Tom Hurley, Director of the Altruistic Spirit Program, states the purpose for these awards:

> "Those gifted with spiritual genius have always taught that human life is an expression of the divine. They have also taught—and the lives of ordinary people as well as saints bear this out—that one of the most profound expressions of the divine light at the core of our beings is creative altruism, or unselfish service motivated by love."[18]

Aquarians strive to make ideals real by carrying them out in the world, therefore, pouring forth the "Water of Life." Being fixed, Aquarians abide by their ideals with rock-like firmness, making lasting contributions to humanity. Unselfish service becomes a way of life once Aquarians realize that all human beings are related. These humanitarian servers do not have to be Mother Teresa's, but can be ordinary citizens who live out the bigger picture. For example, Falaka Fattah and David Fattah, who received one of the four 1990/91 Temple Awards, have been family to more than 2,000 young men who are or were gang members in Philadelphia.[19] They know, like John Donne, who titled one of his poems, "No man is an island." In that poem, he asks, "For whom doth the bell toll? It tolls for thee."[20]

Perhaps more than any other sign, Aquarians realize the need for brotherhood and sisterhood on a planetary level that means tolerating individual differences of opinions and values for the sake of the greater good. Believing in humane treatment for everyone, they embody the Golden Rule which has existed in nearly every major world religion. Abraham Lincoln, U. S. President during the Civil War revealed his Aquarian perspective when he eloquently expressed the need for transcending differences by announcing, "With malice towards none and charity for all."

Subpersonality End of the Continuum

Rebel without a Cause

Rebel learned to shout "No!" as a standard response to life while still a two-year old and never lost the art. As a teenager, he rebelled against rules and regulations as most do, but at forty-two, he still rebels. He led a walkout while still in high school, but no one remembers whether there was a purpose for it other than to have a day's vacation from classes. He swaggers as he walks, defying anyone to get close to him. Once he participated in a riot and cursed the authorities, along with others, but he remained detached from what caused the disturbance.

By solidifying his identity around the role of rebel, he protects himself from examining his own insecurities. He maintains distance from his own inner polarities by seeing the world as "me against them" and never examines the creative tension that exists within himself. The value of the gift of fighting against injustice gets lost because he never struggles with the issues for which he stands. He needs to learn how to take responsibility for creating a better world, and this he can accomplish by coming to better terms with his total identity.

Shocker Sue

Sue's wardrobe resembles the neon lights on the Las Vegas strip: electric blue and green socks; orange T-shirts emblazoned with the words, "After God created me, she threw away the mold!"; pants that would endear most beings from outer space; and psychedelic shoes that will be popular in the next decade. She was the first in her school to color her hair green and the first to sprout a Mohawk haircut. Like her Leo cousin, Gaudy Maudy, she dresses outlandishly. However, Gaudy Maudy loves the feeling of adornment and enjoys having people look at her, but she does not intend to shock as does Sue. Sue does not enjoy setting trends as much as she delights in the look of shock on people's faces when they see her. Sue has stretched the interpretation of uniqueness into a new meaning: defying the standard. Her distortion comes, not from wanting to be different, but from only responding to outer cues on how to be set apart. She remains as controlled by the norm as her peers who follow it, because she uses the norm as a measure of what not to be and how not to act. Only as she tunes into her very own drummer will she learn to express her true individuality. Only then will her gifts inspire others to become authentic.

SUE'S WARDROBE RESEMBLES THE NEON LIGHTS ON THE LAS VEGAS STRIP. . .

Automaton Alvin

A computer programmer in a nuclear physics laboratory, Alvin goes to work, walking as if his head were in a cloud, untouched by human contact. He remains unmoved by news about any of his colleagues—whether they birth babies, marry, move to Africa, or die. Divorced from all of his feelings—feelings which might not even emerge during mid-life crisis!—Alvin protects himself from intimacy. He intensely fears closeness of any kind, yet even this awareness is buried from view. His only friends are co-workers, and they only converse about computer programs and intellectual concepts. Otherwise, Alvin lives alone, reads books for company, and plays computer games in his spare time.

Although frightening, Alvin's first task in his journey to wholeness is to learn why he is so deathly afraid of emotions and to heal those old wounds. Then, gradually, he will need to identify feelings and eventually express them. Although a genius, Alvin's intelligence fails to help him in the healing process, for he must move into the unconscious where nothing is rational or linear.

Aloof Alice

Alice, Alvin's sister, also fears intimacy although she has more friends than her brother, sometimes even acquiring lovers or a spouse. She, too, has submerged her feeling nature and relies upon her detached, intellect to provide clues about what transpires around her. She can be counted on in a crisis to be the one who remains calm and collected. As a teacher, she has opinions but refuses to become embroiled in the politics of whether or not her profession should unionize. She is disgusted by her colleagues who exhibit great emotion about the issue. Detachment becomes a problem primarily in relationships with significant others in which Alice always maintains distance.

Objectivity can be a great gift when appropriately used, and Alice certainly does not have to forfeit this contribution when allowing other dimensions of her personality to emerge. She does need to tap into higher consciousness so that caring surfaces. Learning about transpersonal love can assist Alice in integrating around her true Self.

Eccentric Edgar

Newspaper reporters occasionally write about Edgar, whose habits seem odd. Once he allowed his fingernails to grow two inches long, much to the horror of everyone who saw him. One year he began to create a village for elves behind his house, and the project continued until nearly every square inch of his backyard was filled with miniature houses, bridges, highways and tiny cement elves. Another year he decided to build the largest airplane ever flown and made it entirely out of wood. The plane never flew. Edgar does not necessarily intend to shock anyone; he just becomes lost in bizarre projects which consume his mind for their duration. If a symbolic picture could be drawn of his mind, it would look like a hamster running through one of the twisting,

. . .HE BEGAN TO CREATE A VILLAGE FOR ELVES BEHIND HIS HOUSE. . . UNTIL NEARLY EVERY SQUARE INCH OF HIS BACKYARD WAS FILLED WITH MINIATURE HOUSES, BRIDGES. . .

turning tubes on top of its cage. He forgets about all other dimensions of his existence: body, emotions, spirit. He forgets about life in the real world.

In order to return to an integrated existence, Edgar first needs to discover enticing enough reasons to live a multi-dimensional life rather than just in the mind. If so, then some type of mindfulness training might enhance his ability to be present in the here and now. Eventually, he could use his gift of innovation and creative thinking in more worthwhile projects.

Free-Spirited Frieda

Frieda values her freedom above all else in the universe. Once upon a time she married, thinking that she might be able to live in the suburbs for awhile. She had not tried that experience yet. She earned money as a children's story teller at the local library, but the marriage ended when she had the opportunity to crew on a sailboat to the South Seas. Like a will-o-the-wisp, she takes off any time she thinks a commitment to anyone, any place, or any thing might stifle her freedom. She fears her individuality might be compromised, so she keeps on the move, never allowing herself be become too involved for long.

LIKE A WILL-O-THE-WISP, SHE TAKES OFF ANY TIME SHE THINKS A COMMITMENT TO ANYONE, ANY PLACE, OR ANY THING MIGHT STIFLE HER FREEDOM.

Her distortion arises from her hidden fear, a fear of losing herself. Yet, she does not realize that by constantly running she loses her Self-direction. When she learns new ways to feel intact as a whole being no matter how deeply she is involved with others, then she can be truly free. Then, she can freely choose whether or not she becomes involved with certain people or experiences rather than always leaving to protect that illusory sense of self.

Anarchist Amanda

Amanda has been involved in several violent campaigns against the established order. Once she built bombs in a basement with other revolutionaries, and they intended to destroy the headquarters of a major computer company. They said that the corporation was ruining the environment and deserved to be bombed. Another time, she and a group of her friends assembled an arsenal of weapons and intended to blockade the White House. Amanda graduated Phi Beta Kappa in philosophy from the university, and she has written a multitude of papers expressing her anarchist views. Unfortunately, Amanda never used her brilliance to provide a vision for what could replace the old.

Amanda would have to find other ways to vent her hostilities and to meet her need to be special in order for her to experience a greater wholeness. With a humanitarian perspective that includes more than her own one-pointed hate, she could then more constructively use her gift of justice.

Arrogant Astor

Astor espouses opinions on every political and intellectual situation that arises, and he never fails to present those ideas, as if platters of gold, to anyone who will listen. He displays his conviction of rightness with such fervor that others sometimes call him pompous. Once he was elected to the Senate because of his oratory skills. That election occurred before people became disgusted with his inflexibility and inability to compromise on important issues. He would rather lose a political battle all together than concede one inch on his views.

At some point, Astor began to believe that he was his ideas and, therefore, he had to staunchly defend them. The ideas became his front to the world covering any insecurities he might have. If Astor realizes the rich resources within himself to add to his repertoire of getting along in the world, he will be able to begin to loosen up and to relate to people in a more genuine way rather than through a string of words. As he develops the ability to listen to others, he will become more effective as a thinker, speaker and politician.

References for Chapter 11

[1]. Eichler, 1986.
[2]. Saradarian, 1980, p. 260.
[3]. Spangler, 1980, pp. 84.
[4]. Bailey, 1951.
[5]. Yeomans, 1989.
[6]. Bohm, 1990.
[7]. Anderson, 1989, p. 1.
[8]. Rudhyar, 1970, p. 106.
[9]. Hickey, 1970, p. 27.
[10]. Oken, 1990, p. 235.
[11]. Dobyns, 1972, p. 25.
[12]. Huber, 1984, p. 206.
[13]. Rudhyar, 1970, p. 101.
[14]. Jocelyn, 1966.
[15]. Assagioli, 1965.
[16]. Bailey, 1951, p. 135.
[17]. Huber, 1984, p. 210.
[18]. Miller & Luck, Winter 1990/91, p. 35.
[19]. Miller & Luck, Winter 1990/91, p. 36.
[20]. Donne, 1958.

PISCES

Ann Nunley

February 21 - March 20

CHAPTER 12

PISCES

Their inner work is not always visible to the rest of us, but is quite visible to the Divine and those who benefit from their unselfish love.—Kathleen Burt[1]

Every transpersonal Way begins from a state of incompleteness and has as its goal the achievement of unity. In this endeavor, the Way of Devotion is based on the feeling which, more than any other, personifies desire for unity—love.—Piero Ferrucci[2]

Affiliated House:	12
Ruling Planets:	Neptune and Jupiter
Element:	Water
Quality:	Mutable
Polarity:	Yin
Dates:	February 21 - March 20
Key Words:	I BELIEVE
Symbol:	Two fish; dolphin
Anatomy:	Feet

Imagery Experience for Pisces

Imagine sitting beside the ocean. The sun shines brightly, and the gentle breeze carries the smell of the sea. Begin to synchronize your breath with the sound of the ocean waves gently crashing on the shore below. ... With each breath, you become more and more in tune with the rhythm of the waves ... until you become one with the water. ... Allow yourself just to sense being the sea ... beyond time ... and duality ... just being the sea. ... Allow this experience for several minutes. ... Returning to the present time and space, again feel your own body touching the chair or floor. Experience yourself fully present back in the room. As you are ready, dance or move or draw to express your imagery experience.

Essence End of the Continuum

As the twelfth sign of the zodiac, Pisceans who live at the most integrated and whole end of the continuum experience "going home" to pure Being, to spirit, to the Source. In essence, they represent the potential for all human beings to eventually merge back into the Great One. From this perspective, duality is a mere illusion. The two fish, symbolic of Pisces, one going one direction and the other another direction, yet tied together, represent the journey from duality to unity. At first, the little fish which symbolizes the physical, emotional, and mental realms of the personality self, precedes the big fish or Self. That is, the personality self remains unaware of the Self, although the Self stays present with the little fish. Then, as consciousness increases, the little fish begins to be aware of the duality and, at times, tries to swim away from the big fish. Later, as consciousness reigns supreme, the big fish swallows the little one, so that the personality becomes "soul-infused." Einstein also talked about attaining liberation from the (little) self.[3]

In the journey to wholeness, the personality surrenders—sometimes gracefully and sometimes not—to the higher, divine Will: "Not my will, but Thine." Everyday concerns that once seemed so important such as developing individuality, creating family, and attaining success in the world fade as the soul-infused personality becomes receptive to the higher spiritual energies. However, the spiritual energies may still be expressed in everyday life. The focus changes from outer diretion to inner diretion. Illusions are shattered, and darkness turns to light. Rudhyar speaks about this journey as "Transcendence, overcoming, piercing through illusions and false security, severance of social ties, embarking for the great adventure with utter faith and in denuded simplicity of being."[4]

In the process of returning home, Pisceans manifest selfless, inclusive love. Whereas Leos learn to open their hearts, Pisceans become open hearts. In transcending the little self, they simply become pure compassion, merged with the divine Spark. The ability to just BE epitomizes Pisces at its best.

Middle of the Continuum

Moving from self-assertiveness and individuality in Aries to selflessness and merger into the One in Pisces, each sign of the zodiac represents a natural evolutionary progression in terms of life lessons. However, no one person is more evolved than another simply because his or her sign appears later in the zodiac. The choices individuals make, no matter what the construction of their natal chart, ultimately determine their evolution on their own continuum of possibilities.

Pisces represents the following qualities:

- Yearning-for-the-divine versus escapism;
- Compassionate and empathetic;
- Imaginative and creative;
- Motivated by the unconscious;

- Psychic and impressionable;
- Boundless and non-materialistic;
- Service-oriented and prone to suffering;
- Solitary, introspective and emotional;
- Devotional and serene.

Yearning-for-the-divine versus escapism

Whether or not Pisceans consciously yearn for the divine, they all long for the infinite "home." They undergo divine discontent until they realize a higher purpose. Some peacefully turn their awareness more and more to the transcendent, attuning to the rhythm of spirit. These souls verbally express their urge for divinity in many different ways. For example, they say, "searching for peace;" "being at one with God;" "uniting with the infinite;" "enjoying the serenity of nature;" "not feeling at home anywhere;" or "experiencing oneness with everything." Others only dimly sense that something is missing. This latter group often unwittingly ascribes the sometimes vague and sometimes stormy discontent to conditions or persons that they perceive of as causing pain and suffering rather than their own separation from Self.

THESE SOULS VERBALLY EXPRESS THEIR URGE FOR DIVINITY IN MANY DIFFERENT WAYS.

Some Pisceans respond to the call consciously and choose methods to bring them closer to Self and to the Source. They pray, meditate, chant, walk in the woods, go on retreats, write, dance, create music, join monasteries and ashrams, or selflessly serve. Even so, this path contains obstacles such as chattering minds and restlessness which even long-term meditators experience. Other Pisceans choose to escape the vague feelings of discomfort, not realizing the true origin of their discontent. Many, many forms of escapism exist ranging from harmless pleasures to deadly, self-destructive acts. Watching too much television, reading too many novels, or day-dreaming away the afternoon may harm no one if done in moderation. On the other hand, severe addiction to alcohol, drugs or other substances often destroys families and even kills the addicted. The diversionary path also takes other forms such as psychosomatic illness or, in some cases, psychosis, though the underpinnings of these paths usually remain unconscious. Nevertheless, illness carries its own metaphors and meaning which provide seeds for healing and becoming whole.

The return to wholeness and to Self requires surrendering to something bigger than personality. The little self must surrender control to the Higher Self in order to truly live. Huber says that "In order to attain the vibrational field of the ONE LIFE, we need the metamorphic force of the esoteric Ruler Pluto. He destroys the tie which chains us to matter."[5]

Yet the very act of surrendering and leaping into the void, as frightening as it sometimes seems, creates deeper meaning and peace. Eventually, Pisceans can surrender even the fear of death when they realize that death merely represents a transition from one state of consciousness to another. They continue their journey "home" to the One.

Compassionate and empathetic

Pisceans are very sensitive, allowing them to understand the most subtle nuances of feelings and inner emotions. They are soft and gentle-hearted on the inside no matter how they express on the outside. Indeed, Pisceans' feeling nature contributes to their ability to "walk in someone else's moccasins," as the saying goes, empathetically soaking up others' experiences. Sensing the connectedness of all life, they cannot harm even a flea.

> . . .PISCEANS' FEELING NATURE CONTRIBUTES TO THEIR ABILITY TO "WALK IN SOMEONE ELSE'S MOCCASINS". . .

Pisceans do not choose to be tender-hearted; they simply are. However, they can choose how to express this quality, depending upon their place on the continuum. Some try to block out such enormous receptivity and present a protective, gruff front, while others respond immediately to those in need. Those closest to the most integrated end of the continuum love selflessly, yet do not martyr themselves in the process. They intuitively know, as Rudhyar stated, that "Compassion is the absolute Law of a universe in which there is order and harmony."[6] These types discern when it is more loving to reach out a helping hand and when to stand back.

Those closer to the subpersonality end of the continuum seem to believe they must respond, often sacrificing themselves for the sake of others and becoming martyrs. When they do attempt to take care of themselves, they feel guilty because others still suffer. Then they may even lash out in anger at those in need, so great is their own feeling of responsibility and guilt. Such sensitivity provides both a blessing and a curse to Pisceans, depending upon how they handle the gift.

Imaginative and creative

The more that Pisceans tap into spirit and integrate around their Self, the more they freely and spontaneously express creativity. Superconscious realms—or the "higher unconscious" as Assagioli called it—replete with visions, wisdom and imagination, offer rich reservoirs of inspiration whether in art, music, dance, photography, poetry, or film making, romance, or just being. Many people who choose these careers or ways of being abound in Piscean energy. Ferrucci comments on the transformation that comes from theater, another Piscean arena, by saying, "Acting stands on the indefinable ground between two major aspects of the Self: the beautiful and the sacred" and that acting creates a field in "which time, space, events, and emotions are different from those in our ordinary world."[7]

The dolphin, symbol of Pisces at the most integrated end of the continuum, represents agility, grace and intelligence, all qualities valuable in creative expression. Dobyns talks of the Piscean "hunger for infinite love and beauty."[8] Those most successful at tapping into this realm maintain a childlike wonder which "requires a relaxed attitude, receptivity, an intuitive sense, a delight in juxtaposing and savoring particulars, sensuousness, openness, and participation,"[9] according to Rico.

THE DOLPHIN REPRESENTS AGILITY, GRACE AND INTELLIGENCE, ALL QUALITIES VALUABLE IN CREATIVE EXPRESSION.

Those closer to the subpersonality end of the continuum may not benefit from the riches of the superconscious but nevertheless still tap into visions and imagination. Some lead an active fantasy life, and some harbor illusions and hallucinations. Whether generating ballets, paintings, photographic essays or devious con-artist plans, their imagination soars. No matter where they play out their energies on the continuum, Pisceans need an outlet for creativity.

Motivated by the unconscious

By definition, the unconscious simply means that which is not immediately available to awareness. Ferrucci referred to the unconscious as "energies and feelings that mysteriously motivate our lives."[10] Yet, for Pisces, the veil between consciousness and unconsciousness seems to be thinner and the pull from that underwater sea stronger. Whether accessing creativity from the "higher conscious," or monsters from the shadowy realm of the "lower unconscious," or feelings from mass consciousness, Pisceans seem to perceive what many do not. They operate subliminally as if always seeing beyond the eternal mist that separates everyday reality from their more ethereal world.

Assagioli differentiated between the "higher," "middle," "lower," and "collective" unconscious.[11] He defined the collective unconscious much like Jung and believed that people absorbed impressions from others and the environment much like osmosis occurs at the cellular membrane level. He saw the higher unconscious as the region from which "we receive our higher intuitions and inspirations . . . the source of the higher feelings such as altruistic love . . . higher psychic functions and spiritual energies."[12] Ordinary thoughts and perceptions close to the surface compose the middle unconscious, and the lower unconscious contains experiences and underlying beliefs from early conditioning as well as autonomic systems that govern body processes.

How much should the unconscious be probed? Assagioli did not approve of indiscriminately roaming through this realm for years out of idle curiosity. He said, "When the unconscious disturbs, it has to be dealt with; if it keeps quiet, we do not make a systematic offensive against it."[13] Primarily, he supported bringing unconscious material to consciousness to prevent being at its mercy. Assagioli and many transpersonal therapists since have developed innumerable methods for accessing the unconscious: dream work, myths, free drawings, journal writing, guided imagery, spontaneous movement, body work, special breathing practices, meditation, and many more. Most Pisces people prefer these modes of learning to more linear, logical processes such as talking or listening to lectures.

Marks warns that "We are prisoners of the energies in ourselves which we fail to acknowledge and integrate."[14] When too strongly influenced by unconscious processes, Pisceans respond impulsively or compulsively without thinking through actions. Unaware of their needs and wants, they often send mixed messages to others, not even realizing the ambivalence. They may attract people and circumstances which represent the Pisceans' projected, unconscious patterns. The twelfth house traditionally has been known as the house of "hidden enemies," and usually the enemy is within—the unconscious shadow. As long as fears, inferiority feelings, shame and guilt remain repressed, the shadow dominates, creating havoc in the life. As fears and insecurities are confronted, healing begins. Marks concurs: "Aware of our fear, we are able to experience it, define it, assess it realistically, and make choices which honor it or transcend it."[15] Then the gifts from the unconscious can shine forth.

AS LONG AS FEARS, INFERIORITY FEELINGS, SHAME AND GUILT REMAIN REPRESSED, THE SHADOW DOMINATES, CREATING HAVOC IN THE LIFE.

PSYCHIC AND IMPRESSIONABLE

With such receptivity to realms beyond the five senses, Pisceans sometimes excel as clairvoyants and psychics, although this skill may lie dormant. Others fear this ability and deny the veracity of any impressions they receive. The more highly integrated the person, the more that this gift can be transmuted into finely tuned receptivity to higher states of consciousness. This kind of intuition requires self-trust.[16] The closer to the subpersonality end of the continuum, the more that the person tunes into lower frequency astral and emotional fields. Although psychic impressions from these realms may prove accurate, they also may not. At this level, the psychic merely picks up thoughts, desires, and emotions from others which naturally fluctuate and change.

Associated with the element of water, Pisceans absorb much from the environment—especially all kinds of feelings and emotions. Oken says that "Pisces is one of the most magnetic signs. It seeks to attract everything within its auric force field, as there is a need to gather and unify all currents and streams."[17] Pisceans have to learn to discern which impressions come from themselves and which emanate from others. They can even absorb other people's headaches and ailments if not careful. They so closely attune themselves to their environment, that they sometimes resemble chameleons as they change from one group or place to another. Loud and raucous in a sportsmen's bar, quiet and compassionate in a support group, giggly and silly in a gathering of early adolescents, they shift like the sand on a windy desert. The gift of receptivity and impressionability also makes them great actors who can play any role whether on stage or in the theater of life. Elizabeth Taylor exemplifies a Piscean actor.

Boundless and non-materialistic

Pisceans need banks to contain their river waters that otherwise spill out over the surroundings. Without some internal or external structure, they sometimes mutably drift with the current, unable to find a focus for their life. Their very being seems to be in constant flux. They must find their center or Self provide a safe anchor rather than losing themselves in the boundless sea.

More than any other sign, Pisceans transcend time and space much to their joy or dismay, depending upon their place upon the continuum. Those most integrated are the true mystics who find liberation from the material world. They can be in this world, but not of it. The world is not their habitat, and they learn to live in the eternal now or kairos, that long-sought-after goal of so many religions. Kairos has nothing to do with chronological time; rather it is that space in which artists forget dinner, children unself-consciously play for hours, and saints pray, all oblivious to the outer world.

KAIROS IS THAT SPACE IN WHICH ARTISTS FORGET DINNER, CHILDREN UNSELF-CONSCIOUSLY PLAY FOR HOURS, AND SAINTS PRAY, ALL OBLIVIOUS TO THE OUTER WORLD.

For others who lack a cohesive, integrated sense of self, the journey through the cosmic ocean is fraught with problems. Rather than mystically realizing the Great Oneness, they simply possess inappropriate boundaries, seeping into others' spaces and lives. They cannot discern where they end and other people begin. Rather than receiving great insights, they swim helplessly through the murky fog and remain confused. They show up three hours late for meetings and appointments, oblivious to anything linear or material.

Pisceans realize the transitory nature of life in the material world. Huber says, "Everything terrestrial is transient."[18] Money, possessions, formal degrees and credentials, possessions all have little relevance in the transcendent, and Pisceans understand better than many the wisdom of this insecurity. Many "starving artists" possess considerable Pisces energy, for the call to the creative or compassionate beckons stronger than the call to possess worldly goods. For others, the non-materialistic path leads to impracticality and drifting aimlessly through life. Sometimes the line is thin between spiritually transcending reality and simply being out of touch with reality. Pisceans must learn to listen to the inner voice, and they lead more purposeful lives when they learn to discern between the voice of the Self and the voice of illusion, a never-ending task. Dissolving structures and boundaries, Pisceans swim through life.

Service-oriented and prone to suffering

Hickey says that "when they are true to their real nature, Pisceans have a high and holy destiny and are the true saviors and servants of mankind."[19] Willing and inspired to help, they either serve or suffer, no matter where they are on the continuum. Therefore, human service occupations such as social workers, pastors, nurses, other medical practitioners including physicians, massage therapists, and psychiatric workers, and many other types of healers frequently have Piscean energies. They often work in prisons, nursing homes, and other institutions helping the sick, lonely and downtrodden. Although some successfully and happily manage businesses, most Pisceans value service and creativity far more than money or other material possessions. Many Piscean entrepreneurs give freely to those in need and have very soft hearts for employees with problems, almost always extending the second or third chance, sometimes to their own detriment.

> ". . .Pisceans have a high and holy destiny and are the true saviors and servants of mankind."

The dilemma all Pisceans face concerns when to give and when not to give. Some provide more than needed, subtly controlling others through their generosity. They may do too much for others, depriving them of the opportunity to do things on their own. Popular psychology literature abounds with information about this issue of co-dependence. Pisceans are called to serve; they must decide how to best minister in a way that honors the highest good in themselves and others.

Certainly Pisceans are not required to suffer, for those most in tune with Self live joyfully. However, many do experience loneliness and depression. They often feel misunderstood and out of place and perceive themselves as victims. Others anguish because of their enormous sensitivity, soaking up the pains of the world. War in an unheard-of country causes them heart pain, and they cry at Bambi movies, hurting for all of the homeless and parentless of the world. Self-undoing, which often results in suffering, connotes one of the meanings of the twelfth house. They may wallow in self-pity, indulgently overspend to compensate, or sabotage themselves through many varieties of addictions. When living in the victim or martyr role, Pisceans may wonder why God does not rescue them. Yet, through their suffering, they develop greater compassion and ability to serve and eventually move closer to the Self end of the continuum.

Solitary, introspective and emotional

No matter whether Pisceans choose the cloistered life of monk or nun or the professional work of nurse or physician in a busy suburban hospital, they almost all need chunks of privacy in which they shake off the vibrations of their environment and return to themselves. They may need to go on silent, meditative retreats from time to time or spend an hour alone each day, or occasionally just soak in a long, hot bath. Solitude enriches their lives unless they are frightened of what might emerge from the subconscious while quiet, in which case they may avoid aloneness.

> SOLITUDE ENRICHES THEIR LIVES UNLESS THEY ARE FRIGHTENED OF WHAT MIGHT EMERGE FROM THE SUBCONSCIOUS WHILE QUIET. . .

Many spend hours silently mulling over things within their inner world, mostly unaware of anything external. At other times, when they feel really safe with certain persons, they may talk nonstop for hours as if they were a bottle whose cork popped out, spilling forth the long pent-up contents. As superb actors, they may appear quite gregarious, while at heart remaining timid and quiet. Rich resources of strength and wisdom often emerge from this deep, inner communion. They can cleanse and purge old, outworn residue, creating space for new life, or they may just wallow in murky waters.

As a water sign, Pisces represents emotions and feelings. Like their Cancer and Scorpio cousins, Pisceans may experience vast mood swings, and they certainly identify far more with emotions than with mental processes. Like a river, they gradually erode away rocks or opposition rather than confronting anything directly. They may send mixed messages, afraid of being pinned down if too direct. Whenever in the presence of overwhelming, fiery people, they retreat into their own world pretending they are alone and hoping the loud noise goes away. The great waters of life may purify or swamp, depending upon the Piscean's choices.

Devotional and serene

True serenity and freedom for Pisceans can only be attained by surrendering to a power greater than their personality self, whether that be God, the Source, the universe, or their own Self. They must be willing to turn their little will over to a Higher Will, as taught in Twelve-Step traditions, many religions and spiritual paths.

Burt calls Pisces the "search for the castle of peace,"[20] and many Pisceans become devoted to something as part of this process. Many paths exist to the divine, some mystical, some religious, and some nature-oriented. Others experience the Source through creativity, music, art, or service. A variety of religious and spiritual ways exist that appeal to people at all places on the continuum. The main danger from the devotional path is fanaticism, and Ferrucci suggests that devotion can be directed to "an unrecognized aspect of oneself projected onto the cosmos."[21] He continues, "Only devotion to a boundless, infinitely loving, beatific, and luminous being can truly liberate."

BURT CALLS PISCES THE "SEARCH FOR THE CASTLE OF PEACE". . .

Serenity and a sense of wholeness emerge for those have learned to trust in Self and the Source and who have healed or are healing past wounds. Transformation often occurs unnoticed, much like a rose bud very gradually opening. Over time, Pisceans slowly realize that they are funded by inner resources from which to draw upon during times of crises. Through devotion, faith and surrender, Pisceans eventually know peace.

Subpersonality End of the Continuum

Gullible Greta

Greta sometimes appears as an innocent little fawn, trusting everyone. Once she gave $5,000 to someone collecting money to feed the poor only to discover later that the "poor" was just the con artist who asked for money. She believes everything people tell her and rarely discerns between truth and fiction. She trusts that her lover tells the truth when he says that he has to work out of town four nights a week when, in truth, he stays at another woman's house. Easily swayed, Greta has lost track of her own center which could provide wisdom and discernment. Therefore, she trusts what others say rather than listening to her own inner voice.

Her gift of trust is the very quality that has become distorted. By learning to tune into the wisdom of her Self, she can resurrect faith and trust into its proper place. Then she will be able to know when to believe others and when not, for she will be grounded through her own faith in Self.

Drifter Doug

Doug can never quite make up his mind what he wants out of life. Even when he dreams of doing something, he lacks the ability to make it reality. With a strong compassionate and artistic bent, he sometimes thinks about being an art therapist, but he never enrolls in classes. He practiced guitar for awhile and has a natural flair for music, but no one pointed the direction for how his talent could be used in other ways. Listing priorities or creating a plan for how to make something happen seem so foreign to Doug that he does not take action. When someone else creates the banks to provide a course for his river, he channels his energies and talents better. Although he becomes bored with routine jobs, they at least provide structure.

As long as he drifts, Doug misses opportunities to share his ample gifts in meaningful ways, and his great potential remains latent. Doug needs to develop a connection to his higher Will which could motivate him and provide direction. Only then can his talents properly serve himself and others.

Low-grade Medium

Medium could place a "psychic reader" sign in front of her house, for she wants to tell everyone's fortune. She is enamored with her gift and builds her self-esteem by providing this service to everyone she meets whether or not asked. Now and then, she just absorbs the feelings of another person and shares those with her listener. Occasionally she sees clairvoyant images in her mind which she gleans from the other's aura, and she provides interpretations. And sometimes, she just reads body language for her "psychic" information. Generally, Medium wants to help, but her information is not always accurate.

OCCASIONALLY SHE SEES CLAIRVOYANT IMAGES IN HER MIND WHICH SHE GLEANS FROM THE OTHER'S AURA, AND SHE PROVIDES INTERPRETATIONS.

In order to upgrade her gift and to receive impressions from the highest spiritual dimensions, Medium must become disidentified from being a psychic. That is, as she aligns with her Self, she can allow intuition to flow through her rather than thinking, "I am a channel." The spiritual path requires long, hard work to purify motivations for using talents. If she is willing to do that, she, indeed, has a great gift to share.

Con-artist Conrad

Conrad uses his creative genius to plan all kinds of schemes. His incredible ability to act makes him even more believable. Even those far less naive than Gullible

Greta fall for his plans, so skillful is he in weaving magic. Even if convicted and sent to prison, he continues his wiles, duping those on the outside through phone calls and those on the inside from his glib tongue. Conrad long ago forgot his motivation for conning people, but his identity is so absorbed in this role that he knows no other way to live. Many times, he even believes his own stories, making his lies more difficult to detect.

If Conrad could ever find sufficient satisfaction by using his genius and ability to persuade people in honest pursuits, he could start organizations to feed the hungry of the world or to solve difficult societal problems. He would then be able to relate authentically to his loved ones. First he must develop the capacity to be honest with himself and to call upon the integrity that abides, even for Conrad, within his core.

Verna Victim

Verna's sense of being a victim started in childhood. She may have lived in an abusive home, or maybe her parents lacked self-esteem and passed on that belief. In any case, Verna now believes that she is a victim and lives from that premise. She unconsciously attracts people to her who abuse her or take advantage of her, perpetuating the belief. Even when she leaves a cruel partner, she still fails to exert her own power in new situations. Instead, she complains helplessly to others about her plight.

> . . .VERNA NOW BELIEVES THAT SHE IS A VICTIM AND LIVES FROM THAT PREMISE. SHE UNCONSCIOUSLY ATTRACTS PEOPLE TO HER WHO ABUSE HER OR TAKE ADVANTAGE OF HER, PERPETUATING THE BELIEF.

If Verna can retrieve her buried anger, new energy will be released so that she can assert herself as a whole person. Verna will have to explore and dig to bring her beliefs into the open so that they can be revamped. As she begins to experience the light from her inner core, she gradually will be able to believe in herself. Then she will be able to present herself as a capable, strong, resilient woman who deserves a good life, and others will respond accordingly. Her gift of passivity can be transmuted into gentle vitality.

Romantic Ray

Violins, candlelight, and flowers appeal to Ray's yearning for sentimental encounters. He writes poetry to his lover shortly after meeting, and he dreams of the sweet, loving things he will do for his partner. Had he been born in another century, he might have chosen troubadour as his career, singing of his unrequited love to his lady.

So what amorous person could be disappointed with Ray, the gentle and attentive man who always thinks of the loved one? Ray's distortion lies in the fact that he idealizes love so much that he often does not see the true person behind the poetry. Although many of the qualities he cherishes in his lover may be true, he sees a mirage, never allowing love to deepen beyond infatuation. The partner never becomes truly human to Ray.

In order to transmute the gift of love from pure romanticism to genuine love, Ray needs to become more grounded in reality. He needs to realize that his loved one deserves to be more than an icon and that he benefits from relating to a human being. Ray can also celebrate some of this gift by turning his devotion to the spiritual. Then Ray can love devotedly from a deep, spiritual core rather than a subpersonality.

Mystical Marla

Marla, the Mystic: she almost emblazons this message on her forehead for all to see. Being mystical represents her claim to importance and undergirds an illusory self-esteem. Without this pseudo-spiritual quality, she feels useless and empty. Following one guru or spiritual path after another, Marla seeks solace for what is lacking in her daily life. Justifying whatever decisions she makes, she tells others that her Higher Self told her to take certain action, or maybe that she was doing God's will. In truth, Marla is out of touch with her own center.

Her distortion of the spiritual yearning that genuinely resides within her lies in her pretense in being something that she is not. Also, by so strongly identifying as "The Mystic," Marla limits her life by insisting that she play that role in all situations. She needs to go deeper for an understanding of spirituality that transcends roles and identifications. She may still visit ashrams and read holy literature, but she will not need to wear them as garments for all to see.

Escapist Edward

Even as a little boy, Edward ran away from his feelings by living in a dream world. His wistful tales about princes and princesses, dragons and magic kingdoms could have filled volumes. As he grew older, he read science fiction voraciously. Whenever anything painful happened in the outer world, Edward retreated to his books and videos, forgetting anything else existed. He has cousins who drink excessively and those who work day and night to cover up fears and pains, but Edward remains ensconced in his own world ignoring any discontent.

WHENEVER ANYTHING PAINFUL HAPPENED IN THE OUTER WORLD, EDWARD RETREATED TO HIS BOOKS AND VIDEOS, FORGETTING ANYTHING ELSE EXISTED.

Edward escapes from his own insecurities and fears through fantasy. He also fails to recognize his own inner yearning for perfect peace which comes through an attunement to Self. Instead, he immediately covers up those feelings of vague longing, keeping them submerged in the unconscious. Edward needs to deal with past hurts and wounds, and he also needs to listen to the murmuring from his inner wisdom that "call him home." As he both heals and reunites with his spiritual dimension, Edward finds new fulfillment. His gift of imagination can be now used creatively for the service of others rather than just his own escape.

References for Chapter 12

[1]. Burt, 1988, p. 505.
[2]. Ferrucci, 1990, p. 241.
[3]. Einstein, 1984.
[4]. Rudhyar, 1970, p. 109.
[5]. Huber, 1984, p. 227.
[6]. Rudhyar, 1970, p. 113.
[7]. Ferrucci, 1990, p. 189.
[8]. Dobyns, 1972, p. 33.
[9]. Rico, 1983, p. 50.
[10]. Ferrucci, 1982, p. 37.
[11]. Assagioli, 1965.
[12]. Assagioli, 1965, p. 17.
[13]. Assagioli, 1965, p. 100.
[14]. Marks, 1989, p. 140.
[15]. Marks, 1989, p. 135.
[16]. Eichler & Halseth, 1992.
[17]. Oken, 1990, p. 247.
[18]. Huber, 1984, p. 223.
[19]. Hickey, 1970, p. 28.
[20]. Burt, 1988, p. 487.
[21]. Ferrucci, 1990, 252.

EPILOGUE

Each of us contains a radiant Self, emanating light from our deepest core, like the hub of a wheel. At the same time, we all embody many facets of our personalities, each facet a different spoke on the wheel. We can choose to embrace all of our multi-facets or we can reject some of them. We can choose to take responsibility for our lives, or we can blame others for our plight. Choices, choices, and more choices provide our gateway to freedom. How we respond to these choices determines whether we grow, stagnate or regress. As we choose to respond to life in healthy ways, we move down the spoke towards greater harmony and wholeness, towards the Self. At times we fall back into old patterns and ways of being, and then we remember again to choose new, more freeing ways. Progress is not measured by perfection but by having the old debilitating patterns occur less often, and when they do occur, staying in the old way for shorter periods of time, remembering to choose the new way of responding sooner.

Blessings to each of us as we all move towards remembering who we truly are.

COPYRIGHT ACKNOWLEDGMENTS

The author gratefully acknowledges the permission to use quotations from the works listed below. In every case, diligent efforts were made to obtain permission to reprint selections from previously published works. In a few instances, permission was not received in time for formal acknowledgment. Any omissions will be corrected in future printings upon notification. All published citations have been, however, formally cited and listed in the references.

American Federation of Astrologers for citations from *Reflections and Meditations on the Signs of the Zodiac* by Louise Huber.

Joann Anderson for a citation from *Basics of Group Psychosynthesis.*

Aquarian Educational Group for a citation from *The Symphony of the Zodiac* by Torkom Saradarian.

Bear & Co. for a citation from *Meditations with Teilhard de Chardin* by B. Gallagher.

Molly Young Brown for a citation from *The Unfolding Self.*

CCRS Publications for citations from *Astrology, Psychology and the Four Elements* by Stephan Arroyo; and from *Your Secret Self: Illuminating Mysteries of the Twelfth House* by Tracy Marks.

Zipporah Dobyns for citations from *Evolution Through the Zodiac.*

Findhord Press for a citation from *Explorations: Emerging Aspects of the New Culture* by David Spangler.

John Firman for citations from *"I" and Self: Re-visioning Psychosynthesis.*

Group for Creative Meditation for citations from *"The Pilgrimage of Necessity,"* a talk given by Frances Moore.

Institute of Noetic Sciences for a citation from *"The 1990 Temple Awards for Creative Altruism,"* an article by J. Miller and M. Luck in *Noetic Sciences Review.*

Little Brown, a Time Warner Company for a citation from John Donne's poem, *"For Whom the Bell Tolls"* in *Atlantic Book of British and American Poetry.*

Llewellyn for citations from *Archetypes of the Zodiac* by K. Burt.

Leyla Rael for citations from *From Humanistic to Transpersonal Astrology* by D. Rudhyar.

Routeledge & Kegan Paul for a citation from each of the following books: *Personality Types* by C. G. Jung; *The Portable Jung* by J. Campbell; *A Psychology with a Soul: Psychosynthesis in Evolutionary Context* by J. Hardy.

Shambhala for citations from the following books: *The Holographic Paradigm and Other Paradoxes* by K. Wilber; *Mandala* by J. & M. Arguelles; *Voices of Our Ancestors: Cherokee Teachings form the Wisdom Fire* by D. Ywahoo.

Edith Stauffer for citations from *Unconditional Love and Forgiveness.*

J. P. Tarcher for citations from the following books: *Beyond Ego: Transpersonal Dimensions in Psychology* edited by R. N. Walsh & F. Vaughan; *Inevitable Grace* and *What We May Be* by P. Ferrucci; *The Possible Human* by J. Houston; *Writing the Natural Way* by G. L. Rico.

Theosophical Publishing House for citations from the following books: *"Male and Female Polarity in Oriental Thought,"* by H. Guenther, an article in *A Spiritual Approach to Male-Female Relationships* edited by S. Miners; *The Atman Project: A Transpersonal View of Human Development* by K. Wilber.

Frances Vaughan for a citation from *The Inward Arc: Healing and Wholeness in Psychotherapy.*

Samuel Weiser, Inc. for citations from the following books: *The Astrology of Fate* and *Relating: An Astrological Guide to Living with Others on a Small Planet* both by Liz Greene.

John Wiley & Sons for citations from *"Psychosynthesis,"* an article by M. Crampton in *Innovative Psychotherapies* edited by R. J. Corsini.

Thomas Yeomans for quotations and ideas from his training programs.

REFERENCES

Anderson, J. (1989). *Basics of Group Psychosynthesis*. Edmonds, WA: Joann Anderson.

Arguelles, J. & M. (1972). *Mandala*. Berkeley, CA: Shambhala.

Arroyo, S. (1975). *Astrology, Psychology, and the Four Elements*. P. O. Box 1460, Sebastolpol, CA 95473: CRCS Publications.

Assagioli, R. (1965). *Psychosynthesis.* New York: Penguin Books.

Assagioli, R. (1973). *The Act of Will.* New York: Viking Press.

Aurobindo, S. (——). *On Yoga II,* Tome 2, p. 689.

Bailey, A. A. (1951). *Esoteric Astrology.* New York: Lucis Publishing Co.

Bohm, D. (1990). Personal conversation in Kalamazoo, MI.

Brown, M. Y. (1983). *The Unfolding Self: Psychosynthesis and Counseling.* Los Angeles: Psychosynthesis Press.

Burt, K. (1988). *Archetypes of the Zodiac*. St. Paul: Llewellyn Publica tions.

Byrom, T. (Renderer). (1976). *The Dhammapada: The Sayings of the Buddha*. New York: Alfred A. Knopf.

Campbell, J. (Ed.). (1971). *The Portable Jung*. New York: Viking Press.

Cavanaugh, J. (1970). *Some Men Are Too Gentle to Live Among Wolves*. New York: E. P. Dutton.

de Chardin, T. (1968). *Letters from Two Friends 1926-1952*. New York: New American Library.

Crampton, M. (1981). Psychosynthesis. In R. J. Corsini (Ed.), *Innovative Psychotherapies* (pp. 709-723). New York: John Wiley & Sons.

Dobyns, Z. (1972). *Evolution Through the Zodiac.* Los Angeles: T.I.A. Publications.

Dobyns, Z. (1973). *Finding the Person in the Horoscope.* Los Angeles: T.I.A. Publications.

Donne, J. (1958). *Hymn to God, my God, in my sickness.* In E. Sitwell (Ed.), *Atlantic book of British and American poetry.* Boston: Little, Brown & Co.

Dychtwald, K. (1982). Reflections on the holographic paradigm. In K. Wilber, (Ed.). *The Holographic Paradigm and Other Paradoxes.* Boston: New Science Library, Shambhala. pp. 105-112.

Eichler, R. (1983). The four elements: life lessons and relationships. American Federation of Astrologers, Inc. Bulletin: Today's Astrologer, 45(4), pp. 123-126.

Eichler, R. (1984). Pluto, the bulldozer. Lecture given at American Federation of Astrologers Convention in Chicago, Il.

Eichler, R. (1986). The meaning of the Aquarian Age. Lecture given at Unity Church, Wichita, KS.

Eichler, R. & Halseth, J. (1992). Intuition: Enhancing group work. *Social Work with Groups, 15*,(1).

Ferrucci, P. (1982). *What We May Be*. Los Angeles: J. P. Tarcher, Inc.

Ferrucci, P. (1990). *Inevitable Grace*. Los Angeles: J. P. Tarcher, Inc.

Firman, J. (1991). *"I" and Self.* 459 Hawthorne Avenue, Palo Alto, CA 94301: John Firman.

Gallagher, B. (1988). *Meditations with Teilhard de Chardin.* P. O. Box 2860, Santa Fe, NM 87504: Bear & Company.

Green, A. (1978). The integral yoga of Sri Aurobindo. *In Synthesis 2: The Realization of the Self.* (Revised). Redwood City, CA: The Synthesis Press. pp. 41-48.

Green, E. (1980). Personal conversation.

Greene, L. (1978). *Relating: An Astrological Guide to Living With Others On a Small Planet.* New York: Samuel Weiser.

Greene, L. (1980). *Star signs for lovers.* New York: Stein & Day.

Greene, L. (1984). *The Astrology of Fate.* York Beach, Maine: Samuel Weiser.

Guenther, H. (1984). Male and female polarity in Oriental thought. In Miners, S. (Ed.). *A Spiritual Approach to Male-Female Relationships.* Wheaton, Il: Theosophical Publishing House.

Hand, R. (1981). *Horoscope Symbols.* Rockport, MA: ParaResearch, Inc.

Hardy, J. (1987). *A Psychology With a Soul: Psychosynthesis in Evolutionary Context.* New York: Routledge & Kegan Paul.

Hickey, I. M. (1970). *Astrology: A Cosmic Science*. Bridgeport, CN: Altieri Press.

Houston, J. (1982). *The Possible Human: A Course in Enhancing Your Physical, Mental, and Creative Abilities.* Los Angeles: J. P. Tarcher, Inc..

Huber, L. (1984). *Reflections and Meditations on the Signs of the Zodiac*. Tempe, AZ: American Federation of Astrologers.

Jocelyn, J. (1966). *Meditations on the Signs of the Zodiac.* San Antonio, TX: The Naylor Company.

Jung, C. G. (1971). *Personality Types.* London: Routledge & Kegan Paul.

Keen, S. (1982). Self-love and the cosmic connection. In Wilber, K. (Ed). *The Holographic Paradigm and Other Paradoxes*. Boston: New Sci ence Library, Shambhala. pp. 116-118.

March, M. & McEvers J. (1977). *The Only Way to Learn Astrology, Vol. II.* San Diego: Astro Computing Services.

Marks, T. (1989). *Your Secret Self: Illuminating Mysteries of the Twelfth House.* P. O. Box 1460, Sebastopol, CA 95473: CRCS Publications.

Maslow, A. *Toward a Psychology of Being*. New York: Van Nostrand.

Miller, J. & Luck, M. (Winter 1990/91). The 1990 Temple Awards for Creative Altruism. *Noetic Sciences Review, 17,* 35-37. (Institute of Noetic Sciences, 475 Gate Five Road, Suite 300, Sausalito, CA 94965)

Moore, F. A. (no date given). The pilgrimage of necessity. (Talk given at the New Age Bible and Philosophy Center, Santa Monica, CA). Ojai, CA: Group for Creative Meditation.

Oken, A. (1973). *As Above, So Below*. New York: A Bantam Book.

Oken, A. (1990). *Soul-Centered Astrology.* New York: Bantam Books.

Ornish, D. (1990). *Dr. Dean Ornish's Program for Reversing Heart Disease.* New York: Random House.

Rico, G. L. (1983). *Writing the Natural Way.* Los Angeles, CA: J. P. Tarcher, Inc.

Rodegast, P. & Stanton, J. (Compilers). (1985). *Emmanuel's Book.* New York: Some Friends of Emmanuel.

Rudhyar, D. (1970). *The Pulse of Life.* Berkeley: Shambhala.

Rudhyar, D. (1975). *From Humanistic to Transpersonal Astrology.* Palo Alto, CA: The Seed Center.

Saradarian, T. (1980). *The Symphony of the Zodiac.* Agoura, CA: Aquarian Educational Group.

Sat Prem. (1984). *Sri Aurobindo: or the Adventure of Consciousness.* New York: Institute for Evolutionary Research.

Spangler, D. (1980). *Explorations: Emerging Aspects of the New Culture.* Findhorn Publications Lecture Series.

Stauffer, E. (1987). *Unconditional Love and Forgiveness*. Burbank, CA: Triangle Publishers.

Szent-Gyorgyi, A. (1977, revised). Drive in living matter to perfect itself. In Vargiu (Ed.). *Synthesis 1: The Realization of the Self.* Redwood City, California: The Synthesis Press. pp. 14-26.

Vaughan, F. (1994). *The Inward Arc: Healing and Wholeness in Psychotherapy and Spirituality.* Nevada City, CA: Blue Dolphin Publishing.

Walsh, R. N. & Vaughan, F. (Eds). (1980). *Beyond Ego: Transpersonal Dimensions in Psychology.* Los Angeles: J. P. Tarcher, Inc.

Welwood, J. (1982). The holographic paradigm and the structure of experience. In Wilber, Ken (Ed.). *The Holographic Paradigm and Other Paradoxes.* Boston: New Science Library, Shambhala. pp. 127-136.

Wilber, K. (1980). *The Atman Project: A Transpersonal View of Human Development.* Wheaton, IL: The Theosophical Publishing House.

Yeomans, T. (November 1989). Psychosynthesis for professionals. (Lecture given during a year training course). Toronto.

Ywahoo, D. (1987). *Voices of our Ancestors: Cherokee Teachings from the Wisdom Fire.* Boston: Shambhala.

Index

V

W

Y

Z